Junípero Serra, the Vatican, and Enslavement Theology

D1615831

Santa Clara County
LIBRARY

Renewals:
(800) 471-0991
<u>www.santaclaracountylib.org</u>

Junípero Serra, the Vatican, & Enslavement Theology

by Daniel Fogel

ism

press

San Francisco

Library of Congress Cataloging-in-Publication Data

Fogel, D. (Daniel), 1953-
    Junípero Serra, the Vatican, and enslavement
theology.

    Bibliography: p.
    Includes index.
    1. Serra, Junípero, 1713-1784.   2. California—
History—To 1846.   3. Franciscans—California—Missions—
History—18th century.   4. Indians of North America—
California—Missions—History—18th century.   5. Slavery
and the church—Catholic Church—History—18th century.
6. Church and social problems—Catholic Church.
7. Catholic Church—History—1965-   . I. Title.
F864.S44F64   1988   266′.2′0924 [B]   87-32489
ISBN 0-910383-25-1

Ism Press, Inc.
P.O. Box 12447
San Francisco, CA 94112

Correspondence and criticism welcome.

Manufactured in the United States of North America

4i

Cover Graphics

Front cover: *"The Man of Sorrows," pinewood sculpture, two feet high. This painted sculpture, made by an unknown artist in the late 1800's, was found in Aguilar, southern Colorado.* Courtesy of the Taylor Museum of the Colorado Springs Fine Arts Center.

Back cover: *Portrait of friar Junípero Serra at the age of 60, in 1774. This painting, depicting Serra without his customary spectacles, was based on a sketch by Pedro Pablo Conto de la Cruz.* Courtesy of Harry Downie and the Academy of American Franciscan History.

Table of Contents

List of Illustrations *8i*

Acknowledgments *9i*

Introduction 1

How Jesus Became the Christ (4) — *How Christianity Became
an Empire* (5) — *Racial Politics of the Virgin Mary* (7) — *The
Totalitarian Church* (9) — *The Rise of Islam* (10) —*The Muslim
Conquest of Spain* (11) — *Saint James against the Peoples of
Color* (15) — *Three Great Spanish American Catholics...* (17)
Bartolomé de las Casas (17) — *Bernardino de Sahagún* (25) —
Miguel Hidalgo (27) — *...Who Never Made it to Beatification,
Far Less Sainthood* (32) — *How Catholicism Penetrated Mexico*
(33) — *The Pueblo Indian Uprising of 1680* (35) — *Englishmen
against Spaniards, Yankees against Indians* (38).

1. Junípero Serra and the California Missions 41

The Apostle Arrives in Mexico (43) — *His Mission in the
Sierra Gorda* (44) — *Serra's Work for the Inquisition* (45) — *His
Masochism* (47) — *King Carlos Expels the Jesuits* (48) — *Serra
Leads the Franciscans into California* (50) — *Early Hardships* (51)
— *The Mission as a Social System of the Imperial Frontier* (52) —
The Missionaries and the Soldiers (54) — *The Indian Revolt at
San Diego, 1775* (62) — *Asylum, Punishment, and Pardon* (66) —
A Hard-Headed Zealot, a Serene Fanatic (69) —*Serra's Conflicts
with the Military Commanders* (71) — *Pueblo San José vs.
Mission Santa Clara* (72) — *The Dispute over Self-Government*
(74) — *More Soul-Saving than Life-Giving* (76) — *Serra's
Confirmation Campaign...* (77) — *...and his Happy Death* (81).

2. The Indians of California 83

Gatherers, Fishers, Hunters (86) — Environmental Management (92) — Property Relations (93) — Kinship, Marriage, and Divorce (94) — Sex Separation and Women's Autonomy (98) — Sexual Relations (99) — Reproductive Rights and Childbirth (103) — Kindness Towards Children (104) — Justice without Shackles (104) Chiefs, Councils, and Shamans (105) — Warfare and Restraint (107) — Life's Joys (109) — The Communal Impulse and the Selfish Impulse (110) — The Dead and the Historical (111) A Vulnerable Balance (112).

3. The Missions, Culture Shock, and European Invasion 114

A New Way of Life... (115) — ...and New Ways of Death (120) Medical Conditions at the Missions (121) — Bells of Joy, Bells of Sorrow (123) — The Whip and the Cross (129) — A Setback for Women (132) — Indian Resistance and Rebellion (137) — Toypurina the Sorceress and the San Gabriel Uprising (138) Soldiers/Colonists vs. Indians (140) — Persistence of Indian Customs and Beliefs (141) — Turn of the Century, Turn for the Worse (147) — The Mission Indians under Mexican Rule (151) The Chumash Uprising of 1824 (152) — Secularization and Dispersal (156) — The Gold Rush and Yankee Invasion (158) Indian Slavery in the Free Republic (160) — Yankee Genocide (161) — Was Serra a Racist? (163) — An Apprenticeship for Feudalism (164).

4. The Vatican vs. the People's Movements: Reconciliation or Liberation? 165

Catholic Democracy, Liberation Theology (166) — John Paul 2's Counter-Reformation (167) — The Pope in Chile and Argentina (169) — The Struggle within the North American Church (173) — Catholic Women Advocates against the Vatican (173) — The Case of Archbishop Hunthausen (178) — The Gay Question (179) — 'I Cannot Continue to be Silent...' (180) — He Who Pays Peter's Pence Doesn't Call the Tune (184) — On the Ordination of Women (185) — Serra vs. Liberation Theology (186).

Reference Notes 189

Bibliography 207

Index 211

List of Illustrations

Santiago, the Spanish warrior/saint 16
The German Franciscans win one for the virgin Mary 19
Death Cart, by Nasario López 34
La Santísima Trinidad, the Holy Trinity 37
Statue of Junípero Serra 40
Indian women carrying grass seeds and water 55
"The California Indians' Way of Fighting" 60-1
Death of friar Luis Jayme, mission San Diego 65
Visiting friar arrives at a mission 78-9
Indian women cleaning grass seed 82
Map of California's tribal groups and missions 84
Map of known Ohlone tribelets 85
Hupa woman preparing acorn meal 87
Indian woman carrying root-digging stick 88
The basket weaver 89
The sweat lodge 100-1
Mission Indians' construction work 116
Neophyte men plowing mission fields 124-5
Declining percentage of women among mission Indians 133
Gambling games at mission San Francisco 143
San Francisco mission Indians dance, by Louis Choris 144-5
Indian dance at mission San José, by Wilhelm von Tilenau 146
Map of Chumash territory and its missions 154
Ishi, one of the last Yahi Indians 162
General Pinochet greets pope John Paul 2 170
Jeannine Gramick, co-founder of New Ways Ministry 176
John J. McNeil, apostle of gay liberation 181

Acknowledgments

Jeannette Henry Costo of the American Indian Historical Society was generous in explaining to me the experiences of Native American catholics and the reasons for her strong opposition to the canonization of Junípero Serra. Noel Francis Moholy, O.F.M.,* who has been leading the campaign for Serra's canonization for three decades, was equally generous in explaining the religious viewpoint that has motivated his work.

Professors Norma Alarcón and Francisco X. Alarcón helped fill some of the woeful gaps in my knowledge of Mexican history.

Randy Milliken, anthropological researcher at the University of California at Berkeley, discussed several questions relating to the California Indians and the mission period at length with me, providing information and valuable insights. Polly Quick, former anthropology professor at UC Berkeley, was helpful in referring me to source materials. Malcolm Margolin was insightful in answering my questions about his book on the Ohlone Indians. Jeffrey Burns, archivist of the archdiocese of San Francisco, acquainted me with sources of information on today's catholic church and periodical literature on the mission period.

Dr. Günter Risse, chairman of the department of history of the health sciences at the University of California at San Francisco, took a good deal of time and effort to provide me with some medical historical background, helping me get a handle on the medical problems faced by California's Indians under the mission system.

---

*O.F.M. is a Latin abbreviation for the Order of Friars Minor. It refers to members of the Franciscan order of the catholic church.

Thanks to the following publishing companies for permission to reprint excerpts from the works cited:

Academy of American Franciscan History, Box 34440, Bethesda, Maryland 20817:
Writings of Junípero Serra, four volumes. Antonine Tibesar, O.F.M., editor. © 1955.

Monthly Review Press, 155 West 23rd St., New York, NY 10011:
Guatemala: Occupied Country. Copyright © 1969 by Eduardo Galeano. English translation by Cedric Belfrage. Reprinted by permission of Monthly Review Foundation.

National Catholic Reporter, weekly newspaper, P.O. Box 419281, Kansas City, Missouri 64141.

New Catholic Encyclopedia, Catholic University of America, Box 45, Cardinal Station, Washington, DC 20064.

Oxford University Press, 200 Madison Ave., New York, NY 10016:
The Creation of Patriarchy, by Gerda Lerner. Copyright © 1986.

Random House, Inc., 201 East 50th St., New York, NY 10022:
The First Coming: How the Kingdom of God Became Christianity, by Thomas Sheehan. Copyright © 1986.

University of California Press, 2120 Berkeley Way, Berkeley, CA 94720:
The Conflict Between the California Indian and White Civilization, by Sherburne F. Cook. Copyright © 1976.

University of Nebraska Press, 901 North 17 St., Lincoln, Nebraska 68588:
Indian Life at the Old Missions, by Edith Buckland Webb. © 1952.

Introduction

The controversial campaign to declare Junípero Serra a saint raises a cluster of questions about the catholic church, human freedom, and the native peoples of America.

Junípero Serra (1713-1784) was a Franciscan catholic missionary from Spain, who founded missions among the Indians along the Pacific coast of California from San Diego to San Francisco. Serra and his franciscan colleagues saw their mission as one of winning pagan souls for the kingdom of God in heaven. The military authorities whom the franciscans had to work with were out to conquer fresh territory, prestige, and riches for the earthly kingdom of Spain's Carlos 3.

The franciscan missionaries were mostly self-sacrificing men, dedicating their lives to what they viewed as the spiritual salvation of the Indians. The Spanish military leaders were ambitious men, aiming to advance in the military hierarchy and hoping for a comfortable retirement as ranch owners in California or Mexico. Both groups of Spaniards were loyal servants of the king, and dogged partisans of Spanish catholic social values. Neither group of Spaniards respected the societies which the Indians of California had evolved over thousands of years.

The campaign to canonize Junípero Serra, initiated by U.S. franciscan priests, has been in motion for over 40 years. In 1985, pope John Paul 2 declared Serra "venerable," meaning that Serra had led a life of heroic virtue; this is the first step on the road to sainthood. Beatification, in catholic tradition, is the next and penultimate step. When the Vatican announced, in the summer of 1986, that pope John Paul would call at mission Carmel during his 1987 visit to California, the franciscan partisans of Serra predicted that the pope would beatify Serra on that

coming occasion. Mission Carmel, founded by Serra and his companions in 1770, became the capital of the California mission system, and
the burial place of Serra 14 years later.

A few weeks before the pope's 1987 visit to the U.S., the Vatican made
a surprise announcement that John Paul would not beatify anyone
during his visit. Vatican officials cited technical reasons, involving
difficulties in documenting a miracle that Serra must have performed
(whether on earth or from heaven), to qualify for beatification. But a
more compelling reason for the pope's hesitation was sharp protest by
Native American catholics against elevating Serra to sainthood. In
March 1987, the Tekakwitha Conference, the organization of Native
American catholics numbering over 4,000 members, issued a statement
criticizing as "grossly inaccurate" official church reports on Serra's
treatment of California's Indians, charging that they "totally misrepre-
sent the native understanding of their own history and cultures."[1] And
Native American catholics leading the campaign against Serra's
canonization filed an official complaint with the Vatican.

In his speech before 12,000 Native American catholics in Phoenix,
Arizona on 14 September 1987, the pope revealed his leanings in the
Serra controversy: "...I wish to recall the work of the many
missionaries who strenuously defended the rights of the original
inhabitants of this land. One priest who deserves special mention
among the missionaries is the beloved friar Junípero Serra, who
traveled through lower and upper California. He had frequent clashes
with the civil authorities over the treatment of Indians."

The pope, who no doubt read his speech from drafts presented him
by interested U.S. priests, neglected to add that both Serra and the
"civil authorities" (i.e., Spanish military commanders), despite their
disagreements, worked together to impose the same social system and
spiritual regime upon the California Indians. John Paul went on to
acknowledge the negative aspects of European contact and conquest
of the Native Americans, while carefully exempting European catholic
missionaries from his critical remarks: "...The early encounter
between your traditional cultures and the European way of life... was a
harsh and painful reality for your peoples. The cultural oppression, the
injustices, the disruption of your life and of your traditional societies
must be acknowledged."[2] Yet he claimed that, on balance, the missionaries improved the Indians' living conditions, and "...above all, they
proclaimed the good news of the salvation in our Lord Jesus Christ.
Your encounter with the gospel has not only enriched you. It has
enriched the church..."

Three days after this sermon to Native American catholics, the pope paid his visit to mission Carmel. Laying a wreath on Junípero Serra's grave, he praised Serra as a model for catholic priests today: "The way in which he fulfilled [his] mission corresponds faithfully to the church's vision today of what evangelization means. He not only brought the gospel to the Native Americans, but as one who lived the gospel he also became their defender and champion."[3]

John Paul 2 is a highly political pope. He chooses his saints and sermons carefully, with a sharp eye for political angle and nuance. Is there a logical connection between his praise for Serra during his 1987 North American trip, and his stonewalling against appeals by women, gay and lesbian catholics for equality within the church?

Three key areas of controversy within the catholic church worldwide have been *social revolution*, *women's role*, and *sexual freedom*. The church's efforts to reach the rural majorities in third world countries over the past 25 years have thrust many priests, nuns, and church layworkers into the struggle of the poor against the rule of the big landowners, corporations, and repressive military forces. Liberation theology, preaching salvation for the masses *on earth* through common struggle against exploitation—including even armed insurrection against tyranny—has enlightened and encouraged this dynamic new trend in third world catholicism.

Meanwhile, in the "first world" countries of North America and western Europe, the church has had to face the rising demands of catholic women—both religious and secular—for equal rights in the church and in society. Vatican decrees against contraception and abortion have been rejected, in practice, by millions of catholic women—raising the question of whether the hierarchy can keep trying to impose its patriarchal dogma without losing moral authority, and many members to boot. And the homosexual rights movement has impacted the church, as catholic gay and lesbian groups have emerged and some gay priests have boldly stepped forward, struggling to reconcile gay rights with christian values.

In the midst of these swirling controversies challenging church tradition and Vatican authority, the figure of Junípero Serra emerges as a solid partisan of tradition and obedience.

The pope, the apostles of liberation theology, and the liberal North American catholics all claim to be true christians, and all uphold the catholic church as an institution. What would Jesus of Nazareth have thought of their disputes? Oddly enough, a study of Jesus' actual life and mission reveals that Jesus himself was not a christian: He *rejected* the designation of messiah (christ). Nor did he intend to found a new church.

How Jesus Became the Christ

Jesus' mentor, John the baptist, denounced the selfishness of the rich towards the poor, the corruption of the tax collectors, and the abuses of the Roman soldiers in occupied Palestine (Luke 3.10-14). John did not challenge the division of society into rich and poor, nor did he question the social source of the power of tax collectors and soldiers. He preached that people should treat others, whatever their social station, with fairness and compassion.

John the baptist, a radical Jew, chafed against jewish religious orthodoxy and ethnic complacency. He rejected the messianic notion that the god of the jews would destroy the gentiles and bring on his kingdom for the exclusive enjoyment of his own people. He railed against those who carefully observed religious ritual, while treating their neighbors inhumanely. John declared that god's final judgment would cut through pious hypocrisy and condemn all those—whether jew or gentile—who lacked grace and charity in their treatment of others. The only way for sinners to avoid god's terrible judgment was to repent, cleanse themselves of sin and change their ways.[4]

John's message was a stern and demanding one. Focusing on the wrath of god's judgment, he was ascetic and pessimistic. Jesus took the core of John's preaching and gave it an upbeat accent. Proclaiming, "The kingdom of God is at hand!" (Mark 1.15), Jesus invited all those who heeded god's desires to share in the fruits of the kingdom. "Whereas John had emphasized the woes of impending judgment, Jesus preached the joy of God's immediate and liberating presence."[5]

Jesus proved to be a worldlier preacher than John. He kept company and shared meals and wine with all those men and women who would hear his message. He continued to denounce greed, selfishness and religious hypocrisy, pointing to positive examples of humble gentiles acting more humanely than priestly jews. He tried to respect and protect women, embracing even prostitutes among his converts.

His railing against the men of wealth irritated the religious establishment, and frightened the Roman rulers of Palestine. But Jesus, like John before him, was no revolutionary: If he did not investigate the social roots of greed and injustice, far less did he attempt to rally the masses to overthrow the unjust social and political system. After all, since the kingdom of god was already at hand, what would have been the point of a revolt of the oppressed?

Unable to really change society through moral preaching and exorcist displays, Jesus finally slid into pessimism and despair, resigning himself to a martyr's end. When Jesus was arrested and dragged before the religious authorities, his closest disciples fled in confusion and terror. Nothing in his preaching or actions had prepared them for the terrible struggle that was to come. Far from publicly defending Jesus against the religious bigots and the Roman executioners, Simon Peter denied any connection with him. In so doing, Simon cut himself off from the only force that could have saved Jesus from the cross: the assembled throng. And apparently, neither Simon nor the other male disciples even bore witness to Jesus' public humiliation and death. On the other hand, several of Jesus' women followers—Mary Magdalene, Mary the mother of James, Salome, and others—followed him to the cross.

Ironically, the movement that was to become christianity—first proclaiming the dead Jesus as the soon-to-return messiah, and later merging Jesus with God himself—was started by those disciples who had denied and abandoned Jesus in his hour of anguish and death. Jesus had probably never claimed to be the messiah*; the whole thrust of his preaching was for a direct connection between the individual and a loving god, thus shortcircuiting the need for a messiah.

How Christianity Became an Empire

Any social movement that challenges the oppressive *status quo* must contend with powerful material forces dragging it back into an accommodation with the status quo. Christianity's first accommodation to the status quo was its elevation of Jesus to the false role of messiah. The yearning for a messiah grows out of the despair of the oppressed masses. Lacking confidence in their own ability to overthrow tyranny and social injustice, widening layers of the masses may embrace and exalt a savior figure as a spiritual salve for their suffering. The more perfect and charismatic their savior, the more impotent are the masses in intellect and initiative.

---

*According the jesuit theologian Thomas Sheehan, Mark's account of Jesus embracing the designation of christ/messiah before the religious tribunal (Mark 14.61-2) was not factual; rather, it was inserted into the gospel by early christian evangelists after having elevated the late Jesus to the role of messiah.[6] Sheehan also holds that the accounts of the jewish crowd clamoring for Jesus to be crucified (Mark 15.12-13) and of the supposedly bloodthirsty people declaring, "His blood be upon us, and on our children" (Matthew 27.25), were false insertions into the gospel, with no basis in historical fact.

Yet christianity, as it spread from Palestine into southern Europe and northern Africa, retained a radical edge. The early apostles did not preach a merely passive awaiting of the second coming of christ: They preached and practiced a new way of life. Better put, they tried to revive the *old*, communal values of sharing, humility and brotherly love that class society was wrenching apart. Everyone joining the christian movement, whether rich or poor, had to cast his or her entire fortune into the common fund. The christians lived in communal households, sharing out food and clothing according to the modest needs of all. A christian traveller, unburdened by provisions, was guaranteed hospitality by his fellow christians at his city of destination.

The young christian movement irritated the Roman emperors and the big landowners around the Mediterranean. The empire, which had ruined the free peasantry even within Italy, was relying more and more on slave labor. Slaves of all colors flocked to the new religion. So did many of the marginal laborers (lumpenproletarians) languishing in the cities. Few rich men took kindly to the apostles' denunciation of their greed and moral appeals upon them to renounce luxury and join the christian brotherhood. Not religious, but social bigotry was behind the cruel persecution of the early christians.

Even so, the christian movement could not overturn slavery, nor create a liberating new social order. The christian community, radical in its *distribution* of collective wealth, was not based on any new system of *production*—nor could it conceive of one, given the lack of a coherent revolutionary class in those days. Its pacifist dogma of universal love guaranteed that the ruling minorities would maintain a monopoly on armed power. In their treatment of women, the apostles lost ground over Jesus, with Paul in particular stressing woman's submission to man in the family, church, and society.

And inevitably, the material and social inequalities plaguing society at large gained a foothold within the christian movement itself. The clergy, at first, were elected by their local communities, and subject to recall; they enjoyed no special privileges or material rewards. As the movement grew and the tasks of administering the communities' daily affairs got more complicate d, the clerics more and more became full-time officials, paid a salary from the common fund. To organize and unite the far-flung movement, the most prominent local clerics, the bishops, gathered themselves into councils. The bishops from the stronger and richer communities set the pace at the councils. They now had a chance to garner wealth as well as prestige. The upper clergy gelled into a caste, separating themselves from the common christians and from the people. As long as christianity remained a persecuted movement, the trend towards hierarchy was held in check. But the existence of a privileged clergy gave the secular rulers of the empire a group they could bargain with, to turn christianity to their own ends.

The turning point came in the year 312: Constantine, who had proclaimed himself emperor in Gaul (now France) and was marching his troops to Rome to oust the reigning Maxentius, embraced christianity. As promised by his legendary vision of the cross, Constantine went on to conquer Maxentius and take over the Roman empire. His conversion to christianity may have been more an astute political decision to secure popular support, than a purely religious revelation. At any rate, Constantine in power ended the persecution of the christians. Christian captives were freed from the mines and prisons. From the catacombs where many had taken refuge, christians returned to the cities, where they found that their religion was not only tolerated, but officially endorsed. The clergy regained possession of the many church buildings and properties confiscated during the persecutions.

The pope who presided over this decisive change in the fortunes of christianity was Miltiades, a black African. Miltiades had suffered under the persecution, before becoming bishop of Rome (pope) in 311.* Now, with Constantine's help, he started merging the catholic church with the Roman empire.

Racial Politics of the Virgin Mary

In its struggle to convert the "pagan" masses of the Roman empire, christianity was by no means dealing with a blank religious slate. The peoples of the Mediterranean had created and embraced a colorful array of local cults and regional religions. Their worship of a variety of goddesses and gods, animals, and more distant forces of nature, was rooted in cultural traditions going back centuries, in some cases millennia. How was this newcomer cult of Jesus, inspired by a radical jewish preacher whose mission had lasted roughly two years and ended

---

*Miltiades, who died in the year 314, was the second of three black popes, all of whom were later canonized: Victor 1, a black African, was bishop of Rome from 189 to 199, and Gelasius 1, born of African parents in Rome, served as pope from 492 to 496.[7] In later centuries, the Vatican and its artists "bleached out" these and other black saints, depicting them as white Europeans. Saints Augustine (AD 354-430) and Benedict (480?-543?) were also black, and also won sainthood only to lose their color. Civilization and christianity must have been a good deal less racist over 1700 years ago, than they are today.

in his humiliating death, to compete successfully with the existing, deep rooted cults which the people so cherished?

The early christian evangelists did not merely persuade and spiritually conquer the pagan masses. To gain a mass following, they cleverly *adapted* their doctrine to the prevailing mass cultural environment, co-opting key elements from the most popular cults. Probably the strongest of these was the cult of Isis, the black mother goddess, which spread from her birthplace in Ethiopia into Egypt, and across the Mediterranean into Europe.

Isis, who became the prime goddess of the Egyptian pantheon, was worshipped as the virgin mother of Horus. After the infant Horus was killed by a scorpion's sting, Isis brought him back to life. She was the moon goddess reigning in heaven, and the goddess of grain. The Egyptians venerated her for teaching women to grind grain, spin flax and weave cloth, and teaching men to cure disease and settle into married life.[8]

The cult of Isis was carried east through Palestine into Asia, and north into Europe, by African immigrants. It took hold in Greece and Italy, whose peoples embraced several other black goddesses imported from north Africa. The cult promised future salvation through fasting and abstaining from sensual pleasures.[9]

The early christian evangelists blended Isis, mother of Horus, with Mary, mother of Jesus. For those north Africans, west Asians and south Europeans already influenced by the Isis cult, it took no great leap of faith to accept Mary as the virgin mother, or to believe in the resurrection of the dead Jesus and his ascent into heaven. As they converted to christianity, they transformed christian belief along African cultural lines. The virgin Mary became the black Madonna.

The Roman emperors at first persecuted the Isis cult movement. But Caligula, who ruled as emperor from AD 37 to 41, acknowledged the popularity of the cult and allowed the building of a temple for Isis in Rome.[10] Many of his successors also tolerated the cult, while continuing to persecute the christian movement.

With the establishment of christianity as the official religion of the empire, this situation was reversed. The Vatican came to look with horror upon the "pagan" influences that christianity had absorbed. And even as the state-supported catholic church expanded, worship of Isis and other goddesses remained popular in many parts of Europe. In the iconoclasm campaign begun in the AD 600's under emperor Leo, catholic fanatics destroyed many black Madonna, Isis, and other goddess icons and images. Goddess worshipers resisted by hiding their beloved images in forests and caves. When the iconoclasm ended, the Madonna images were restored, but often without their original dark skin tones.[11]

In 431, the council of Ephesus convened by Europe's christian leaders declared that the virgin Mary was the Mother of God. By this time, Jesus had drifted from being a radical preacher (which he was in reality), to being the awaited messiah (which he had not claimed to be), to being the human form of god. The church leaders had prudently decided to stop pinning all their followers' hopes on an imminent second coming of the christ. A godly Jesus ruling human affairs from on high is a far more solid foundation stone for an established church than is an activist Jesus christ poised to intervene directly in human affairs and sweep away the pious hypocrites.

Neither the cult of Isis nor the cult of Mary was liberating for women. In both cases, the virgin mother is also a faithful and loving wife. She is a domesticated woman, and she knows her place in society. When men worship the virgin Mary, they do not worship female power, but rather male power reflected back to them in a maternal embrace. They also use the virgin image to sanitize and ennoble their sexual drive to possess women. Just as belief in the all-powerful messiah Jesus reflects the powerlessness of the masses, belief in the all-loving virgin Mary, mother of god, reflects the powerlessness of women.

On the other hand, it seems likely that, the farther back one traces Isis through history into pre-history, the closer one will approach to real female power. Many of the goddesses created by horticultural societies were sensual, dynamic, and independent from men. As horticulture (gardening) gave way to agriculture (plow cultivation) and men for the first time settled into major productive roles, the goddesses—like the women—were hemmed in. Now they were glorified as mothers (notably of sons), faithful wives and providers—no longer as women for themselves and for other women.

The Totalitarian Church

After becoming the official religion of the Roman empire, christianity was transformed from a religious and social movement of the oppressed into a church of the oppressors. The loving and forgiving god of Jesus became the terrible and punishing god of the empire. The upper clergy put an end to the communal christian fund, and indulged in the riches they skimmed from the fabulous church treasury. Their imposition of a battery of rituals and restrictions on church members outstripped the pious hypocrisy of the jewish high priests against whom Jesus had railed. Christian community gave way to catholic feudalism.

Jesus and his disciples had embraced the poor, the outcast and despised people of all colors as equal members of the community of believers (although the women always held a lower status than the men). The Vatican *coerced* the poor into unconditional obedience, and slid heavily into cultural and racial bigotry. As the black Madonna lost her color, the line of black saints and popes came to an end. Jesus had preached "turn the other cheek" in the face of violent attack. The Vatican endorsed wars to conquer, and even exterminate infidels and heretics—i.e., those who followed rival religions, and those christians who rejected Vatican dogma and practice.

The rise of Islam in Arabia and its lightning spread westward across north Africa in the AD 600's revealed the deep alienation of the peoples of color from official christianity.

The Rise of Islam

Muhammad was a far worldlier prophet than Jesus had been; he never held any illusions that his movement could spread by purely peaceful persuasion. If his teachings lacked the radical humanitarian trend and utopian vision of Jesus', nonetheless they contained many aspects that appealed to popular desires for social justice and solidarity (at least among the Arab peoples). Muhammad banned infanticide, which had victimized many newborn girls in Arabia due to poverty and the degraded status of females among the nomadic pastoralists. Insisting that the wealthy give generously to the poor, he tried to remove the stigma from poverty. And he banned capture and enslavement of Arab by Arab.

Compared to what institutional christianity had become, the muhammadan movement was dynamic, even liberating. It renounced an ordained priesthood and ritual sacraments: The common man was free to interpret the Koran as he saw fit, in accord with public consensus. This flexibility was just what was needed by a young religion being spread far and wide by nomads and merchants.

The islamic movement, while trampling underfoot the freedom of many local societies and cultures (and probably setting women back a good deal in the process), brought the benefits of literacy, higher education, and a wide range of scientific and technical inquiry. And so it was muslim north Africa and Spain that took the lead in mathematics, astronomy, and development of the mechanical arts, while christian Europe lapsed into its "dark age" (really a *white* age, in the sense of slamming the door against peoples of color). In AD 389, a christian mob incited by Theodosius, head of the eastern Roman empire, had wrecked the library of Alexandria in Egypt—destroying the historical records, scientific knowledge, and religious and artistic creations bequeathed by African and Mediterranean civilizations over several thousand years. Muslim scholars, scientists and artists now had to pick up the pieces.

The Muslim Conquest of Spain

In 711, the black muslim general Tarik ibn Ziad led an army of 7,000 men—most of them Moors like Tarik, while the rest were Arabs[12]—from the northern tip of Morocco, across the straight of Gibraltar and into Spain. Sent by the Moorish governor Musa Nosseyr, their mission was to dethrone the upstart Visigoth king Roderick.

The Visigoths, a Germanic people, had plundered Rome in 410 and a few years later moved into Spain, where they established an elective monarchy based on their minority ethnic group. In 418, the Visigoth rulers of Spain submitted to the supreme authority of the Roman emperor. But they spent nearly two centuries trying to impose their Aryan culture on the unwilling Spanish majority (many of whom were descendants of Roman colonists), and banning marriage between Visigoths and Spaniards—before giving in and converting to Roman catholicism themselves. They tried to convert Spain's Jews to christianity, or reduce them to slavery. By the early 700's, the Visigoth rulers, having done practically nothing to develop industry and commerce, were imposing a crushing tax burden upon the Spanish peasantry, reducing many to serfdom.[13]

The Moorish general Tarik had actually been invited into Spain by a Visigoth leader engaged in a civil war for the throne against king Roderick. Once the African forces landed in Spain and began moving north, they were welcomed as liberators by many native Spaniards as well as Jews. The war within the Visigoth ruling circles was transformed into a kind of people's war against the entire Visigoth regime, as Tarik's army swelled with Spanish volunteers.[14]

The Moorish/Arab/Spanish coalition under Tarik, advancing north to Toledo and beyond, won a stunning series of victories over king Roderick's forces. Governor Musa, joining the struggle himself, brought 18,000 more soldiers from Morocco—mostly Berbers—to help Tarik. In 713, Tarik crushed the last of Roderick's forces, and islamic rule in Spain began.

The victorious Moors carried out land and tax reforms, easing the burdens on the peasants and allowing them the right to sell their property. Serfs who converted to islam were declared freed men. Thus the Moorish and Arab conquerors won a big majority of the Spanish people to islam, while fashioning themselves into a new aristocracy, based on the date of their arrival in Spain.[15]

Social mobility was increased, providing a stimulus for bourgeois commerce and industry. Moorish and Arab scholars collected as many works of Greek, Egyptian and Indian science and philosophy as they could find, and translated them into Arabic. Astronomy and medical science flourished, with women as well as men participating in the cultural ferment.[16]

Aside from their economic inducements to the peasantry, the Moorish leaders did not attempt to force their muslim religion or Arabic language on the Spanish people. They assumed the right to approve bishops, but otherwise let the catholic church coexist peacefully with islam. Muslims, christians and jews had equal rights.

The slave trade became the blight of muslim Spain. Starting in the late 700's, Slavs and Germans taken prisoner in the Frankish (French) territories were herded into Spain by Frankish and Jewish traders. If Spain's Moorish and Arab rulers did not initiate this white slave trade, they certainly benefited from it. The enslaved men were bought as laborers or servants, the women as housemaids or concubines.[17] A great racial mixing took place in southern Spain—more coerced than free, to be sure.

Meanwhile, the defeated Visigothic nobles had regrouped in the northern mountains of Asturias. Joining forces with the local people, they began a counteroffensive against the muslim regime, under the banner of christianity. Their kingdom in Asturias expanded, and the battles between the northern christian kingdoms and the southern muslim kingdoms raged on and off, back and forth for over 750 years.

The christian rulers, learning some key lessons from their defeat in 711, allowed muslims and jews to practice their religions and govern themselves according to their respective laws within the reconquered christian territory—as long as they paid regular tribute (taxes) to the christian rulers. Still lacking economic initiative, these rulers easily slid back into their old ways of exploitation, setting up big landed estates, where they saddled the resident peasants with rents, services, and even outright serfdom.[18]

In their struggle to reconquer Spain, the northern catholics faced the problem of having too small a population of the faithful to settle securely those lands which their armies had occupied. So they annexed only those lands they could repopulate and garrison, carefully fortifying their settlements and cities against muslim attack. They also evolved the *mission system* for the spiritual reconquest of the muslim peasantry. This meant resettling freshly baptized people into compact villages under the close supervision of specially trained priests. The new converts not only received regular religious instruction at the missions, but also labored at ranching, farming, spinning and weaving tasks in the mission quadrangle and on its surrounding lands. The missions could thus support themselves, and any surplus food and clothing produced by the new converts could support the christian soldiers.

A key factor in the struggle between the christian north and the muslim south was the inner rivalry, fragmentation and even civil wars that took place *within* each of the two religious camps. Whichever camp could achieve unity and a strong sense of purpose would get the upper hand. By the early AD 1000's, many Moorish and Arab nobles had become corrupted by idle luxury, contending among themselves as heads of petty states. The advancing christian armies forced them to buy peace by paying annual tribute. This was an economic boon to the christian states, and it sharpened the class tensions within the muslim states. The muslim rulers, instead of abandoning their lavish lifestyles, tightened the tax burden on their own subjects to pay the christians. The christian king Alfonso 6 conquered Toledo, the geographical center of Spain and the old Visigothic capital, and vowed to drive the muslims into the sea. The muslim nobles made a desperate appeal for help from Yusuf ibn Tashifin, the black Moroccan leader of the rising Almoravid muslim movement.[19]

Amassing a huge army drawn from the west Saharan peoples and throwing camel-mounted cavalry into the fray against the christians' horse-mounted cavalry, Yusuf drove the christian forces out of southern Spain and Portugal. Appalled at the corruption and self-indulgence of the muslim nobles who had begged him for salvation from the christians, he kicked them out of power and appointed his own governors in their place. Yusuf ruled both northwest Africa and southern Iberia until his death in 1106.[20]

The Almoravid empire gave rise to a renaissance in commerce, industry and culture in muslim Spain. But it also gave spur to the slave trade. Ironically, now black African as well as white European slaves were herded into southern Spain.[21] Racial mixing continued apace, and slavery was not a permanent and hereditary condition; a slave might attain free status by marrying her master or his master's daughter, and a slave man might set up his own trade and even inherit part of his master's estate.

As the Almoravid dynasty gave way to the Almohad dynasty, the muslim rulers again became demoralized and corrupt. The christian states regrouped and, under the banner of the crusades, renewed their assaults against the muslim realm. By the end of the 1200's, the christians had reconquered all but the muslim kingdom of Granada in far southern Spain.

The Spanish Catholics Get Back in the Saddle

As they approached total victory, the christian rulers dropped their facade of tolerance towards jews and muslims. In 1391, they incited the masses, devastated by a plague and frustrated by their low wages, to massacre jews in many parts of Spain and Portugal. The surviving jews had to choose between death, flight, and conversion to catholicism. Many chose conversion and intermarried with "old" catholics, achieving prominence in business, academia, government, and even the catholic hierarchy. Yet this did not save them from the flames of the inquisition, which exerted itself to root out, destroy, and seize the property of converted jews accused of secretly practicing their old religion.

In 1492, the christian forces finally conquered Granada, destroying the last outpost of islam in Spain. Massacres of defeated African troops became all the rage. The remaining jews were expelled from Spain that same year. And the booty that the catholic monarchy seized from Granada was used to finance Columbus' expedition to America.

The archbishop of Granada, Hernando de Talavera (from a converted jewish family), tried to convert the Moorish population to catholicism by gradual persuasion. Queen Isabel's confessor, Francisco Jiménez de Cisneros, had other ideas: He introduced forced mass conversions.[22] Jiménez, rising to the rank of cardinal, also ordered the destruction of the Moorish libraries—wiping out centuries of the most advanced knowledge and artistic expressions.

In 1499-1500, the Moors rebelled, but were defeated. They were given the choice of conversion or expulsion. The elaborate racial caste system rigged up by the Spaniards to rule their vast American empire made it practically impossible for those Moors who remained to assimilate into the mainstream of Spanish society.

Saint James against the Peoples of Color

The patron saint of the christian reconquerors of Spain was James, one of the twelve apostles of Jesus and the first to suffer martyrdom. According to legend, between Jesus' death and his own execution in Palestine, James visited Spain, and his reputed relics were preserved at Santiago de Compostela in Spain's northwest corner. So ¡*Santiago!* became the battle cry of Spain's christian warriors as they assaulted the Moorish troops and citadels. The humble and gentle saint James now became known as *Santiago Matamoros,* "Saint James the killer of Moors." Both the battle cry and the patron saint were dragged across the Atlantic to America, where saint James became *Santiago Mata- indios,* "Saint James the killer of Indians."

Hernando Cortés and his small team of freebooting soldiers raised the banner of Santiago in their war to conquer Mexico. They destroyed a Mexican state that was more advanced than the Spanish state in its handicrafts, irrigation, public sanitation and hygiene, justice system, social welfare, social mobility, and—despite its notorious use of ritual human sacrifice—its tolerance for cultural and religious diversity. The Spaniards accomplished their seemingly impossible feat by playing on the resentment felt by those neighboring societies which had been conquered by the Aztecs (relative newcomers to the region) and forced into paying annual tribute.

Besides their terrifying horses, steel swords and firearms, the Spanish *conquistadores* brought unfamiliar moral qualities into Mexico. The Aztecs had developed an elaborate code of honor in the way they conducted their warfare: When they planned to annex a rival city-state, their ambassadors would announce their intentions to their rival leaders, trying to persuade them, through repeated negotiations, to surrender without a struggle; only after their rivals refused to submit after three consecutive negotiating sessions would the Aztecs initiate hostilities, thus depriving themselves of the advantage of surprise. The Spanish warriors, by contrast, were devious: They gained emperor Moctezuma's favors and a privileged entrance into the capital city by talking peace—and then massacred the dancing Aztec nobles in their sacred courtyard.

Moreover, the Aztecs had no way of understanding the Spaniards' insatiable greed for gold. For the Mexicans, gold was one of many esteemed products of nature, used to fashion art works, ornaments, and objects for religious worship; there was no intrinsic value attached to plain bars of gold. The idea of a man amassing great wealth by piling up gold, or of an empire supporting itself on the basis of gold reserves,

*Santiago (St. James), the Spanish warrior/saint, trampling
the conquered. Painting attributed to Pedro Fresquiz, late 1700's.*
(courtesy of the Taylor Museum of the Colorado Springs Fine Arts Center)

was incomprehensible to the Aztecs. The idea of men melting down, for their own enrichment, the painstaking handiwork of generations of highly skilled artisans, was absurd.

Betrayed and outmaneuvered by the Spaniards, devastated by a smallpox epidemic, driven to starvation and thirst by the merciless siege of their city, the Aztecs fought heroically against the Spaniards and their Indian allies, till they were overwhelmed in 1521. "At last, when all was over," wrote Jacques Soustelle, "the Mexican rulers could have expected a bitter bargaining that would fix the amount of the tribute to be paid to the conquerors. They were incapable of imagining what was to come: the overthrow of their entire civilization, the destruction of their gods and their beliefs, the abolition of their political institutions, the torture of the kings for their treasure, and the red-hot iron of slavery."[23]

Unlike the Moorish conquest of Spain, there was nothing liberating about the Spanish conquest of Mexico. The native cultures and languages were scorned and suppressed, the Aztec and Mayan historical and religious chronicles burned. Mexican industries were banned by law, to guarantee a captive market for Spanish industries, which in turn were retarded due to lack of competition. While introducing their diseases to the peoples of Mexico, the Spaniards introduced practically no medical science. They enslaved hundreds of thousands of Indians in the gold and silver mines, and on the big colonial plantations.

In 1524, Spanish priests from the largest catholic order, the franciscans, arrived in Mexico to evangelize the Aztec priests who had survived the conquest.

Three Great Spanish American Catholics...

Bartolomé de las Casas (1472-1566) was born in Sevilla in southern Spain, into a middle class family; while both his parents were catholic, his father was descended from jewish converts.[24] As a young man in 1493, he witnessed Columbus' triumphant return to Sevilla. His father, now an impoverished merchant, joined Columbus' second voyage to America later that year. While his father was profiting from native labor on an estate he was issued on Española (the island now divided between the Dominican Republic and Haiti), Bartolomé served in the christian militia against Moorish rebels in Granada. He attended the cathedral academy in Sevilla, studying Latin and theology, and later law. When his father returned to Sevilla in 1497, he brought along an Indian servant, whom he gave to Bartolomé. But soon queen Isabel issued a decree ordering the *conquistadores* to return all those Indians they had brought to Spain, back to their native lands—so Bartolomé had to set his Indian servant free.[25]

Having qualified as a lay teacher of christian doctrine, Las Casas sailed for America in 1502 with Nicolás de Ovando, governor designate of Española. Arriving in Santo Domingo, Las Casas took part in the military repression of native uprisings. He was rewarded with an *encomienda*, a "trusteeship" giving a colonist control over the labor of the Indians living on a tract of land, who in return were supposed to receive religious instruction. Thanks to this forced labor, Las Casas' plantation prospered. But he gave up his *encomienda* in 1506 to voyage to Rome, where he took religious vows before returning to Española.[26] Touched by the humanistic sermons preached by the dominican Pedro de Córdoba to Indian churchgoers every Sunday, Las Casas interpreted the sermons into the Indians' language. In 1512 he entered the priesthood, becoming the first priest ordained in America.

Shortly afterwards, Las Casas went to Cuba, serving as chaplain for the Spanish conquest. This time, he tried to persuade the Indians to submit peacefully. Around 1513 at Caonao, he appealed to the Spanish soldiers to restrain themselves; but they paid him no heed, and Las Casas had to witness the resulting massacre of the Indians.[27] Once again, he received an *encomienda* in the wake of the conquest, employing some of his new Indian laborers as miners. Again he concentrated on making profits, preaching only occasionally.

As Easter 1514 approached and there was only one other priest in his region, Las Casas decided to leave his estate to hold mass and preach. "...He began, I say, to consider the misery and servitude that those [Indians] suffered. He drew on what he had heard and seen on the island of Española, where the priests of Santo Domingo were preaching that one could not, in good conscience, own Indians, and that they did not want to take confession from or absolve those [Spaniards] who owned Indians... He became convinced of the same truth, that the treatment of the Indians of the [west] Indies was unjust and tyrannical. Finally, he determined to preach this truth; and, as he himself owned Indians, he presently had the reproach of his sermons at hand. So he resolved, in order freely to condemn the *encomiendas* as unjust and tyrannical, to give up his Indians and place them in the hands of governor Diego Velázquez..."[28] This is from Las Casas' later account of his own life.

Las Casas' passionate sermons denouncing exploitation of the Indians shocked congregations of *conquistadores*. But he could not convince them to change their ways. Within a few years, only a tenth of the native population of Cuba remained alive, and they continued to labor under the *encomienda* yoke. Las Casas decided to return to Spain to inform the king. He was accompanied on his voyage by two dominican priests, including Antonio de Montesinos, who had been the first to preach for freedom for the Indians.[29]

Upon arrival in Spain, Las Casas began his career of shaking up the religious and royal establishment with his fervent exposure and denunciation of the colonists' abuses of the Indians. By his audacity, energy, and force of will, he gained audiences in the upper circles of

The German franciscans win one for the virgin Mary, 1509: The franciscans were pushing the still controversial theory of immaculate conception, which holds that the virgin Mary was herself uniquely free from original sin. The dominicans, a rival catholic order, opposed this notion as heresy. In Heidelberg, the franciscans, rallying the masses to their side, accused the dominicans of signing a pact with the devil, tortured them into confessing, and had them burned. (from Rossell Robbins, The Encyclopedia of Witchcraft & Demonology, *Crown Publishers, 1959). Around the same time in Spanish America, franciscans and dominicans pursued more worldly disputes over the status and rights of American Indians.*

the Spanish church and state that no simple priest could have the right to expect. In 1516, cardinal Jiménez, nearing death, sent a commission to the west Indies to investigate and correct abuses; he appointed Las Casas special adviser to the commission, with the title, "protector of the Indians."

The commission was not long at its work in Santo Domingo before Las Casas realized that his fellow commissioners had no intention to help the Indians. His own efforts provoked hostility among Española's wealthy colonists, bringing his life into danger. His only supporters were the dominican priests, in whose convent he sought refuge from the threat of physical attack. In 1517, he returned again to Spain.[30]

This time, Las Casas put forth a grand scheme to liberate the Indians without overturning the colonial system, and campaigned for it before the royal court. In the west Indies, some *encomienda* owners had responded to Las Casas' preaching by saying they would need twelve African laborers as compensation for freeing all their Indian laborers. Las Casas now proposed to the court, along with the abolition of Indian slavery, the right of each Spanish colonist to import twelve African slaves. Soon he repented this error and struggled fiercely to correct it, extending his freedom campaign to include Africans. But the monarchy liked the idea of African slavery, which it had introduced in America as early as 1501, and seized on Las Casas' original proposal to further the slave traffic to America.[31]

To abolish the *encomienda* system, Las Casas proposed that he administer a defined area of land in Española, where men of war would never be allowed to enter; he would admit only those Spaniards who came to promote agriculture, commerce, and evangelization of the natives. After a long campaign, Las Casas got the king to approve his plan, with some modifications, in May 1520. Then he returned to Española to implement it.

Again, Las Casas' utopian scheme chafed against the entrenched interests of the *encomienda* owners (*encomenderos*), who were not about to give up their command over the Indian labor that had made them rich. They soon disrupted his attempts to set up the free and peaceful christian community. Frustrated and saddened, Las Casas again took refuge in the dominican convent, where in 1523 he joined the dominican order. He spent some eight years in study, serving as a prior of the convent.

On one occasion, Las Casas learned that a parish priest was giving the last sacraments to a gravely ill Spaniard who held many Indians on his *encomiendas*. He collared the priest in an adjoining room, and warned the dying man that he would be condemned to hell if he did not set his Indians free. The man consented, and Las Casas let the final sacraments proceed.[32]

Sympathizing with the enslaved Indians of Peru in the wake of Pizarro's destruction of Inca civilization in the 1530's, Las Casas travelled secretly back to Spain, again pressing the king to declare complete freedom for the Indians. He got the king to approve his declaration of freedom and landownership rights for the Indians within the Spanish empire, as part of the Laws of the Indies. Las Casas returned at once to America, where he ranged from Española to Mexico to Peru, in his efforts to humanize the Spanish empire.

In Española, Las Casas had to subdue the native rebel leader Enriquillo. Baptized and educated by the dominicans, Enriquillo had turned against Spanish rule in 1520. Rallying the Indian masses to insurrection, Enriquillo became a popular hero, and his forces won a series of stunning victories against the Spanish soldiers.[33]

Las Casas put his method of peaceful persuasion to the test. He got the king to send Enriquillo a personal letter, guaranteeing freedom for him and his comrades, including full rights to the lands they held. Las Casas thus persuaded Enriquillo to end his insurrection, bringing him by the hand to the local colonial government for a peace treaty. Ironically, he proved far more able to persuade Indian fighters to lay down their arms, than to persuade his own countrymen to stop fighting to enslave the Indians.

In 1536, Las Casas petitioned pope Paul 3 repeatedly to intervene on behalf of the American Indians in the catholic theological debate raging over them. Las Casas, and his fellow partisans of Indian rights among the clergy, insisted that Indians were rational beings with human souls; their opponents, providing theological cover for the *conquistadores* and *encomenderos*, denied the Indians both reason and soul. The pope, shrewdly opting to spread his church among the American Indians, sided with Las Casas: In June 1537, he issued a bull rebuking those who justified the enslavement of Indians by insisting they lacked reason. Declaring that the Indians had reason and souls and were thus equal to other men, pope Paul upheld the Indians' right to receive the catholic faith and instruction.[34]*

*Pope John Paul 2, in his 14 September 1987 sermon before Native American catholics in Phoenix, Arizona, noted that "Already in 1537, my predecessor pope Paul 3 proclaimed the dignity and rights of the native peoples of the Americas by insisting that they not be deprived of their freedom or the possession of their property."[35] John Paul neglected to mention Las Casas, whose persistent efforts persuaded Paul 3 to issue his enlightened bull.

Back in Spain, Las Casas campaigned for stronger legal protection for the Indians. His moral pressure led to the New Laws of the Indies, issued by the monarchy in 1542. These laws ordered the release of Indian slaves to whom legal title could not be proved, and barred compulsory personal service. They did not abolish the *encomienda* system, as Las Casas was demanding. Rather, they declared that the *encomienda* was not a hereditary grant: After one generation, the owner had to free his Indians. To help enforce the new laws, Las Casas was named bishop of Chiapas (today in southern Mexico). His first act of enforcement came in his home city of Sevilla, Spain, as he freed several Indians brought there as slaves. In July 1544, at the age of 70, he set sail for America, along with 44 fellow dominicans.

They arrived in Santo Domingo in September. The publication of the new laws created a furor among the *encomenderos*, who vented their rage against Las Casas and the dominicans in general. The *conquistadores* of Peru launched a military revolt against the crown. The dominicans now found allies among the franciscan priests, many of whom had previously supported the *conquistadores* against the Indians.[36]

Upon his arrival in Chiapas in early 1545, Las Casas issued strict regulations to priests receiving confessions from Spaniards: No absolution could be given to those who held Indians in *encomienda*. During the Lent season, when all practicing catholics traditionally came to church for confession, the *encomenderos* with their dependents and partisans now bitterly resisted condemnation by their priests. Many priests, not so willing as Las Casas to antagonize their Spanish flock for the sake of Indian freedom, refused to follow his regulations. Las Casas set up a council of bishops to support his campaign. The *encomenderos* sent envoys to the king, demanding that the new laws be struck down. By the end of 1545 the king gave ground, recognizing the right of an *encomendero* to pass his estate on to an heir. The legal ground was cut out from under Las Casas. He returned to Spain in 1547, this time for good. He had crossed the Atlantic 14 times.

Was Las Casas' campaign on behalf of the Indians now over? By no means. He continued to shower the monarchy with petitions for Indian rights. While having long since renounced luxury and adopted a humble lifestyle, he wielded influence at the royal court and at the Council of the Indies. He took on the Aristotelian scholar Juan Ginés de Sepúlveda in a grand philosophical debate over the nature of the American Indians. Sepúlveda had gained prestige at the royal court by publishing an apology for the conquest of the Indians, asserting that the Indians "are inferior to the Spaniards just as children are to adults, women to men, and indeed, I might even say, as apes are to men."[37] Las Casas confronted him at the council of Valladolid in 1550, with famous theologians presiding. The king agreed to suspend further conquests of American Indian peoples, pending the outcome of the debate.

In his arduous written and oral reply to Sepúlveda, Las Casas praised the human capacities of the American Indians he had known. The Indians, he asserted, were "very talented in learning, and quite ready to accept the christian religion."

> Furthermore, they are so skilled in every mechanical art that with every right they should be set ahead of all the nations of the known world on this score, so very beautiful... are the things these people produce in the grace of their architecture, their painting, and their needlework. But Sepúlveda despises these mechanical arts, as if these things do not reflect inventiveness, ingenuity, industry, and reason itself.
>
> ...In the liberal arts which they have been taught up to now, such as grammar and logic, they are remarkably adept. With every kind of music they charm the ears of the audience with wonderful sweetness. They write skillfully and quite elegantly... [These are things] I have seen with my eyes, felt with my hands, and heard with my own ears while living a great many years among those peoples.[38]

Sepúlveda had never been to America, and his arrogant scorn lent a bitter edge to Las Casas' defense of the Indians' cultures. "They [the Indians] are not ignorant, inhuman, or bestial," Las Casas continued in his formal contribution to the debate, written in Latin. "Rather, long before they had heard the word Spaniard, they had properly organized states, wisely ordered by excellent laws, religion, and custom..."[39]

Perhaps the most remarkable aspect of Las Casas' arguments was his plea for religious pluralism and tolerance—not only towards Indians, but also towards Jews and Muslims—at a time when the inquisition was raging in Spain. Sepúlveda argued that the practice of human sacrifice among American Indian peoples justified religious war to conquer them. Las Casas objected: "Between two evils, one must always choose the lesser, and the sacrifice of a few innocents by the Indians will always be a lesser evil than the destruction of whole kingdoms and cities."[40] The Indians, he insisted, "are not obliged to abandon the religion of their forefathers until they come to know another which they find better..."[41] Las Casas summed up his case:

"The Indians are our brothers, and Christ has given his life for them. Why, then, do we persecute them with such inhuman savagery...?"[42]

Las Casas carried the day, and the debate had a big influence, especially in church policy. Yet the nagging gulf between enlightened formal policy and exploitative practice continued, under the pressures of colonial empire.

Now Las Casas plunged into the task of condensing his life's work in writing. In 1552, he published a pamphlet titled, *Brevísima relación de la destrucción de las Indias*, his "Most Brief Account of the Destruction of the Indies." It was a scathing exposé of the cruel deeds of the *conquistadores*, and an indictment of the entire Spanish colonial policy in America. "The reason why the christians have killed and destroyed such an infinite number of souls," he wrote, "is that they have been moved by their wish for gold and their desire to enrich themselves in a very short time."[43] The *Brevísima relación* was soon translated and widely circulated in French, English, and several other European languages.

In 1562, Las Casas published the final draft of his preface to the *Historia de las Indias*, his major written work. Three years earlier, he had left written instructions that the book itself should be published only "after 40 years have passed, so that, if God determines to destroy Spain, it may be seen that it is because of the destruction that we have wrought in the Indies..."[44] As it turned out, the Spanish state survived, and the *Historia de las Indias* was not published for over 300 years. At the age of 90, Las Casas completed two more works on the Spanish conquest in America. Two years later, he died in a dominican convent in Madrid.

Las Casas has been much maligned for providing propaganda ammunition to the imperial rivals of Spain. His detailed and uncompromising exposé of Spanish atrocities against the Indians gave rise to the "black legend," in which Spanish catholics were depicted as especially cruel, greedy, and bloodthirsty. French, English, and Dutch propagandists had a field day with Las Casas' material, which they cited lavishly in their polemics against the Spanish empire. In my opinion, Las Casas is not to be blamed for this undesired outcome. The tragedy is that there were no equally dedicated partisans of the Indians among French, British, or Dutch missionaries or colonists, to expose the equally cruel assaults committed against the American Indians by their own countrymen.

King Carlos 1's halfbaked use of Las Casas' plans to protect the Indians flowed from contradictions peculiar to Spain's American empire. Not the royal army, but freebooting Spanish warriors had established Spanish power in Middle and South America, laying their hands on fabulous riches. The monarchy needed to get and keep the gold, silver, and other products of Indian labor flowing into its own coffers. It could not allow the *conquistadores* to entrench themselves as an independent power in America. The king decided to use the Indian rights question to undercut their legal and moral position. King Carlos 1 was also holy Roman emperor Charles 5, and his declaration of the Laws of the Indies provided a gloss of christian compassion.

If Carlos truly abolished Indian slavery, the whole source of his dynasty's wealth and power would be disrupted. And if he pushed the *encomenderos* too hard by enforcing his enlightened laws in America, he would soon have a colonists' revolt on his hands, and probably a civil war within Spain as well. So the king's policy involved a clever balancing act between colonial exploitation and Indian rights—with Indian rights always existing far more on paper than in reality.

A cynical view sees Bartolomé de las Casas as a hapless pawn in this royal balancing act. A more optimistic view sees Las Casas' passionate appeals for human rights for the indigenous peoples outliving the decrepit dynasty of the catholic kings.

Bernardino de Sahagún (1499-1590), born in León, Spain, became a priest of the franciscan order. Trained for evangelizing work in America, he arrived in Mexico in 1529, eight years after the conquest.

Suppression of the native peoples' languages, and forced assimilation of Spanish and Latin, were official crown policy. Sahagún rejected this approach. He learned Nahuatl, the Aztec language, thoroughly, and took a keen interest in the Indians' culture. He saw that the rapid conversion of masses of Indians to christianity was superficial, as the Indians' own religious beliefs persisted strongly. "... The native culture was estimable," in Sahagún's view, "and in certain aspects superior to that being imposed upon the natives; it was necessary to study and to know this culture thoroughly, not only in order to combat the pagan beliefs successfully, but also in order to be able to preserve it and to integrate it in the common heritage he foresaw would be the national culture of Mexico."[45] He was incensed at the wholesale destruction of Aztec and Mayan hieroglyphic books by the *conquistadores* and religious authorities, who denounced the Aztecs' and Mayas' literary creation as the work of the devil.

Sahagún spent practically his entire adult life gathering information on the culture, religion, and history of the Aztecs and neighboring peoples, and setting it to writing in Nahuatl. He prepared a detailed questionnaire about the peoples' customs and beliefs, and presented it to older Indians well educated and versed in their people's traditions. They wrote out their answers in hieroglyphics, which Sahagún then translated into Nahuatl, which had been given a Latin alphabet. He also spoke tirelessly with his Indian informants in their own language, taking notes on their conversations in Nahuatl. He used these notes to check the accuracy and consistency of the written responses he had derived through the hieroglyphic format.

Sahagún helped found the college of Santa Cruz at Tlaltelolco, twin city of the Aztec capital of Tenochtitlán, to educate and evangelize the sons of Indian chiefs and nobles. There he placed Nahuatl on a par with Spanish and Latin, as a language of general study. As teaching tools, he produced several works of sermons and psalms in Nahuatl translation, a Nahuatl grammar text, and a "Trilingual Vocabulary" of Nahuatl, Spanish, and Latin. In 1545, Sahagún placed most of the teaching and administration of the college in the hands of its native graduates.

With the Laws of the Indies now directing missionaries to teach Indian converts in their native languages, Sahagún pushed ahead with his anthropological labors. The literary fruit of his half century of work was the *General History of the Affairs of New Spain (Mexico)*, 12 volumes of manuscript written in Nahuatl and illustrated by Indian scribes.

Sahagún's work invoked the wrath of many royal and church officials, who opposed the perpetuation of "pagan"* beliefs and felt he was building an obstacle in the path of complete christian conversion of the natives. The catholic inquisition arrived in the Yucatán peninsula in the 1560's, and proceeded to investigate apostasy among Mayas who had outwardly converted to christianity. Finding that the Mayas had retained many of their old beliefs, the inquisitors burned all the hieroglyphic books they could lay their hands on. They dug up and burned the skeletons of dead Mayas deemed "false christians" who could not remain buried in consecrated ground. And they imprisoned,

---

*The word "pagan," from the Latin *pagus*, means "peasant" or "country-dweller." It is ironic that Spanish catholics considered the Aztec religion pagan, since the Aztecs were probably a more urbanized people than the Spaniards and other Europeans: The population of the city of Tenochtitlán prior to its conquest was estimated at 300,000—whereas the population of London in the early 1500's was about 120,000.

tortured, and burned at the stake living Mayas denounced as apostates. After the terror subsided, Mayan intellectuals, having learnt the Spanish alphabet, rewrote their holy books, adding a chronicle of the Spanish conquest and a passionate critique of Spanish rule.

The inquisition also turned its attention to the Aztecs. In their campaign to destroy the remnants of the old Aztec religion, the inquisitors attacked the efforts of Aztec intellectuals to preserve Nahuatl as a written language, either in its hieroglyphic or latinized alphabetic form. Sahagún's work verged on apostasy, in the eyes of the inquisition. His papers were seized in 1571, but he continued his work. In 1578, as he was nearing the age of 80, a royal decree confiscated all his texts and documents.

The final years must have been bitter for Sahagún. His desire to redeem all the Indian souls for christianity while respecting their rich and diverse cultures, had sustained him during his decades of patient and systematic work. Now he came round to feeling that his life's work had been in vain, and that the christians should have left the Indians alone.[46] Bidding farewell "to his children, the Indians," Bernardino de Sahagún died in Mexico in 1590.[47] His *General History of the Affairs of New Spain* was not published until nearly 300 years later. He has since earned a reputation as the first American ethnologist, and a precursor of modern cultural anthropology.

Miguel Hidalgo y Costilla (1753-1811) was born in Guanajuato, northwest from Mexico City. Educated at a catholic academy, he graduated from the University of Mexico in 1773. He was ordained as a priest in 1778, and taught philosophy and theology until 1782.

In 1784, Hidalgo presented his "Dissertation on the True Method of Studying Scholastic Theology." In it, he criticized the sterile convolutions of a self-enclosed theology ensconced in the church's institutional authority. Instead, he proposed a "positive" and "historical" approach to theology, referring directly to the bible and tradition. Hidalgo showed that any correct historical analysis required a concrete sequence of events, geographical setting, and a critical approach to texts, ideas and interpretations.[48]

Hidalgo's dissertation, bold and fresh in its substance, was cloaked in catholic orthodoxy: He carefully supported his thesis on the work of enlightened theologians who had preceded him, and framed his historical method in terms of understanding god and his relation to mankind. The young scholar won the prize of 12 silver medals offered by the dean of the cathedral of Valladolid for the best thesis on the study of theology.[49] He seemed to have a splendid church career before him.

But Hidalgo was not the churchy type. He avidly read Diderot and the French encyclopedists, cultivating a broad field of learning and free thinking under his priest's garb. He hated the Spanish colonial regime, which tried to repress every form of creative thought and enterprise. He resented the Spanish-born ruling caste in Mexico, which not only oppressed the Indian and *mestizo* (mixed race) majority, but also stifled the white, Mexican-born *criollos*.

Hidalgo was accused of heresy for his radical intellectual leanings, and of immorality for his apparent refusal to submit to priestly celibacy (he is said to have fathered several children). He was banished from Valladolid to distant parishes. Denounced as a partisan of the enlightenment, he was tried by the inquisition in 1800, but received no sentence. In 1808 he was transferred to the parish of Dolores, not far from his home town of Guanajuato.

The misery of the poor Indian peasants in this dry region impressed Hidalgo deeply. Hidalgo's own salary was barely enough to support him and his dependent sisters and cousins. Yet, along with his spiritual ministry, he tried to enrich the material and cultural life of his parishioners. He organized an orchestra, and helped the peasants expand their cultivation of grapes, olives, and mulberry trees for raising silkworms. He set up small industries to cultivate honeybees, tan hides for leather, bake bricks, and manufacture earthenware. This got him into trouble with the law, which continued suppressing Mexican industry to the benefit of Spain. Hidalgo had to watch while constables came to chop down his parishioners' trees and uproot their vines.[50]

The middle and upper classes of Mexican society, the *criollos*, were now in political ferment. Napoleon had just conquered Spain, installing his brother on the throne. The Spanish colonial regime in Mexico was in disarray, as the people of Spain began their tough and bloody struggle to oust the French army. The Mexican *criollos* sensed that their hour had come to seize power. They formed into secret societies to plan a course of revolutionary action. The conspiracy came to involve thousands of people, making compact organization and real secrecy a problem. The leading conspirators were betrayed to the authorities in late 1809, so their first plan to launch the revolution was blocked.

Hidalgo eagerly joined in the conspiracy. He discussed goals and plotted tactics with two young army officers prominent in the conspiracy, Ignacio José Allende and Juan de Aldama. Allende wanted a swift and surgical coup, based on *criollo* elements in the army. Hidalgo argued that the revolution must depend on the people, not the army.

Allende planned to start his coup in December 1810. But again, the conspiracy was betrayed, and its leaders faced imminent arrest and execution. At 2 o'clock in the morning of 16 September 1810, Aldama rushed to Hidalgo's house in Dolores, woke him and his visitor Allende, and proposed that they go into hiding. According to one account, Hidalgo, as he was dressing, interrupted Aldama's entreaty: "Gentlemen, we are lost, there is no alternative but to go and seize *gachupines.*"[51] *Gachupines* was their scornful term for the Spaniards living in, and ruling Mexico. Hidalgo was 57 years old, Allende 31.

Summoning his brother Mariano and a dozen armed men along with Allende and Aldama, Hidalgo seized the local jail, forcing the warden to free his political prisoners. His revolutionary band thus swelled to 80 men, and they filled the jails with Spaniards they arrested. As dawn broke that Sunday morning, the bells of Hidalgo's church rang to gather the people from the countryside.

Hidalgo's sermon was a fiery call to mass insurrection. He denounced the *gachupines* for plotting to recognize Napoleon's rule over Spain and turn church and state over to the French. He called upon all patriotic Mexicans and loyal catholics to raise the banner of the beleaguered Spanish king Fernando 7 and drive the traitors out of America. Ironically, Hidalgo's famous "cry of Dolores" was not a cry for the independence of Mexico, nor did he rally the masses behind his enlightenment ideals. As soon as he called the people into the struggle, he seemed to get swept up in the tidal wave of their passions and prejudices—so that he found himself *following* the people as much as leading them.

The *criollo* revolutionary band now became a surging revolutionary army of Indian and *mestizo* peasants. They overran plantations, smashed property, and seized cattle, corn, and weapons. Liberated plantation workers—men, women, and children—joined the revolutionary army as it moved on to the next plantation or town. After taking the town of San Miguel, the rebel fighters broke down the doors of the rich and looted their homes. In choosing their targets to attack, they made no neat distinction between Spanish- and Mexican-born whites. After three centuries of slavery, cultural contempt and racial humiliation, the oppressed were taking their revenge.

Allende was furious over the rioting in his home town of San Miguel. Brandishing his sword, he tried to disperse the looters. Hidalgo urged him to be more patient with the rebels, arguing that some excesses were unavoidable. While Hidalgo did not condone looting, he stressed to Allende that this was the only revolutionary army in the field.[52]

As his army was on the move again through the countryside, Hidalgo stopped at the sanctuary of Atotomilco. There he brought out a small image of Our Lady of Guadalupe, the beautiful brown virgin Mary,* and raised it high on his lance. A great emotion swept through the ranks, as soldiers wept and knelt before the image. Hidalgo declared the virgin of Guadalupe as the banner of his army, and his soldiers fastened images of the virgin to their sombreros.[54] The Spanish king Fernando 7 was fading fast.

On 28 September, the rebel forces, now numbering about 50,000, entered the silver mining town of Guanajuato. The small Spanish army detachment, overwhelmed by their numbers and energy, decided to make a desperate stand from a grain storage tower, firing cannon volleys down upon the rebels. Through a stubborn frontal assault costing many of their lives, the rebels finally conquered the tower and killed all its remaining defenders. The victorious rebels rampaged through the town, wrecking and looting the shops and houses of the wealthy, burning taverns, and smashing the machinery of the mines. White townspeople were assaulted and massacred, despite the efforts of the white *criollo* revolutionary leaders to stop the rioters. Hidalgo was now appalled at the excesses committed by his soldiers in his town of birth.[55] Even so, he set up a cannon factory at Guanajuato, before moving on to Valladolid.[56]

The next day, 11 October, archbishop Lizana excommunicated the priest Hidalgo from the catholic church. On 19 October, Hidalgo published a decree abolishing slavery in Mexico, and assumed the title of *generalísimo* of the revolutionary army. With his forces in power in Valladolid, he set up a new government that tried to conciliate the *criollo* upper classes. Proclaiming his political goal of an elected

---

*According to legend, in 1531, an elderly Indian named Juan Diego saw the virgin Mary at Tepeyac, a hill northwest of Mexico City. Speaking in Nahuatl, she directed him to have the bishop build a church on the site. The first sanctuary to Our Lady of Guadalupe was built in 1533. The image and cult of the virgin of Guadalupe spread from Mexico to El Salvador, Puerto Rico, Spain, and the Philippines.[53] In Mexico, the brown Madonna was often worshipped as a modified form of the native people's fertility goddesses.

For an insightful feminist critique of the cult of the virgin of Guadalupe, see Norma Alarcón, "Chicana's Feminist Literature: A Re-Vision through Malintzin...", *This Bridge Called My Back: Writings by Radical Women of Color*. New York: Kitchen Table Press, 1983, pp. 187-9.

Mexican congress that would govern in the name of Fernando 7, he offered high military and civil posts to several prominent *criollos*. But the *criollos*, terrified by the rioting in Guanajuato, refused to participate, and went over to the side of the Spanish viceroy.

Even if Hidalgo had been able to educate and discipline his forces in time to prevent their cruel excesses against the white population, there is no way he could have reconciled the interests of the insurgent masses with those of the *criollo* elite. The arming of the Indian and *mestizo* peasants and workers, and their crushing triumph over the plantation owners and colonial armed forces, meant the overthrow of the exploiting minority by the exploited majority. Hidalgo had to meet the social demands of the victorious people—and he did, abolishing all payment of tributes to landowners and restoring the Indians' rights to their communal lands. The lands and towns liberated by the Mexican people's army formed the embryo of the dictatorship of the proletariat —some 40 years before Karl Marx was to coin the term.

On 30 October 1810, the people's army, numbering over 80,000, routed the Spanish armed forces at Monte de las Cruces. Now the road to Mexico City lay clear, with no Spanish forces standing in the way. Allende wanted to march swiftly into the capital and take power. Hidalgo hesitated, for three fateful days.

Hidalgo feared that his soldiers would do to Mexico City what they had done to Guanajuato. He also feared that, once occupying the capital, they would be assaulted from the rear and massacred by the elite Spanish force rushing back from San Luis Potosí. His soldiers were tired and nearly out of ammunition. The rebel councils that had sprung up in the course of the people's war were divided over how to proceed. The three days of indecision sapped the morale of many people in the army: When Hidalgo finally gave new mobilization orders, about half of them had left and gone their own way.[57]

Meanwhile in Mexico City, as the white residents were gripped by fear of the coming rebel onslaught, the Spanish viceroy led a procession to the cathedral. There he invoked the Virgin of Remedios, a white-skinned, blue-eyed version of the virgin Mary.[58] If the struggle involved rich against poor on a social level, and European against Indian on a cultural level, it also involved the white virgin Mary against the brown virgin Mary on a symbolic level.

But Hidalgo did not march on the capital. He turned his army around and headed back north, toward Querétaro. On 7 November, they were surprised and routed by the Spanish force under Félix María Calleja. Hidalgo gathered all the forces he could salvage, and retreated to

Valladolid. Allende, furious over the defeat and upset with Hidalgo for not letting him exercise any military command, retreated to Guanajuato. When Hidalgo learned that Guadalajara had been liberated by local rebels, he moved there with a thousand soldiers, set up a revolutionary government, and sent an ambassador to the United States to negotiate its recognition.[59]

The counterrevolution, now gaining ground, punished the insurgent masses. In Alhóndiga, Calleja, in Roman imperial fashion, ordered the *decimation* of the Indian and *mestizo* population: Every tenth man of color was arbitrarily executed. Hidalgo's forces in Guadalajara retaliated by decimating the city's Spanish population.

With Calleja's force moving on Guadalajara, Allende proposed confronting him with only the best of the revolutionary soldiers, leaving the rest behind in the city to cover their retreat in the event of defeat. Hidalgo disagreed, and massed some 100,000 soldiers for the decisive battle. On 17 January 1811, the rebel army fought heroically, but were badly outmaneuvered by Calleja's compact and well disciplined forces. Calleja won the day, and the rebel army collapsed. Hidalgo, Allende, Aldama, and other leaders fled north, hoping to reach the U.S. and plan a new campaign. En route, they were betrayed to the Spanish forces and arrested.

At his trial, Hidalgo accepted full responsibility for what he had done. Whereas Allende asked for pardon, Hidalgo declared: "Pardon is for criminals, not for defenders of the country."[60] He did express deep remorse for the loss of life which the revolution had brought in its wake.

Feeling he had struggled to do god's will towards the humble and the downtrodden, Hidalgo still considered himself a loyal catholic. But he was finally convicted of heresy and officially defrocked. His religious superiors then turned him over to the royal authorities for execution. At dawn on 30 July 1811, Miguel Hidalgo y Costilla was shot by firing squad. His severed head, along with those of Allende and Aldama, was placed on display at the fateful grain storage tower in Guanajuato—until 1821, when Mexico gained its independence from Spain.

... *Who Never Made it to Beatification,*
far less Sainthood

And why not—especially since several fools and scoundrels *have* been elevated to sainthood by the Vatican? A parallel way of phrasing this question is: Why have the faces of Harriet Tubman, John Brown, and chief Joseph never been carved into the rock of Mount Rushmore?

How Catholicism Penetrated Mexico

By the mid-1700's, there were over 4,000 catholic friars at work in Spain's American colonies.[61] They were not uniformly successful at converting the native peoples to Roman catholicism. The peoples of Incasic Peru, e.g., tended ideologically to reject the Spanish conquest and the foreign culture imposed upon them. According to Inca cosmology, the conquest had plunged their carefully ordered world into chaos, absurdity and injustice—so that they've been living, ever since, in a world turned upside down, a world moving "in reverse." This world must be set right through the emergence of a new Inca (warrior king) to expel the foreign rulers.[62] As long as this messianic belief system held sway among the Peruvian masses, traditional catholic teaching, with its emphasis on submission to the (white) lord's will, could not penetrate very deeply. Moreover, many native peoples of Peru, and especially women, continued to worship their local goddesses and gods from before both the Inca and Spanish conquests.

In central Mexico, the missionaries seem to have been more successful in winning real mass acceptance of catholic dogma. This was due, in part, to some key aspects common to both the Aztec religion and Roman catholicism.

Aztec priests and monastery students, like the priests and novices of the more zealous catholic orders, imposed harsh discipline and punishment upon themselves. An Aztec priest in training had to rise in the middle of every night and hike to the mountains, where he offered incense to the gods and drew blood from his ears and legs with agave thorns. He had to fast frequently, and labor hard on the temple land.[63]

Aztec women could become priestesses by entering the temple during adolescence and taking a vow of celibacy. They were instructed, supervised, and guarded by old priestesses, and they did the domestic work of the temple, weaving clothing for the priests and idols.[64] From this system to the catholic sisterhoods of nuns, no great leap was required. On the other hand, Aztec women could also become magicians, and those who continued to practice their magical arts after the conquest no doubt risked collision with the inquisition.

The Aztecs used to confess, through a priest, to Tlazolteotl, the goddess of carnal love and of sin. But unlike the catholic practice, Aztec confession took place only once in a person's lifetime—usually in old age.[65] While Aztec religion had no notion of original sin, its stress on personal predestination meshed with catholic fatalism. The Aztecs also divided their afterworlds into the realms of a blissful heaven (Tlalocan)

Death Cart, a New Mexican adaptation of Jesus' journey to Calvary. Cottonwood and pine sculpture by Nasario López, around 1860.

Taylor Museum of the Colorado Springs Fine Arts Center. Gift of Alice Bemis Taylor.

and a murky underworld (Mictlan)—although the latter held little of the terror, and none of the torture of the catholic hell.

The sacrament of the Eucharist, so crucial to catholic worship, must have held a psychological attraction for devout Aztecs. In the eucharist ritual, the holy wafer and wine symbolize the flesh and blood of Jesus, and the worshipper who partakes of them becomes one with christ.* In certain Aztec rituals, the faithful actually ate the flesh of a sacrifice victim, who was viewed as the incarnation of a particular god; far from insulting or degrading the sacrificed man, the Aztecs viewed themselves as *honoring* him by consuming his flesh, as they thus assimilated his godly qualities.[66]

The Aztec regime applied the death penalty against adultery and homosexuality, and also imposed death on women who induced abortions (unless done to save the pregnant woman's life). Divorce, while possible, was very difficult to obtain. On these questions of sexual policy, the Spanish catholic regime brought no big changes.

The Pueblo Indian Uprising of 1680

As the Spanish soldiers and missionaries with their christian Indian protégés pushed the frontier of New Spain north, they encountered communal Indian societies with no rigid social hierarchy, where women enjoyed social equality with men, and where sexual expression was relatively free.

The peoples living along the Rio Grande in what is now New Mexico were dubbed Pueblos for their compact villages surrounded by fields of corn, beans, squash, and cotton. The Spaniards conquered many of them in the early 1600's through vigorous colonial settlement, ruthless siege and attack, and mass enslavement. The Spanish governor, Juan de Oñate (later fined and stripped of his honors by a Spanish court for enslaving the Indians), was out for gold and silver. When none was found, he would have called off the whole project as unprofitable. But the missionaries, having baptized thousands of Pueblo Indians, insisted these new found souls could not be abandoned.[67]

The clash between Roman catholicism and the Pueblos' native belief systems was sharp, and the arrogance of the franciscan missionaries turned it violent. For the Indians, their ritual dances with elaborate masks and impersonation of the sacred spirits were bound up with the

*The gospel of John has Jesus saying: "Whoever eats my flesh, and drinks my blood, has eternal life; and I will raise him up at the last day. For my flesh is meat indeed, and my blood is drink indeed. He who eats my flesh, and drinks my blood, dwells in me, and I in him..." (John 6.54-6).

cycles of farming and human fertility, securing the wellbeing of the whole society. To the missionaries, the dances were devil worship, and had to be suppressed. Trying to break the moral power of the deeply respected shamans, they had some of them publicly whipped, at times to death. The Indians retaliated by murdering some missionaries. Finally the Spanish governor arrested 47 shamans, hanged three of them, and imprisoned the rest at Santa Fe.

One of these was Popé, an elder shaman from the Tewa pueblo. Released after several years, he went into hiding in Taos. Along with Domingo Naranjo, born of a Tlaxcalan* Indian mother and a mulatto father, Popé plotted revolt.

Joint action by all the Pueblo societies was very hard to attain, since their governing councils of elders tended to rule by unanimous decision, allowing a single dissenting voice to block a proposed action. But anti-Spanish feelings were running deep and wide, and the organizing skills of Popé and Naranjo bore fruit.

On 10 August 1680, the uprising began. Indian runners carried the attack orders from pueblo to pueblo on knotted strings. Nearly all the pueblos joined in, and the revolt spread west to embrace the Hopis, and perhaps some Navajos and Apaches as well. The insurgents killed franciscan friars in their missions, piling their corpses upon the altars. Spanish families in outlying plantations were killed off, and the colonial capital Santa Fe besieged. After several days, the Spanish residents broke out of Santa Fe and fled down the river, as the Indian rebels jeeringly chanted Latin liturgy they had learned from the friars. The Spaniards left some 400 dead, including 21 of the 33 missionaries.[69]

Rejoicing in their victory, the Indian rebels burned the property left behind by the Spaniards: churches, houses, pigs, sheep, and cattle. Popé ordered that nothing brought by the Spaniards and Mexicans must ever be used again, including even the plants they had introduced: wheat, onions, chilis, peaches and watermelons. But the Indian people, revering every flower and plant, refused to destroy the seeds they had learned to sow.[70]

Popé now became arrogant and abusive. Trying to usurp the power of the free river peoples, he demanded unconditional obedience and ordered the execution of dissenters. The region divided into pro- and

---

*Tlaxcala was an independent city-state bordering on the Aztec empire, whose leaders made a firm alliance with Cortés to destroy the Aztec state. Early converts to christianity, Tlaxcalan Indians often accompanied Spanish missionaries into the northern frontier regions, where they helped convert the "pagan" Indians.[68]

La Santísima Trinidad, *by an unknown artist of New Mexico, early 1800's. The holy trinity bears the unrelenting image of the Spanish friar. Though repeatedly banned by the catholic church, such realist renditions of the trinity persisted in isolated regions like New Mexico. For Junípero Serra and the franciscan friars, the holy trinity was, in effect, Jesus, Mary and Joseph: They began all their letters with the salutation, "Viva Jesús, María, Joseph!"*

anti-Popé factions, and battles broke out along these lines. Popé was removed from power, but the trauma of the internecine struggles caused many people to pack up and move north. In 1692, the Spaniards returned and reconquered the region through heavy fighting.

Englishmen against Spaniards, Yankees against Indians

In Florida, meanwhile, the Spanish catholic missionaries were trying to win Indian souls without subjecting the Indians' bodies to colonial exploitation. They set up a mission system, where no European colonists were allowed to settle. Their missions became a refuge for runaway slaves, whether Indian or African. Spanish law declared that any foreign slave became free upon reaching Florida.

The English slave-owners could not tolerate this situation, which threatened to disrupt their tobacco and cotton plantations in the southeastern colonies. English soldiers, along with Indian warriors they could goad into an alliance against fellow Indians, made slave raids against the Spanish missions. In 1704, some 50 English and 1,000 Creek Indian fighters overran the northeast Florida missions. They took over 6,000 mission Indians captive, and burned three franciscan friars at the stake. The English then enslaved some of the captured Indians, paying their Creek allies in the bargain. The franciscans had refused to allow the mission Indians to own and use firearms.[71]

The Europeans who first colonized along the east coast of North America, ill suited to farm the unfamiliar soil, were time and again saved from starvation by groups of Indians offering gifts of food and showing them how to cultivate corn, squash and pumpkins. Later the English colonial leaders, pursuing their petty and scattered economic interests in rivalry with the French, took direct inspiration from the powerful Iroquois confederation of five Indian nations: In 1754, they met in an intercolonial conference to work out a plan for colonial union.[72]

The English speaking colonists, as they grew more self confident and prepared to cast off the royal yoke of their mother country, showed no gratitude for the solidarity and guidance the Indians had given them. Part of the declaration of independence written and signed by the coalition of slave-owners and wealthy merchants on 4 July 1776, read: "He [king George] has excited domestic Insurrections amongst us, and has endeavoured to bring on the Inhabitants of our Frontiers, the merciless Indian Savages, whose known Rule of Warfare, is an undistinguished Destruction, of all Ages, Sexes and Conditions." The Founding Scoundrels neglected to mention the punitive massacres of

Powhatan Indian men, women and children by English colonists in Virginia in the 1620's; the night attack and massacre of 600 Pequot Indians in Connecticut by the English colonial army in 1637; the issuance of *scalp bounties* by several colonial governments in the 1700's, paying frontiersmen handsomely for every scalp of an Indian man, woman or child they turned in; and the widespread kidnapping and enslavement of Indians, especially their children—among the many other acts committed by merciless European savages against the aboriginal peoples.

1776 was also the year that the franciscan missionary Francisco Palóu, a lifelong spiritual companion of Junípero Serra, founded mission San Francisco de Asís, the sixth Spanish mission established along the coast of California. Which brings us to one of the central themes of this book.

Junípero Serra, statue in San Francisco's Golden Gate Park.

Chapter 1

Junípero Serra and the California Missions

Junípero Serra was born in the village of Petra on the Spanish island of Mallorca on 24 November 1713. A few hours after birth, he was baptized in the village church, and named Miquel Joseph Serra (Miguel José in Castilian Spanish). His parents, like their neighbors, were humble farmers and devout catholics. His mother Margarita had lost her first two children in their infancy. When the midwife brought her baby Miguel back from the church, Margarita kissed him, perhaps for the first time. Many Mallorcan mothers, by custom, refrained from kissing their babies until after baptism—since an unbaptized child was considered *un moret*, "a little Moor."[1]

By the age of seven, Miguel was working in the fields with his parents, helping cultivate wheat and beans, and tending the cattle. But he showed a special interest in visiting the local franciscan friary; the friars taught him reading, writing, religion, mathematics, and liturgical song. At the age of 15, his parents enrolled him in a franciscan school in the capital city, Palma de Mallorca, where he studied philosophy. At the age of 16, he became a novice in the franciscan order.

The slight and frail Miguel now entered his rigorous year of preparation to become a full member of the order: the novitiate. His daily routine at the convent was rigidly structured: prayers, meditation, choir singing, physical chores, spiritual readings, and instruction. He had to wake up every midnight for another round of chants. His superiors discouraged letters and visits.[2]

In his free time, Miguel avidly read the stories about franciscan friars roaming the provinces of Spain and around the world to win new souls for the church, often suffering martyrdom in the process. He followed the news of famous missionaries winning beatification and sainthood. He probably formed a slow burning desire, from this early age, to become a missionary, to win large numbers of pagan souls for god's kingdom in heaven, to risk martyrdom, and to merit the title of saint. But he would have to spend a long and scarcely eventful apprenticeship in Mallorca, before he got his chance.

Upon taking his vows as a full fledged franciscan, Miguel decided to change his name to Junípero, after a close companion of saint Francis of Assisi, founder of the franciscan order. The 17-year-old Junípero, along with his fellow novices, vowed to obey pope and god, to scorn property and comfort, and to be chaste. He still had seven years to go before he could be ordained as a priest. He immersed himself in rigorous studies of logic, metaphysics, cosmology, and theology. In 1737 he became a priest, and three years later was commissioned to teach philosophy at the convent. He then taught over 60 students a course in philosophy, which lasted three years.

At the end of the course in 1743, Serra told his students: "I desire nothing more from you than this, that when the news of my death shall have reached your ears, I ask you to say for the benefit of my soul: 'May he rest in peace.' Nor shall I omit to do the same for you so that all of us will attain the goal for which we have been created."[3] Among his students were Francisco Palóu and Juan Crespí, who were later to join him in founding and developing the California missions. Crespí was to die in Carmel 39 years later, with his companion Serra singing the final lullaby at the requiem mass the next morning. Two and a half years after that, Palóu was to arrive at Carmel to receive Serra's final confession, give him the last sacraments, and intone the final prayer at Serra's burial.

In 1748, Serra and Palóu confided to each other their secret desires to become missionaries. Serra, now 35, was assured a prestigious career as priest and scholar if he stayed in Mallorca; but he set his sights firmly on pagan lands. Applying to the colonial bureaucracy in Madrid, Serra requested that both he and Palóu embark on a foreign mission. After weathering some administrative obstacles, Serra and Palóu got permission, and set sail for Cádiz, a Spanish port of departure for America.

While waiting to set sail for America, Serra wrote a long letter to a colleague back in Mallorca, urging him to console Serra's parents—

now in their 70's—over their only son's pending departure. "They [my parents] will learn to see how sweet is His yoke," Serra wrote, "and that He will change for them the sorrow they may now experience into great happiness. Now is not the time to muse or fret over the happenings of life but rather to be conformed entirely to the will of God, striving to prepare themselves for that happy death which of all the things of life is our principal concern."[4] Just as the atheist philosopher Denis Diderot* and his team of scientists and humanist writers were struggling to rid France of catholic fatalism, compiling their bold encyclopedia whose ideas were to inspire the French revolution, Junípero Serra and his franciscan comrades voyaged to America to win pagan souls for the counter-reformationist church.

The Apostle Arrives in Mexico

After a brief stopover in Puerto Rico, during which Serra led his comrades into the streets to rouse the people in a fervent impromptu mission, the franciscan missionary team arrived in Mexico. Serra refused to ride by carriage from Veracruz into Mexico City, insisting on walking up the steep mountain trail through tropical forests into the capital. On the way, he suffered a leg infection, breaking out into sores which were to give him much pain in his future journeys.

In Mexico City, Serra and his companions entered the college of San Fernando, a specialized training center and regional headquarters for franciscan missionaries. Serra humbly asked to do his novitiate year again—despite his academic prestige, and the fact that the college's novices were far younger men. Though his request was declined, Serra insisted on living as a novice at San Fernando: "This learned university professor...would often eat more sparingly in order to replace the student whose turn it was to read to the community. Or he would humbly carry trays and wait on table with the lay brothers..."[5]

Besides the heavy routine of prayers, hymns and meditations, daily life at the secluded college included classes on the languages of Mexico's Indian peoples, mission administration, and theology. Before completing his required year of training, Serra volunteered for a mission in the rugged Sierra Gorda, to help replace friars who had recently died there. He was accepted, and fellow volunteer Francisco Palóu became Serra's assistant in his first mission.

*Diderot (1713-1784), coincidentally, was born seven weeks before Serra, and died four weeks before Serra.

His Mission in the Sierra Gorda

The Sierra Gorda mission was about 250 kilometers northeast of Mexico City, in a vast region of jagged mountains, home of the Pames Indians and a scattering of Spanish colonists. The Pames, culturally related to the Chichimecas, lived mainly through gathering and hunting, but also engaged in agriculture. Their social stratification, temples, idols and priests were the waning product of a civilization they had developed centuries earlier. Many groups among them, adopting mobile guerrilla tactics, had eluded conquest by the Spanish military.

Serra and Palóu, arriving at the village of Jalpan, found that the mission was in disarray: The parishioners, numbering less than 1,000, were attending neither confession nor holy communion.[6] The two missionaries set about learning the Pame language (related to Otomi) from a Mexican who had lived among the Pames. Once he had a working knowledge of the language, Serra translated the catechism and prayers into Pame, and began preaching to his Indian parishioners in their own language.

To fire the religious imagination of the Pames, Serra dramatized the ritual reenactment of Jesus' forced death march, involving the Pames in the drama. Erecting 14 stations, Serra led the procession himself, heaving a dreadfully heavy cross. At each station, the procession would pause for a prayer, and at the end Serra would sermonize on the sufferings and death of Jesus christ. During holy week, 12 elder Pames played the roles of the disciples; Serra, starring in the role of Jesus, humbly washed their feet and then dined with them.[7]

Serra also paid careful attention to the practical side of mission administration. Working with the college of San Fernando, he had cattle, goats, sheep, and farming tools brought into the mission. Palóu supervised the farm labor of the mission Indian men; the women were taught spinning, sewing and knitting. The products of their labor were collected and rationed to the mission population, according to personal needs. The christian Pames learned how to sell their surplus products in nearby trading centers, under the friars' supervision to protect them from cheating. Pames who adapted successfully to their new way of life received their own parcels of land to raise corn, beans and pumpkins, and in some cases received oxen and seeds as well.[8]

Within two years, Serra had made inroads against the Pames' traditional belief system. On his 1752 visit from the Sierra Gorda mission to the college of San Fernando in the capital, Serra joyfully carried a goddess statue presented to him by christian Pames. The statue, showing the face of Cachum, mother of the sun, had been erected on a hilltop shrine where some Pame chiefs lay buried. The Pames had prayed to Cachum for rain, good harvests, health, victory in battles, and desirable wives. Now Serra presented her statue to his colleagues in Mexico City, as a "trophy" of his success in evangelizing the pagans.[9]

Back in the Sierra Gorda, Serra cut his teeth on a conflict between Spanish soldiers, settlers, and mission Indians. Not only franciscan missionaries, but also Spanish/Mexican soldiers and their families had been sent into the Sierra Gorda to follow up a Spanish military victory over the Pames in 1743. The soldiers were supposed to pursue runaway mission Indians, and secure the region for the Spanish crown. But the soldiers' land claims clashed with the mission lands that the christian Pames were working.

Some of the soldiers' families tried to establish a town, and the officer in charge of their deployment approved their plan. The Pames objected, threatening to defend their lands by force if necessary. The soldier/settlers, letting their cattle graze on the Pames' farmlands, started bullying the Pames, taking advantage of their labor. Serra and the college of San Fernando sided with the Pames—citing the Law of the Indies, which banned colonial settlements in mission territories.

The viceroy, Spain's highest official in Mexico, suspended the colony. But the townspeople protested and stayed put. The government set up commissions and looked into alternative sites for the town. It ordered the settlers to keep their cattle out of the Pames' fields, and to pay the Pames fairly for their labor (with the friars supervising the payment to prevent cheating). After a protracted legal struggle, the settlers moved out, and in 1755 the Pames and friars reclaimed their land.[10]

Serra's Work for the Inquisition

During his 1752 visit to Mexico City, Serra followed up his delivery of the Pame goddess statue by sending a request from the college of San Fernando to the headquarters of the inquisition. He asked that an inquisitor be appointed to preside over the Sierra Gorda. The very next day, the inquisition appointed Serra himself as inquisitor for the whole region—adding that he could exercise his powers anywhere he happened to be doing missionary work in New Spain, as long as there was no regular inquisition official in the region.[11] On 1 September 1752, Serra filed a report to the inquisition in Mexico City from Jalpan, on "evidences of witchcraft in the Sierra Gorda missions." He stated:

> ... I am in possession of several grave indications that in the district of this mission of mine and its neighborhood there are several persons

of the class known as *gente de razón*,* i.e., they are not Indians, who are addicted to the most detestable and horrible crimes of sorcery, witchcraft and devil worship and who are in league with them [the devils] and others, the inquiry into which appertains to your Venerable Holy Tribunal of the Inquisition. And if it is necessary to specify one of the persons guilty of such crimes, I accuse by name a certain Melchora de los Reyes Acosta, a married mulattress, an inhabitant of the said mission... In these last days a certain Cayetana, a very clever Mexican woman of the said mission, married to one Pérez, a mulatto, has confessed—she, being observed and accused of similar crimes, having been held under arrest by us for some days past—that in the mission there is a large congregation of the said *personas de razón*, who thus are not Indians, although some Indians also join them, and that these persons, not Indians, flying through the air at night are in the habit of meeting in a cave on a hill near a ranch called El Saucillo, in the center of the said missions, where they worship and make sacrifice to the demons who appear visibly there in the guise of young goats and various other things of that nature.

Because of these and various other indications that there are various persons of the class already indicated... engaged in such dreadful crimes, and above all having regard to the fact that if such evil is not attacked the horrible corruption will spread among these poor [Indian] neophytes who are in our charge:
...I notify, denounce and give notice to this tribunal of the faith...so that it may make its decision and give such orders as may seem fitting to it, certifying that the sole object and motive of this notification and denunciation of mine is the desire that offenses against the Divine Majesty be avoided..."[12]

Did Cayetana confess to her fantastic crime under torture (as was standard procedure for the inquisition)? What was her fate, and the fate of Melchora de los Reyes, once Serra had denounced them?

According to modern franciscan historians, this report by Serra to the inquisition is his only surviving letter during his eight years of mission work in the Sierra Gorda.[13] Serra's first biographer, Francisco Palóu, wrote that Serra, in his role of inquisitor, had to work in many parts

---

Gente de razón ("people of reason") referred to christian, Spanish speaking residents of the area surrounding a mission—usually of the lower classes, and usually people of color. Non-christian Indians were called *gentiles*, while mission Indians were called neophytes. Spaniards like the franciscan missionaries did not refer to themselves as *gente de razón*, but rather as Spaniards.

of Mexico and travel long distances. Yet curiously enough, the national archives in Mexico City (Archivo General de la Nación), with over a thousand volumes of indexed documents on the inquisition, apparently contain only two references to Serra's work for the inquisition following his 1752 appointment: his preaching in Oaxaca in 1764, and his partial handling of the case of a Sierra Gorda mulatto accused of sorcery in 1766.[14]

A crowning achievement of Serra's mission in the Sierra Gorda was the construction of a splendid church in Jalpan. Calling on masons, carpenters, and other skilled craftsmen from Mexico City, Serra employed the christian Pames in seasonal construction work over the course of seven years, to complete the church. Serra himself gave the Indian laborers a hand, carrying wooden beams and applying mortar between the stones forming the church walls.[15] In 1758, he returned to the college of San Fernando in Mexico City. Over the next nine years, he worked in the college's administrative offices, and as a missionary and inquisitor in the dioceses of Mexico, Puebla, Oaxaca, Valladolid, and Guadalajara. In his missionary wanderings, Serra often kept travelling on foot, despite painful leg and foot sores.

His Masochism

In imitation of saint Francisco Solano (1549-1610), a Spanish franciscan who did 20 years of missionary work in Peru and Argentina, Serra made a habit of punishing himself physically, to purify his spirit. His nightly self-flagellations at the college of San Fernando caught the ears of some of his fellow friars. They also found that Serra wore his daily punishment close to the skin: He would wear a sackcloth spiked with bristles, or a coat interwoven with broken pieces of wire, under his gray friar's outer garment.[16]

In his austere cell, Serra kept a chain of sharp pointed iron links hanging on the wall beside his bed, to whip himself when sinful thoughts (including, presumably, any sexual impulses) ran through his mind in the night. In his letters to his franciscan companions, Serra often referred to himself as a "sinner" and a "most unworthy priest"—despite the fact that his actual behavior was always, by traditional catholic standards, exemplary. Here we see the fruits of Serra's rigorous training in metaphysics at the convent in Palma de Mallorca: The mere *feeling* of "sinful" urges or *thinking* "sinful" thoughts made him a sinner, worthy of physical punishment—just as Cayetana's (apparent) *subjective sensation* that she and her friends flew through the air at night to attend a witches' coven, meant that the witches' night flights actually took place, so that Cayetana had to be turned over to the inquisition for punishment.

In Mexico, Serra was not shy about taking his masochistic show on the road. In one of his sermons in Mexico City, while exhorting his listeners to repent their sins, Serra took out his chain, bared his shoulders, and started whipping himself. So harsh was his self punishment that the people began sobbing. Finally, a man climbed up to the pulpit, took the chain from Serra's hand, and began whipping *him*self, declaring: "I am the sinner who is ungrateful to god who ought to do penance for my many sins, and not the padre [Serra], who is a saint." The man kept whipping himself until he collapsed. After receiving the last sacraments, he later died from the ordeal.[17]

In the course of other sermons on the theme of repentance, Serra would hoist a large stone in one hand and, while clutching a crucifix in the other, strike the stone against his chest with great force. Many of his listeners feared that he would strike himself dead. Later, Serra suffered chest pains and shortness of breath; Palóu suggests that Serra's self inflicted bruises were the cause.[18] Another preaching technique Serra used, to symbolize hell and damnation, was to sear his flesh with a four-pronged candle flame. Palóu described this as "quite violent, painful, and dangerous towards wounding his chest."[19]

To be sure, Serra was not alone in making self punishment a centerpiece of his sermonizing. The more zealous franciscan and jesuit missionaries did likewise. But few took it to the awful extremes that Serra did. The regulations of the college of San Fernando said that self punishment should never be carried to the point of physically incapacitating oneself.[20] Serra was admonished by some of his colleagues for going too far.

King Carlos Expels the Jesuits

On 24 June 1767, the viceroy of New Spain (Mexico) read a Spanish royal decree to Mexico's archbishop and assembled church officials: King Carlos 3 ordered the seizure and deportation of all jesuit priests. The king gave his officials 24 hours to round up all the jesuits in Mexico and send them, as prisoners, to Veracruz for a forced voyage back to Europe. Within days the jesuits, offering no resistance to the king's soldiers, were removed from their 16 missions and 32 stations. No jesuit, no matter how old or ill, could be excepted from the king's decree. Many of the priests died along the rugged mountain trail to Veracruz. "The people of Mexico, rich and poor alike, thronged the paths, watching with tears and lamentations as the Jesuits made their way to embark on overladen ships. . ."[21]

In 1766, the Spanish and Portuguese governments had ordered the destruction of a thriving mission complex in Paraguay which the jesuits had built among the Guaraní Indians, as a refuge from slavery.* That same year, king Louis 15 had expelled the jesuit order from France, exhorting his fellow Bourbon Carlos 3 to do likewise in Spain. The jesuits had grown quite wealthy and influential in western Europe, even becoming confessors to kings and getting involved in royal court intrigues. The other catholic orders were jealous of them, and the jesuits' reputation for observing strict international discipline under their general in Rome, clashed with the rising sentiments of nationalism promoted by both monarchists and democrats.

In Spain, king Carlos 3 used popular resistance to his regime as a handy pretext to get rid of the jesuits. After sharply increasing taxes on the people, Carlos issued an edict restricting the breadth of the sombreros the people could wear, to a specified diameter. This "sumptuary law" was supposed to prevent the people from wasting too much money, and from imitating the upper classes; Carlos wanted the people to spend their money on his wars and colonial expansion campaigns, not on themselves. Many people defied both the tax hike and the hat-trimming edict, going about in broad brimmed sombreros. When an angry crowd of these resisters converged on the royal palace, king Carlos took off for the countryside. His Flemish palace guard fired warning shots over the people's heads (and hats). A group of jesuit priests appeared on the scene, soothed the protesters with speeches, and sent them home. Carlos decided to rescind the tax hike and hat-trimming edict, and to fire his finance minister.[22]

Far from thanking the jesuits for saving the day for him, Carlos scapegoated them for supposedly orchestrating all the resistance from the start. He ordered his lightning arrest and expulsion of all the jesuits from Spain at the end of February 1767; in the following months, the jesuits in Spain's overseas empire were likewise rounded up and shipped, under horrendous conditions, to Italy. Pope Clement 13, shoved around by west Europe's catholic monarchs and ridiculed by the common people in Rome, asked Carlos, "By what authority? . . .", and threatened him with eternal damnation. But Carlos was not fazed, as the pope had no material means to enforce his protest.

---

*This historical conflict was dramatized in the 1985 film *The Mission*, directed by Roland Joffe.

The vacuum created by the jesuits' expulsion from Mexico was filled by the franciscan and dominican missionaries. Junípero Serra, Francisco Palóu, and their companions moved into the jesuit missions in Baja (lower) California. The jesuits had built up 13 missions on that long and arid peninsula over several decades, losing two of their friars at the hands of Indians in the revolt of 1734-6. The franciscans now found that the Indian population in the Baja California mission territories had dwindled to only about 7,150. When the franciscans moved north and turned the missions over to dominican friars three years later in 1770, the Indian population was down to about 5,000. "If it goes on at this rate," wrote Palóu, "in a short time Baja California will come to an end." Epidemics, especially syphilis introduced by Spanish troops, were wasting the Indians.[23] But Palóu attributed the ravages of syphilis to god's retribution for the Indians' murder of the two jesuit friars.[24]

Serra Leads the Franciscans into California

Now that the king of Spain had destroyed one of his best missionary teams (the jesuits), and the Spanish missions in Texas had been set back by Indian attacks, and the missionized Indians of Baja California were dying off, the time scarcely seemed ripe for a new round of territorial expansion and mission building. But José de Gálvez, the king's inspector general in Mexico, had a burning ambition to secure new lands and riches for Spain. Eying Alta (upper) California, Gálvez got the king's ear by spreading rumors about the British and Dutch rulers' supposed plans to add California to their own empires. Then, when a report arrived from the Spanish ambassador in Russia that the tsar was about to establish settlements down the California coast towards Monterey, Gálvez trumpeted the Russian threat for all it was worth. The king gave the go-ahead, and Gálvez outfitted an expedition of soldiers and missionaries to push north into California.

Gálvez chose Serra to head the missionary team in the California expedition—without bothering to ask Serra if he was agreeable to this new mission.[25] As it turned out, Serra, now 55, was more than willing to go along; at last, he could pursue his youthful ambition to harvest thousands of pagan souls in lands previously untouched by the church.

But as the expedition was getting underway, Serra's foot and leg infections had become almost crippling. So the military commander, Gaspar de Portolá, tried to persuade him not to join the expedition after all, and wrote to Gálvez about Serra's condition. Palóu too became concerned, gently suggesting to Serra that perhaps he should stay in Baja California, and let Palóu make the journey to San Diego in his place. Serra rebuked both Portolá's and Palóu's doubts, declaring that he trusted in god to see him through to San Diego and Monterey.[26]

The expedition set out in the spring of 1769. Two men had to lift Serra onto his mule. Along the way, his leg pains became so excruciating that he called the mule driver for help: "Imagine I am one of your mules with a sore on his leg. Give me the same treatment." Here Serra was strictly following the example of saint Francis of Assisi, who had derided his own body as "Brother Donkey." Shrugging, the mule driver applied his usual remedy of tallow mixed with herbs. The next day, Serra joyfully declared his leg much improved, and resumed the journey at full pace.[27]

The overland party, trekking some 1,500 kilometers from Baja California, suffering dwindling food supplies and carefully trading cloth for food with Indians they met along the way, finally arrived in San Diego on 1 July. Between the overland and seafaring parties of the expedition, about 300 men had started on the trip; but no more than half of them survived to reach San Diego. Most of the christian Indians recruited to the overland parties had died or deserted; the military officers had denied them rations when the food started running low. Half of those who made it to San Diego were too sick to resume the expedition, and many died there of scurvy.[28]

Early Hardships

Serra had a cross erected, celebrated mass, and set up the official records of mission San Diego in anticipation of his first baptism. But the Spaniards could hardly sustain themselves physically, far less sustain the natives spiritually. Unlike the Indians, they did not know how to live from the natural products of the land and sea, and they were dangerously distant from their sources of supply in Mexico. They could not communicate well with the Indians, as the surviving christian Indians they had brought from Baja California spoke an entirely different language.

The Indians were at first friendly and curious, gladly accepting the trinkets Serra offered them as enticements to friendship. But their craving for Spanish cloth irritated the soldiers, who accused them of stealing. To scare them away, the soldiers fired their guns into the air. But the Indians only grew scornful of the sick and helpless strangers.[29]

On 15 August 1769, a large group of Indians made a surprise attack on the fledgling mission. The few soldiers and artisans on hand at the mission met the Indians' arrows with musket and pistol fire. Serra, clutching a Jesus figurine in one hand and a Mary figurine in the other, prayed to god to save both sides from casualties. His servant, badly wounded by an arrow, came running to Serra to receive his final blessing, and died bleeding at his feet. The Indians suffered several dead, and had to retreat, with a new found respect for the power of firearms. Serra was distraught over the possibility of Indians dying unbaptized and thus being eternally damned. It seems those Spaniards who were aware of the Indians' casualties did not inform Serra, knowing the news would cause him great pain.[30]

The whole Spanish expedition to California would have failed and retreated, and Serra and his companion Juan Crespí—determined to stay, no matter what—would have starved to death, had it not been for the arrival of a supply ship from Mexico on 19 March 1770. This seemed a miracle, even to spirits less zealous than Serra's. And it enabled the military/missionary party to push north to Monterey. There, Serra and his companions, sustained by frequent gifts of deer and antelope meat from the local Rumsen Indians, founded mission Carmel, which became the capital of the California mission system.

The Mission as a Social System of the Imperial Frontier

Peaceful conquest of the Indians was the Spanish watchword in California. The vast territory had to be secured for the Spanish empire, yet precious few Spanish and Mexican colonists were available to settle the land. Moreover, the Pacific coast of California was already densely populated with native peoples. The Indians themselves had to become the main population base for Spanish rule over California. The mission system was the key to this transformation.

The number of Spanish and Mexican soldiers deployed to California was less than two hundred. They were supposed to explore the territory, help set up the missions, defend them from attack, and enforce Spanish law; they were not supposed to attack the Indians. The number of franciscan missionaries working in California by the end of Serra's life was 18: two for each of the nine missions set up along the California coast from San Diego to San Francisco. How did such a small team of missionaries and soldiers subdue and drastically change the lives of local native peoples numbering around 72,000 in 1770?

To get started, the missionaries lured the Indians with trinkets. Gifts of brightly colored cloth, glass beads, and metal handicrafts stimulated the Indians' fondness for body ornamentation. The Indians had never seen mules, horses, or longhorned cattle before, and these striking animals must have stirred their curiosity about the strangers' way of life. The friars took care to make friends with the most prominent men of the Indian villages, thus gaining access to their communities. When the soldiers and friars started building the first, modest mission churches, some Indians joined in and helped them carry and assemble the adobe bricks—perhaps out of a mixture of curiosity, respect, and the sheer joy of tackling a totally new task.

The strange and wonderful clangor of the mission bells must have had a magnetic appeal, especially for Indian children, and invested the friars with spiritual power in the people's eyes. Gradually, Indian parents started bringing their children to the missions and offering them for baptism. When they found that this meant their child had to live on the mission premises, it was only logical for them to accept baptism too. The friars trained the brighter mission boys, by rote, to sing catholic songs in Spanish and Latin. These boys could then accompany the friars on their recruiting trips to Indian villages, playing on the people's love for music. Heavy religious indoctrination came later, and its impact was doubtful in most cases, due to the language and cultural barriers between friars and their neophytes. Not catholic doctrine, but rather the superficial charm of the alien culture attracted many Indians to the fledgling missions.

The missions were far more than religious outposts: They were social institutions, designed to transform the Indians from scattered hunting and gathering peoples into disciplined farmers, ranchers, and cloth weavers clustered around, and faithful to the church. While securing territories for the Spanish empire, the California missions did not burden the royal treasury in the least. They were financed by the Pious Fund, raised by the jesuits from wealthy catholics in Mexico prior to their expulsion; the pious fund was even used to pay the soldiers' salaries, much to the annoyance of the franciscans.[31]

Serra and his colleagues viewed the mission lands and property as belonging rightfully to the baptized Indians; but the franciscans were holding the lands, cattle, sheep, and mission buildings in trust for the Indians, until the neophytes could be raised to the level of mature catholics and become full fledged citizens of the empire.[32] In this sense, the mission system was a modified version of the old *encomienda* system of colonial "trusteeship" over Indian lands, labor, and religious education. Yet Indian labor at the missions did not serve to enrich colonial masters, or even the franciscan order taken collectively. The products of the neophytes' labor were carefully collected and rationed back to the neophytes by the friars, who continued to live humbly. The Indians' surplus produce was used to feed and clothe the soldiers, or was traded overseas—with the friars trying to fetch fair prices in both cases.

The physical structure and layout of the mission complex was designed for security, social control and cohesion. The main buildings were arranged in a quadrangle. The two friars dwelled in the front row of rooms, with easy access to the fields, the church, and interior parts of the mission. Adolescent Indian girls, unmarried women, and widows lived in a secluded dormitory towards the inner square of the quadrangle, typically facing onto a patio or courtyard. The adolescent Indian boys' dormitory was placed sometimes inside, sometimes outside the main block of buildings. Married mission Indians lived with their small children in a village near the quadrangle. A handful of soldier/guards assigned to the mission lived in houses within sight of the Indians' village, the church, and the friars' dwelling.[33] The main body of soldiers, along with their officers, lived in a *presidio* (fort) at some kilometers' distance from the mission.

Not only the crops, meat, hides, wool, and clothing, but also the missions themselves were the products of Indian labor. Baptized Indians built the churches, friars' dwelling, female dormitory, kitchens, storehouses, corrals, tanning vats, canals, mills, soldiers' quarters—in short, all the buildings.[34] They were supervised by Spanish and Mexican foremen hired by the friars. These foremen refused to do any work of their own, that could not be done on horseback.[35]

The Missionaries and the Soldiers

The soldiers deployed to California were of uneven moral quality. The elite unit among them were the Catalonian volunteers, from northeastern Spain; they were treated fairly by their Catalonian commander, Pedro Fages. Most of the remaining soldiers came from the lower classes of New Spanish (Mexican) society. They were the unfortunate ones whose families lacked the money to buy them exemption from the military draft. Many were men of color, *mestizos* (of Indian and European parentage) or mulattos—while their officers were white Spaniards or *criollos*. These leather-jacketed soldiers from Mexico were often treated with contempt and abuse by their white officers, including Fages.

In those days, before the discovery of gold, there was no glamor in being assigned to California. The soldiers were deprived of the companionship of wives or lovers during their long and tough assignments there. They seemed to have no prospects for achieving either wealth or sexual gratification. Yet, owing to their horsemanship and command of firearms, they felt superior to the Indians, whether pagan or neophyte. Some of the soldiers carried venereal disease.

Indian women carrying grass seeds and water, San Joaquín valley, central California. Drawn by captain S. Eastman, from a sketch by E.M. Kern. Such women were choice targets for rape, first by Hispanic soldiers, later by Yankee immigrants. (courtesy of Bancroft Library, University of California at Berkeley).

Mission San Gabriel, founded in 1771 in southern California (in what is now the Los Angeles area), soon became a source of tension between soldiers and Indians. Nonmission Indians, who liked to visit their relatives and friends in the mission, found their access to the mission rigidly restricted by the soldier guards—even though they came unarmed. Then, around 1772, a soldier raped the wife of a local Indian chief, who vowed revenge. Gathering warriors from neighboring villages, he advanced towards the mission on foot. His party came upon two soldiers guarding the horses in the pasture; he recognized one of the soldiers as the culprit. Donning their heavy leather jackets, the soldiers levelled their muskets at the Indians armed with bows and arrows. The guilty soldier fired at the chief, killing him. The other warriors fled in terror, leaving the dead chief behind. When the Spanish corporal found out what had happened, he ordered the chief's head cut off, brought to the mission, and mounted on a pole as a lesson to the other Indians. At the time, the dead chief's son was living at the mission, the chief having brought him there a short time before.[36]

The soldiers were now emboldened to abuse the Indians still more. Groups of six or more of them would leave the mission in the morning—with or without their corporal's permission—and ride to distant Indian villages. There, they would lasso Indian women like cattle, and rape them. When Indian men tried to defend the women, several were killed by musket fire. The Indians complained bitterly to the friars, who in turn complained to Serra to correct the abuses.* Some soldiers were caught sexually molesting young Indian boys living in the mission. "... How any conversions were effected under such circumstances is little short of a marvel."[38]

In San Diego in 1773, three soldiers were accused of raping two Indian girls, and murdering one of them. Sent back to Mexico for trial, they were found guilty. But their sentence was a wry and curious one: They were ordered to spend the rest of their lives as citizens of California.[39]

The Spanish military commander, Pedro Fages, abused his Mexican soldiers as they built the Monterey presidio. Corporal Periquez later reported:

---

*Serra wrote to a fellow missionary: "... Since the district [of San Gabriel] is the most promising of all the missions, this mission gives me the greatest cause for anxiety; the secular arm down there was guilty of the most heinous crimes, killing the men to take their wives."[37]

...Another time, [three soldiers] and I fell sick. The captain [Fages] came to see us. The medicine he gave us was a severe reprimand, declaring that we were pretending to be sick so as to get out of work, and that we had better get up and get on the job... I was so mistreated that he made me work all winter, even though I was sick all the time.

When he was taking care of some sailors who were down with scurvy, the surgeon, with tears in his eyes, asked him for some chickens which belonged to him... He was unable to obtain them.

Don Pedro Fages' only comment was that getting the men well again was his own business. The only medicine he ever gave them was a scant supply of food. It was a common saying of all the men that more died by famine than from sickness. The surgeon's tears were caused by this: He saw that he could not get them well again for want of nourishing food; and at that time there were plenty of chickens, belonging to the king. But Don Pedro always maintained that the chickens were his; and so he ate them all himself, one by one. Never was it known that a chicken was killed for the sick...[40]

Fages also sold figs and raisins to his soldiers at exorbitant prices.[41] And once the presidio was build, he forced them to labor unrelentingly to maintain it, punishing them harshly for petty infractions like rolling cigarettes. Even on Sundays, they had to haul a week's supply of wood for his kitchen, fetch their own water from the Carmel river, clean their weapons, and pass inspection. This lasted a year and a half, and the soldiers complained to Serra about the overwork. Finally, Serra told Fages that, as a christian, he had to observe the sabbath, and allow his men to do the same. Sunday became a day of rest.[42]

Distraught over the soldiers' abuse of the Indians, lieutenant Fages' abuse of the soldiers, Fages' lack of cooperation with the missionaries and his refusal to allocate food supplies to needy mission Indians, Serra made the grueling trip over sea and land back to Mexico City in 1773, to appeal to viceroy Antonio María de Bucareli. Serra, now 59, fell ill twice during the trip, once so gravely that he was administered the sacrament of extreme unction.

In Mexico City over a six-month period, Serra presented Bucareli with a rigorous list of proposals to rectify the California presidio and mission system: The soldiers' pay should be raised, and they should have their own storehouse at Monterey so they could buy what they need at fair prices; soldiers who deserted should be granted amnesty; married soldiers in California long separated from their families should be allowed to visit them; more new soldiers deployed to California should be married; bachelor soldiers who marry christian Indian women and settle in California should be monetarily rewarded. Immoral soldiers should be removed from their mission posts, at the request of the missionary in charge; California should not be used as a dumping ground for "insolent and perverse" soldiers banished from Mexico. Serra also specified the number of soldiers needed to perform guard and supervisory duties at a mission, under the friar's direction. And he urged that the friars be granted exclusive charge of the training, education, and punishment of the mission Indians. To help implement these proposals, Serra asked Bucareli to replace Pedro Fages as commander of the Monterey presidio.[43]

Bucareli, deeply impressed with Serra's moral and intellectual qualities, granted most of his proposals, including the replacement of Fages (although Serra did not get the new commander he wanted). Serra's call for a force of 100 soldiers to support and defend the growing California mission system was considered somewhat excessive; the actual number of soldiers deployed remained smaller at that time.

The missions still depended desperately on their supply line from Mexico for food, clothing, tools, building materials, and religious images and implements. So the choice of a supply route was a major question. In his correspondence with Bucareli in Mexico City, Serra argued for maintaining the oversea supply route from Mexico's Pacific port of San Blas—as opposed to shifting to an overland route. The ocean voyage from San Blas to Monterey was dangerous and difficult, as the prevailing winds came from the north. But Serra was keenly aware of the *social* and cultural dangers of the overland route:

> The continual passage of pack trains, one following the other, for a distance of over 300 leagues [about 1,250 kilometers, from Baja California to Monterey] through gentile [pagan] country; the presence of so many mule drivers—men for the most part, from the dregs of society, bereft of high principles and conscience—will not all this occasion the utmost disgust and aversion; will it not be the cause of quarrels and disputes with the poor, downtrodden gentiles? The eagerness our men display to get possession of their potteries and other curiosities, which are quite attractive, would all too frequently bring it about that if the gentiles do not part with them either for nothing or for a trifle, they will take them by force from these pitiable people as happened in the case of the potteries in San Diego...

Then too, the presence of so many women there—it would be a great miracle...if it did not provoke so many men of such low character to disorders which we have to lament in all our missions, they occur every day; it is as though a plague of immorality had broken out. I have seen it myself, and, in the bitterness of their hearts, the religious missionaries have written to me about it in their recent letters...

....To all this there must be added the curiosity and vivacity of the gentiles themselves, especially those [Chumash Indians] living in the Santa Barbara Channel, who want to see everything; and when they get the opportunity of stealing, especially iron, they will not miss it. Now to our men this has been a cause for killing, as has happened many a time. It has been exceptional that, when any of the soldiers passed that way, someone was not killed...[44]

Viceroy Bucareli was swayed by Serra's report, and passed it along to Madrid, where it was favorably received. As a result, San Blas was preserved as the port of departure for the oversea supply route to California.

Returning to a joyous welcome in Monterey in May 1774, Serra learned that the mission and presidio there had suffered from want of food over the past eight months. The friars had to subsist for over a month on crushed peas mixed with milk, and coffee. The mission Indians were subsisting through fishing, hunting and gathering in their traditional ways. The soldiers, facing hunger, had to resort to hunting. Now, a timely arrival of the supply ship from Mexico relieved the situation.[45]

Within a few months, hunger returned to those missions suffering poor harvests. Yet grain, flour, and dry goods were now stacked high in Monterey's warehouse. Despite Serra's requests, the new commander, Fernando de Rivera y Moncada, refused to release these consumer goods for months—even though the soldiers, artisans and friars were eager to pay for them. Rivera seemed to view suggestions from Serra or anyone else in California as a threat to his authority. He also blocked Serra's requests to supply other needy missions with available foodstuffs.[46]

From the standpoint of social ethics, the conquering Spaniards had a lot more to learn from the California Indians, than the Indians had to learn from them. The Indian societies in the mission territories placed a high value on sharing and generosity. A "chief" earned respect and prestige, not by piling up goods and wealth for his own benefit, but by sharing his wealth with the less fortunate members of his community.

"The California Indians' Way of Fighting." Pencil drawing probably by Hispanic soldier's attempt to rape an Indian woman. The Ohlone women in and otter skin robes. (courtesy of Museo Naval, Madrid, Spain).

Tomás de Suria (or José Cardero), 1791. Such a conflict may have ensued from the this picture (in the Monterey area) wear tule front aprons, buckskin rear aprons,

A chief who acted like Fages or Rivera towards his own people would quickly be discredited, scorned, and stripped of authority by the people. For this reason, along with the natural abundance of land and sea food sources and their own flexible subsistence skills, California's Indians very rarely faced hunger, before the Europeans came.

The "missing link" in the chain of missions that the franciscans were establishing along the coast of California was the Santa Barbara channel region, home of the Chumash Indians. The first mission in the region, San Buenaventura, was not founded until 1782. In 1775, Serra related the dangerous tensions between the Chumash and soldiers passing through their territory:

> On 24 May, our famous and much discussed packloads from California, the pack train, the soldiers in attendance, and Fathers Dumetz, Cambón and Lasuén, were passing through one of these pueblos called San Pedro y San Pablo [near present day Santa Barbara]. One of the soldiers saw fit to strike a gentile who, out of curiosity, had tried to take his rifle. All of them took up their arms; arrows flew everywhere, and six gentiles were killed by the soldiers.
>
> Good luck, or to speak more correctly, God's providence, has seen to it that the gentiles have always come off worse, so that their bravado is subdued. But God save us if at any time they should come out victorious or that many should unite against us; were that to happen, who knows what would become of us, or how we would pass through their country.[47]

The missionaries' relationship to the soldiers was equivocal. On the one hand, the soldiers' frequent abuses of the non-christian Indians—criminal abuses, for which they were seldom punished—alienated the Indians, and threatened to sabotage the whole mission project. On the other hand, the missionaries needed the soldiers for protection against those same Indians. Francisco Palóu, writing around 1783, lamented the difficulties the friars had in obtaining a military escort, adding that "no journey is possible without one, even between one mission and its neighbor[ing mission]... In many places the escort has to be of no small proportions because of the menace of the pagans who people the intermediate territory."[48]

The Indian Revolt at San Diego, 1775

At mission San Diego, six years of work by the friars and mission Indians had yielded still meager grain harvests, not enough to support the roughly 400 baptized Indians. So the friars, Vicente Fuster and Luis

Jayme, let most of the Indian converts remain in their home villages, receiving catholic instruction from the trained neophytes among them.

The local Kumeyaay Indians practiced a subtle form of agriculture, which the Spaniards did not understand or appreciate. Selectively clearing fields by burning the brush away, and casting a variety of seeds over them, the Kumeyaays cultivated a mixture of hearty plant foods. Their crops sprouted in overlapping time spans, and did not require continual tending. The Spaniards' introduction of the plow, and cattle, sheep and goat grazing, disrupted the Kumeyaays' native crops. The roaming mission animals ate precious native seeds; the mission's wheat, barley and corn crops, not well fitted into the local ecosystem, were a poor substitute for what the Kumeyaays were losing.[49]

Worse still, as at San Gabriel, Spanish and Mexican soldiers made a sport of raping Indian women. Friar Luis Jayme lamented in a letter to Palóu: "I feel very deeply about the fact that what the devil does not succeed in accomplishing among the pagans is accomplished by christians... The uprisings which have occurred in some of the *rancherías* (villages) closest to us were due to the fact that the soldiers had dishonored the wives of some of the Indians."[50]

In a 1772 letter to his religious superior in Mexico City, Jayme spoke of a large Indian village near the mission, where the natives "many times have been on the verge of coming here to kill us all, and the reason for this is that some soldiers went there and raped their women, and other soldiers who were carrying the mail to Monterey turned their animals into [the Indians'] fields and they ate up their crops..." The abused Kumeyaays "...leave their huts and the crops which they gather from the lands around their villages, and go to the woods to experience hunger. They do this so that the soldiers will not rape their women, as they have already done so many times in the past."[51] In 1773, three soldiers raped two young Indian women with such violence that one of them died.

In early October 1775, two mission Indian brothers, Carlos and Francisco,* did not return from a one-day leave of absence the friars had granted them. Instead, Francisco and Carlos, who was chief of the village nearest the mission, moved from village to village, inciting their fellow Kumeyaay Indians to revolt. The brothers later declared that their motive in rebelling was to live as they had lived before.[52]

---

*Baptized Indians were given Spanish names, and supposed to abandon their own names.

Franciscan historians, on the other hand, claim that, on their day off from the mission, Carlos and Francisco robbed two elderly non-christian Indian women of their netted bags of seeds and fish. The women complained to the friars, and when the brothers heard about it, they fled along with five companions.[53]

At any rate, the brothers' rebellious campaign heightened tensions at and around the mission. In late October, several Indians were flogged at the mission for attending a pagan dance at the village of El Corral. According to Indian accounts, friar Fuster demanded they move their village away from the mission, threatening to burn it if they refused. Angered villagers fled to join the rebels.[54]

Friar Jayme, 35 years old, refused to believe his own intelligence reports that the Indians were preparing to massacre the friars and soldiers. Jayme had translated the catechism into the Kumeyaay language. He still hoped he could win the Indians over with kindness.

Meanwhile, Carlos and Francisco had gathered a force of about 800 Kumeyaay men and women (the women prepared to support the male warriors by carrying the spoils of their attack) from nine villages, including several christian villages. This was quite an accomplishment, as the Kumeyaay villages were autonomous, and not accustomed to banding together for a major action.

The rebels chose the night of 4 November, under a full moon, to attack. Setting their torches to the mission buildings, they barraged the surprised soldier guards, artisans and friars with arrows, firebrands, stones, and adobe bricks. Fuster holed up in a small barricaded structure with the soldiers, praying to God and Mary for a miracle as they fired their muskets upon the attackers.

Luis Jayme, woken by the clamor, calmly walked up to the Indian warriors and greeted them in his customary way: *Hijos, amad a Dios,* "Love god, my sons." They seized and dragged him to a nearby gully. There, they stripped away his outer garments, shot him through with arrows, and pummeled him to death.

The attackers' flames destroyed practically the entire physical structure of the mission. But they could not overcome the soldiers' stubborn resistance. The siege lasted for several hours through the night, and just before the break of dawn the warriors fled. Besides friar Jayme, they had killed the mission carpenter and blacksmith.

The warriors' plan had called for a simultaneous attack upon the presidio, which was about five kilometers from the mission, on the top of a hill. But the presidio was untouched. Friar Fuster, in his post mortem assessment of the struggle, wrote to Serra:

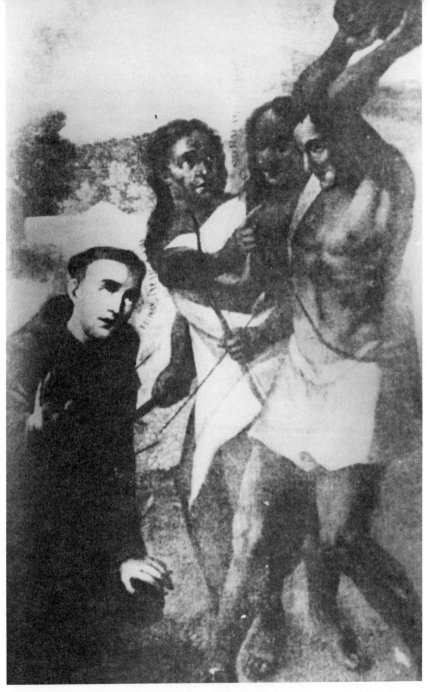

Death of friar Luis Jayme at the hands of Kumeyaay rebels: mission San Diego, early morning, 5 November 1775. In this idealized painting, Jayme pleads, "Love God, my sons"; the Indians reply, "Now there's no love for God." (courtesy of Academy of American Franciscan History, Bethesda, Maryland).

... It was a special act of God's Providence that they did not overwhelm the presidio as well, along with all the people there who were as ill prepared as we were ourselves. An equal number of Indians, or an even greater number, were on their way to accomplish that purpose, and to deal with the presidio in the same fashion as they dealt with us. They had already approached near to it when they saw the mission buildings on fire. They were afraid that the sentinels at the presidio would likewise see the flames, as indeed they could easily be seen. So they retraced their steps to join with those who were fighting us. The impatience of those attacking the mission proved to be a stroke of fortune which saved the presidio. They did not wait for the signal which had been agreed upon for the start of their deadly work. The signal was that, as soon as those who were to attack the mission saw the presidio building in flames, they were immediately to set fire to the mission. And if this had actually taken place, there would scarce be one left to tell the tale.[55]

The Spaniards now had to pick up the pieces of the gutted mission and pursue the rebels. The Indians had not won a decisive victory at San Diego. But if they could spread their rebellion north across ethnic and cultural boundaries, they had a chance to drive the whole Spanish project out of California. There were only 70 soldiers guarding the four remaining missions and the two presidios between San Diego and Monterey.[56]

But the Indians failed to press their offensive, and the Spaniards regrouped. Commander Rivera hastened from Monterey to San Diego, at the head of a team of soldiers. Their campaign to capture Carlos was frustrated three times, as the Indian rebel outwitted them. Finally in March 1776, Carlos startlingly appeared behind the chapel altar at mission San Diego, just as friar Fuster was about to offer mass.

Asylum, Punishment, and Pardon

After hiding Carlos in the chapel, Fuster notified captain Rivera. A few hours later, he received a note from Rivera, directing him to hand Carlos over before sundown. Fuster then warned Rivera against violating the right to asylum in a church, which was part of Vatican and Spanish law. As a christian convert, Carlos may have been aware of this right.

Rivera responded by surrounding the chapel. His soldiers entered and dragged Carlos away, to the stockade. Protesting loudly, Fuster declared Rivera and his soldiers excommunicated.

Rivera, who had been a close friend of friar Fermín de Lasuén (later to succeed Serra as president of the California missions), was deeply distressed by this conflict. Fuster appealed to him to correct his error by returning Carlos to the chapel. Rivera instead rode back to Monterey, to get Serra's opinion. After studying the correspondence of Fuster and other friars, Serra sided with Fuster. As Serra was the highest church authority in California, Rivera accepted his verdict, returned to San Diego, and delivered Carlos back to Fuster's custody in May. Lasuén lifted the verdict of excommunication, and viceroy Bucareli later pardoned Rivera.[57]

Serra, writing to Bucareli months before Carlos appeared in the chapel, urged a pardon for him and all those Indians who had destroyed mission San Diego and killed friar Jayme:

If ever the Indians, whether they be gentile or christian, killed me, they should be forgiven...

While the missionary is alive, let the soldiers guard him, and watch over him, like the pupils of God's very eyes... Nor do I disdain such a favor for myself. But after the missionary had been killed, what can be gained by [punitive] campaigns?

Some will say to frighten them and prevent them from killing others.

What I say is that, in order to prevent them from killing others, keep better guard over [the friars] than they [the soldiers] did over the one who had been killed; and, as to the murderer, let him live, in order that he should be saved—which is the very purpose of our coming here, and the reason which justifies it. Let him understand, after a moderate amount of punishment, that he is being pardoned in accordance with our law, which commands us to forgive injuries; and let us prepare him, not for death, but for eternal life.[58]

Serra wrote to Rivera in the same vein. Yet the military leaders went ahead raiding Kumeyaay villages, capturing "renegade" christian Indians and all those they judged guilty of rebellion. Hauling the prisoners into the presidio, they flogged them 50 times each—an unusually harsh punishment. One christian Indian prisoner died from the whipping.[59]

When Bucareli's order pardoning the Indian rebels arrived, Serra tempered his christian charity with some hardheaded criminology. Writing to Rivera, he suggested that

...the best way to carry out the orders...would be promptly and energetically to set about capturing most of the missing murderers, and the one who was in command of all the enemy forces... You should assemble them, along with those you now hold prisoners, and by means of an interpreter lay the case vigorously yet clearly before them. First of all you should make them reflect on the great amount of evil they have done, then point out the severe punishment they deserve, and the undisputed power which our king and lord has to wipe them out of existence, as indeed they deserve. Point out that new soldiers have arrived and perhaps many more may be on their way, but that the aforesaid king, although mighty beyond compare, is also very christian, that he has taken pity on them, etc.

I do not advocate that they be set free immediately, but that after they have been assured that their lives will be spared they should be freed [after a jail term determined] according to the gravity of their crimes..."[60]

Serra went on to criticize Rivera for his plan to ship the prisoners off to the Mexican port of San Blas; Serra feared this would provoke another Indian rebellion.

Within three years after the Kumeyaay revolt, Serra reported joyfully to the Spanish commander general that "those who had set fire to the mission at San Diego and had most cruelly murdered its principal minister," were now all living at the newly rebuilt mission, and getting along well with the friars.[61] In October 1778, Serra joyfully reported to Bucareli that both Carlos and Francisco had been administered the rite of confirmation, enhancing their catholic status.

Yet a year later, Serra learned from friar Lasuén in San Diego that Carlos and his friend Bernardino had relapsed into disobedience. "I am grieved exceedingly," he replied to Lasuén in January 1780, "at Carlos' and Bernardino's continued bad conduct. I have a particular affection for them, and for the salvation of their souls. With that end in view, I would not feel sorry no matter what punishment they gave them, if they would commute it to prison for life, or in the stocks every day, since then it would be easier for them to die well. Do you think it possible that if they kept them prisoners for a time, and by means of interpreters explained to them about the life to come and its eternal duration, and if we prayed to God for them—might we not persuade them to repent and win them over to a better life? You could impress on them that the only reason they are still alive is because of our affection for them, and the trouble we took to save their lives. Whereas they, because of their criminal conduct, have deserved a cruel death. But, because of our love for God, we set them free, so that they might lead better lives, etc..."[62]

After the rebuilding of mission San Diego, tensions continued between the Spaniards and the local Kumeyaay and Ipai Indians. In March 1778, a report reached the presidio that Indians of the Pamó village (some 50 kilometers northeast of San Diego) and four other villages were making bows and arrows to attack the mission. Sergeant Carrillo launched a surprise attack against Pamó, capturing many men, including four chiefs alleged to be plotting the revolt. The men were flogged, and the four chiefs taken in chains to the presidio. The soldiers also captured a large number of bows, arrows, and clubs from the men of Pamó. It is not clear whether and how the Spaniards proved that these weapons were to be used against the mission. But sergeant José Ortega condemned the four chiefs to death, and summoned the missionaries to prepare them for execution.

This time, even though the convicted prisoners had not attacked the mission or harmed its residents, Serra was not inclined to urge forgiveness. Perhaps his difficulties in rehabilitating Carlos had hardened his attitude towards rebels. At any rate, he resigned himself to helping the condemned Indians die as christians: He urged that they be baptized in prison, given crucifixes and rosaries, and outfitted with tunics of white cotton cloth, "in which they would die and be buried."[63] Here, preparing the Indians for death had merged, in a curious way, with preparing them for eternal life. But the four chiefs' death sentences were later commuted to hard labor terms by the military governor, Felipe de Neve.

"I again shall urge that the guards of your mission be reinforced," Serra wrote to the San Diego friars. "... It is not a little consoling to know that if Your Reverences have to die at the hands of those savages, it will be because you are christians... Still, because we need you alive and robust, it is but right to see that you are well protected and in a condition to increase the number of christians, much as this may displease those [Indian rebels] of Pamó."[64]

A Hard-Headed Zealot, a Serene Fanatic

So fragile and vulnerable were the California missions in their early years, that their survival and growth depended in large measure on the personal qualities of the franciscan missionaries, above all Junípero Serra. By all accounts, Serra was exceptionally zealous and dedicated to his mission. With his motto, "Always go forward and never turn back," his host of patron saints, and his contempt for bodily pleasure and even bodily necessities, Serra blazed a stubborn mission building trail, rallying his less zealous companions behind him.

The hardships of building the missions from scratch, and the military commanders' frustrating refusal to cooperate with the missionaries, demoralized many of the franciscans; some of them repeatedly asked Serra to be permitted to retire to the college of San Fernando in Mexico. Serra, always looking forward to clearing away the obstacles and building new missions, cajoled them to stay and labor for better days. Where others saw only obstacles and fruitless toil, Serra saw the heavenly rewards of the pagan souls he was saving. He fasted often, and ate meat seldom. When he mentioned the hardships of his work with the Indian neophytes, he would be sure to add, "...These poor people cost Our Blessed Savior an incomparably greater price."[65]

Where others saw defeat and disaster, Serra saw god's mercy and a chance to rebuild. When informed by captain Rivera that the Indians had burned down mission San Diego and killed his fellow Mallorcan, friar Jayme, Serra, after a stunned silence, replied: "Thanks be to God. Now that the terrain has been watered by blood, the conversion of the San Diego Indians will take place."[66] Where others saw thieving, disgusting and insolent Indians, Serra saw souls eager for evangelizing. After passing through the vulnerable Santa Barbara channel region, Serra wrote of the local Chumash Indians: "I saw those inhabitants, as I have always seen them, lively, agreeable, and mutely asking for the light of the Gospel."[67] He probably would have been less than amused to learn that many Indians saw the friars and soldiers as sons of the mules they rode—since no women accompanied them, and the mules carried the strangers on their backs as Indian mothers carried their own children.[68]

However, zeal alone could never have made Serra an effective president of the California mission system. Without a firm practical sense, Serra would, sooner or later, have fallen on his face, as so many other missionaries have done in various parts of the world. Along with his soaring zeal, Serra did have a firm and shrewd sense of practical necessity. He devoted painstaking attention to the details of mission administration, and the complicated logistics of procuring supplies from Mexico. His excellent memory, which had distinguished him as a student and professor at Palma de Mallorca, helped him not only to recall appropriate passages of scripture for his sermons, but also to keep track of the varied happenings in the growing mission chain and make daily decisions and proposals based on the quantities of the various grains harvested at the various missions, the number of baptisms recorded at the missions, the physical needs of the mission buildings, the availability of artisans, supervisors and soldiers, the availability of horses, mules and cattle, and the physical and psychological conditions of his missionaries. The mass of paperwork and correspondence that all this required caused Serra to complain that, at times, he felt he was laboring more as a scribe than as an evangelist.

If Serra was a prodigious mission administrator, he was also quite traditional in overall concept. When he had to argue for a policy or proposal, he would typically do so on the basis of church and historical precedent. He rejected innovations tried by some missionaries in Mexico, who allowed their Indian neophytes to come and go to and from the mission as they pleased and encouraged them to mix with Spanish speaking townspeople. Serra and the franciscans in California insisted on observing the law of the Indies which required Indian converts to live at the missions, and they discouraged their neophytes from fraternizing with Hispanic townspeople and soldiers.[69]

Serra's willingness to suffer martyrdom and his zeal to die happily in the arms of the church made him remarkably serene in the face of danger. He fervently believed that, provided he did adequate repentance and self punishment for all of his "sins," his death would usher him into heaven and eternal bliss. So he did not fear death, and in many ways welcomed it. On one occasion, while he was riding with a military escort through pagan territory, a group of Indians attacked the party with a barrage of arrows. Serra joyfully welcomed the prospect of being martyred right then and there—but escaped unscathed.

Serra's Conflicts with the Military Commanders

His serenity in the face of mortal danger contrasted sharply with the jumpiness of the military commanders with whom he had to work. The military leaders, while catholics, were less than devout men. Certainly they valued earthly prestige, wealth, and a comfortable retirement more highly than the prospect of a heavenly ascent after death. Trained to fight and win glory on the battlefield, they fidgeted under the limitations of their role in California, where they simply had to back up the missionaries in peacefully converting the Indians. They resented the prestige that several of the missionaries—above all, Serra—were gaining among the Indians, and even among their own soldiers. Probably more than king Carlos 3's nationalistic scorn for the pope, the California commanders' frustrated personal ambition helps explain their chronic refusal to cooperate with Serra and the franciscans.

Captain Fernando de Rivera, who was commander of the Monterey presidio from 1774 to 1776, set himself stubbornly against founding any new missions. His stinginess in allocating soldiers to accompany the friars in staking out new mission sites vexed Serra. "That military men should move forward with caution is well and good," noted Serra. "But for the kingdom of God, some boldness is more in keeping than all these cautions they are forever impressing upon me."[70]

Rivera, for his part, no doubt saw Serra and the franciscans as throwing stubborn obstacles in the way of *his* carrying out his duties. On one occasion, Rivera requested, on behalf of captain Juan Ayala, that Serra send mission Indians to help unload a ship that had arrived at the port of Monterey. "...This is a very delicate matter that he [Ayala] proposes to me," Serra replied to Rivera. "The work the Indians do here [at mission Carmel] is for themselves, and even though we do not ask them to do it without giving them their maintenance and clothing, they accept it with such haughtiness that at times, out of a group of more than 50, we do not succeed in gathering together more than a dozen. We often find ourselves without firewood to cook the *pozole* [a stew of corns, beans and peas served for lunch] for them, even though it is so easy to collect it. And we continue to tolerate this, waiting for the day when, little by little, they will acquire a better sense of responsibility..."[71] Here it seems that Serra's aim was not so much to protect his Indians against exploitation by the officers, as to husband for the mission what he viewed as their meager capacity for work.

After Rivera was replaced as commander of Monterey, Serra caustically referred to him as "a man who knew very well how to keep his salary of 3,000 pesos intact, while he was eating from [the salary] of the poor friar [at mission San Diego], who got only 400."[72]

In 1777, Felipe de Neve, the military governor of California, installed himself at Monterey, thus coming into close working contact with Serra. Neve ordered his soldiers not to befriend the friars, not to perform any services for them, and not to help them bring back runaway mission Indians.[73] Serra opposed establishing colonial settlements in California—arguing that the missions should first be given more time to develop, provide subsistence for the presidios, and make more land available for settlers. Neve, without waiting for approval from viceroy Bucareli, who was sympathetic to Serra and his aims, broke Serra's opposition and set up the pueblo of San José in November 1777.

Pueblo San José vs. Mission Santa Clara

Mission Santa Clara had just been founded ten months earlier; now Neve decided to set up the new pueblo on the other side of the nearby river. San José was "to be composed of people, as they say, *de razón* ['of reason']—just as if the Indians did not have use of reason too...," Serra later lamented. "As soon as the fathers [at mission Santa Clara] saw what was going on, they protested because of the harm that would come from having their [the settlers'] cattle and horses so near [the mission lands]."[74]

San José was established uncomfortably close to mission Santa Clara. The franciscans, in fact, demonstrated that San José was an illegal settlement: It violated the New Laws of the Indies, which required colonial settlements to be built a minimum distance away from a mission. Since the lands allotted to San José legally belonged to the Santa Clara mission Indians—argued the franciscans—the Indians had the right to slaughter the settlers' cattle wandering onto their lands, without penalty.

"Now the townspeople here ... have, as everyone knows, quantities of livestock, both large and small, and recent history has shown that, besides getting mixed up with the livestock belonging to the Indians from the mission, the animals ... belonging to the townsfolk have caused unceasing damage to the crops put in by the Indians," wrote Santa Clara's friars Murguía and La Peña to Serra. "... The consequence will be, perhaps, that the Indians will have to stop their field work, so as not to labor in vain; and they will have to rely for their food on the herbs and acorns they pick in the woods—just as they used to do before we came. This source of food supply, we might add, is now scarcer than it used to be, owing to the cattle, and many a time the gentiles [nonmission Indians] living in the direction of the pueblo have complained to us about it."[75]

In 1782, Serra's old nemesis, lieutenant Pedro Fages, returned to Monterey, now assuming the position of military governor of California. Instead of correcting Neve's error, Fages aggravated it: He formally divided the lands of pueblo San José and mission Santa Clara according to a line drawn halfway between them; this line fell to the west of the river, i.e., on the mission side. Now the colonists were emboldened to cross the river and graze their cattle on lands the mission Indians had considered theirs. They also prevented the mission Indians from gathering seeds and cutting grass from this land to roof their huts. Serra, frustrated by the viceroy's lack of response to his protests over the situation, appealed to his religious superiors at the college of San Fernando in Mexico City. A decision inclining in favor of the franciscans and mission Indians (but not challenging San José's right to its existing location) finally arrived from Mexico, after Serra's death.[76]

Governor Neve repeated Rivera's tactic of withholding food supplies from the missions despite well stocked warehouses, citing dubious legal technicalities.[77] Besides protesting this policy, Serra tried to protect the mission Indians against unfair pricing in the exchange of wheat between missions and presidios.[78]

In his disputes with Neve as with Fages and Rivera, Serra continued to be restrained by the friars' dependence on the soldiers for protection against rebellious Indians. He had to frame his letters of disagreement and protest to the military commanders with the utmost tact and diplomacy. In 1778 Serra, responding to appeals from friar Lasuén, asked Neve for more soldiers to protect mission San Diego. When Serra reminded Neve of the rebellious history of the San Diego Indians, Neve replied: "Then have them flogged." "That's all very well(!)," replied Serra, "but to carry out such a program with security, troops are necessary. Give that much encouragement to the Padres, I beg of you." Neve repeated that he could not meet Serra's request, nor was there any reason for more troops in San Diego.[79]

The Dispute over Self-Government

According to Spanish law, every mission was temporary. Ten years after its founding, each mission was supposed to be "secularized": The mission lands were to be parcelled out among the christian Indians, and community government was to pass to Indian officials trained for this role. The mission church was to be turned over to parish priests, known as "secular" clergy. The missionaries would then move on to found a new mission and train a fresh batch of neophytes.[80]

Governor Neve insisted on strictly observing the ten-year timetable for self government. At the end of 1778, he wrote to friar Fermín Lasuén, superior of mission San Diego, informing him that an Indian mayor and magistrate must be elected to govern the mission the next year, on its tenth anniversary.

Lasuén objected to this plan, as did Serra. The franciscans wrangled with Neve over the legal technicality of whether the missions were really missions, or pueblos: Since the missions were not yet pueblos, argued the franciscans, the requirement for self government did not apply. But the main substance of the friars' argument was that the Indians were incompetent to govern themselves, and still had to be educated, supervised, and punished by the friars.

Since they could not stop Neve from implementing his legal plan, the friars submitted to the elections of Indian mayors and magistrates as their missions reached the ten-year mark. Neve did not attempt to remove the friars from their missions, but redefined them as parish priests. The friars attempted to reassert their traditional authority. Where the elected mayor agreed to do their bidding, mission affairs carried on much as before. Where the mayor or magistrate tried to exert his own authority and defy the friars, the friars tried to get him disciplined and removed from power.

At mission Carmel, where Serra and Juan Crespí were stationed, the Indians elected Baltazar, a 44-year-old Ohlone of the Rumsen tribelet, as mayor. As soon as he took office, he came into conflict with the friars. Crespí accused Baltazar of seducing his wife's sister Justina, and fathering an illegitimate child by her. Baltazar had probably had three wives before his baptism in 1775, and Justina may well have been one of them. On 24 May 1779, several weeks after his election as mayor, Baltazar's christian wife, Praxedis María, died. A month later, her sister Justina died. Baltazar married again before the church in July, but later fled the mission. Crespí also denounced Baltazar for having beaten with a stick a christian Indian from Baja California who had carried out an order of the friars. Baltazar's desertion, along with a group of followers, to the rugged coastal mountains became a crisis for Crespí and Serra, because the rebels tried to rally other mission Indians to desert. It is not known what became of Baltazar, except that by the end of 1780, he was dead.[81]

Serra's most stubborn objection to the self government scheme was over the friars' loss of the power to punish the mission Indians, including their elected mayors, with the whip. He appealed to the precedent of saint Francis Solano in South America, who had directed his foremen to whip disobedient Indians at his missions. "I am willing to admit," he wrote to Neve, "that in the infliction of the punishment we are now discussing [whipping], there may have been some inequalities and excesses on the part of some fathers and that we are all exposed to err in that regard... [But] the good standing in which we are universally regarded may be gathered from the consideration that when we came here, we did not find even a single christian, that we have engendered them [the Indians] all in Christ, that we, every one of us, came here for the single purpose of doing them good and for their eternal salvation, and I feel sure that everyone knows that we love them."[82]

As we shall see in the next two chapters, the Indians of California had a terrible time understanding this strange and humiliating form of paternal love, when the love they gave their own children was of such a different quality. The friars' insistence on treating Indian men and women — whose peoples had governed themselves freely for thousands of years — as helpless children, guaranteed that the experiments in mission self government would end in fiasco.

The Laws of the Indies provided for mission Indians to receive training in self government; in practice, the California Indians received little or none. The friars did not teach the Indians to read—with the exception of bright Indian boys who were taught the rudiments of Spanish and Latin literacy. Nor did the friars develop written forms for the Indians' own, diverse languages. Few friars mastered the spoken languages of their neophytes. Serra himself admitted to his great difficulties in learning the Indian languages spoken at his mission Carmel—attributing his problems to his own "sinful" nature. No doubt he continued whipping himself to expiate his sins, but this did nothing to stimulate his, or the Indians', cultural development. The friars' imposition of a rigid work, worship and meal routine on their neophytes, without democratic discussion or Indian participation in decision making, stripped the Indians of autonomy and self esteem. Serra's and the franciscans' insistence that the Indians were not ready for self government became a self fulfilling prophesy.

More Soul-Saving than Life-Giving

The nearly devastating epidemics, introduced by the Europeans, that frequented the California mission Indian populations, would have given pause to any secular humanist to question the logic and justice of the whole mission system. But Serra, with his vision riveted on heaven, took the epidemics in stride. "Death might wreak havoc among his hard-won neophytes," franciscan historians have noted, "but he found consolation in his sorrow, for he had prepared them for a future life which, his religious convictions assured him, was worth infinitely more than the life they were leaving and the pain of parting."[83]

In July 1775, Serra wrote to his religious superior in Mexico: "In the midst of all our little troubles, which are plentiful, the spiritual side of the missions is developing most happily. In San Antonio [a mission halfway between Monterey/Carmel and San Luis Obispo] they are faced with two harvests at one and the same time, that is, of the wheat, and of a plague among the children, who are dying. A number of days ago, the surgeon went there to help them. His skill and demeanor are praiseworthy, and he is our greatest comfort."[84] Evidently, the second "harvest" refers to god's harvest of the Indian children's souls in heaven. Note also that Serra calls the doctor "*our* greatest comfort," not the *Indians'* greatest comfort. There was only one Spanish doctor in all of California, and he was helpless in the face of the epidemics.

Francisco Palóu relates that, at mission Santa Clara, the first baptisms took place in May 1777, "for as there had come upon the people a great epidemic, the fathers were able to perform a great many baptisms by simply going through the villages. In this way they succeeded in sending a great many children (who died almost as soon as they were baptized) to heaven."[85]

Serra's Confirmation Campaign . . .

Serra's final struggle with the military leaders came over his authority to administer the rite of confirmation to the mission Indians. Serra had applied to the pope for the official right (faculty) to confirm baptized Indians in California. The pope granted Serra's faculty to confirm in 1774, but it took four years to pass through the creaky Spanish bureaucracy into Serra's hands. Since the faculty expired ten years after its date of issue, he now had six years left to confirm all the neophytes he could reach in California.

He was 64 years old, and his left leg was badly ulcerated. Moreover, governor Neve challenged the validity of the confirmation documents Serra had received, and tried to block him from confirming. Serra plunged ahead, travelling up and down the California mission chain to administer confirmation to thousands of neophytes—while maintaining his regular duties and correspondence. As Neve threatened to physically seize Serra's confirmation papers, Serra had to play a cat and mouse game—with the mouse (Serra) outwitting and outmaneuvering the cat at every stage.

There is irony in Serra's devotion, during his final years, of so much time, energy and suffering to confirm his California neophytes and thus move them—formally—another big step towards becoming full fledged catholics. For he continued to treat them as helpless children, opposing their right to govern themselves. Nor could he offer his more zealous neophytes a future in the clergy, since the franciscan order continued rigidly to exclude Indians from the priesthood. Serra's zeal in confirming his neophytes is, in its way, touching. Yet I have the nagging impression that he was motivated more by desire to secure his *own* place in heaven, than by concern for the happy future of the mission Indians.

In October 1783, Serra prepared to return from southern California to his resting place in Carmel, after thousands of miles of missionary travels by foot and muleback in Mexico and California over 35 years. He wrote to a fellow friar:

Visiting friar arrives at a mission. Note the Indian boy standing at the belfry,

rotating the "joyous bell" to ring it.

... I have felt very deeply the deaths of so many of our brethren [at the college of San Fernando in Mexico]. And the nearness of my own death is constantly before me, all the more so as I find my own health collapsing.

I reached San Diego in excellent spirits. But the 40 leagues [165 kilometers] I had to traverse in coming back here by land made me quite fatigued. And I shudder at the thought of the hundred leagues [400 kilometers] or more that separate me from Carmel—and a great part of it is through desert wastes.

But, should God see fit to allow me to arrive home, I shall certainly try to go to Santa Clara and San Francisco, to administer my last round of confirmations before the time limit expires in which I may use the privilege. My faculty to confirm ceases in May of next year.

I consider this my last pilgrimage. May our Lord be graciously pleased to allow me to finish it, if that be his most holy will. After that, or even right now, [you] may look around for someone to succeed me—a man of more vigorous body and mind than this sinner.[86]

Serra did make it to Santa Clara and San Francisco for his last round of confirmations. Then, he returned to Carmel, in May 1784—just before his faculty to confirm expired.

Taking stock of his 15-year mission in California, Serra rejoiced in the over 6,000 baptisms and 5,300 confirmations conferred to the Indians, in a region "where the name of Jesus was never heard before."[87] There were now nine missions and four presidios in California, staffed by 18 missionaries and 172 soldiers; the mission Indian population numbered about 4,650. The two colonial pueblos, San José and Los Angeles (whose establishment the franciscans had opposed), each contained a few dozen settlers; they could not yet support themselves economically, whereas several of the missions could.[88]

On 31 July, Serra welcomed the long delayed decision by the military governor to found mission Santa Barbara, among the Chumash Indians. "... How many souls from Montecito, and from other places among the pagans in whose midst we live, would not already be in heaven if my proposals had been followed," he declared.[89]

He continued to occupy himself with the practical problems of the mission system. Many franciscan friars were upset over rumors filtering down through the royal hierarchy, that they were about to be removed from California, and replaced by dominicans from Baja California. Serra faced the prospect of his companions having to abandon their 15 years' labor in California with serenity, just as he faced his pending death. As it turned out, the franciscans were to stay on in California.

... and his Happy Death

On 18 August, Francisco Palóu arrived in Carmel from San Francisco, to spend the final days with his companion of 40 years. In May, Palóu had received Serra's general confession in a tearful encounter. Now, he administered all the final sacraments to Serra in the mission Carmel church.

On Friday, 20 August, Serra painfully walked the weekly stations of the way of the cross with his neophytes. On 28 August, he died peacefully in his austere cell.

So, what of beatification? And what about sainthood? Clearly, if sainthood means self sacrificing devotion to harvesting pagan souls for the kingdom of god in heaven, then Junípero Serra deserves to become a saint.

But, if neither god, nor heaven, nor hell, nor the devil exist (and, in my view, they do not), then we must radically shift our angle of inquiry. We must hew to the unforgiving soil of human social relations. And this means judging the Spanish mission experience by its impact on the lives and worldly destiny of the native peoples of California.

Cleaning and sifting grass seed, to prepare it as food: Indian women in the San Joaquín valley, central California. Drawn by captain S. Eastman, from a sketch by E. M. Kern. (courtesy of Bancroft Library).

Chapter 2

The Indians of California

The native peoples of California numbered perhaps 300,000, at the time of the Spanish incursion in 1769. They consisted of over 100 ethnic groups, each with its own sense of identity and territory, and its own language or dialect. There were eight or nine major language stocks, as different from one another as English is from Chinese. Altogether, over 100 languages were spoken in California, about 70% of them mutually unintelligible. California was home to a greater variety of language and culture groups than any region of similar size in North America, or perhaps in the world.[1]

While the peoples were scarcely conscious of their own history, their diversity implies a complex story of overlapping waves of their ancestors' migration from Asia through Alaska and down the Pacific coast, followed by westward migrations by other native peoples from different parts of North America, combined with northern migrations by still other native peoples from Mexico. The archeological record is scarce, but it seems reasonable to infer a long process of culture evolution involving both convergent and divergent trends: intergroup contact, competition over resources, conflict, trade, partial amalgamation through intermarriage, diffusion of new discoveries and techniques among neighboring peoples, and relative isolation in distinct local habitats.

By permission of Smithsonian Institution Press.
From *Handbook of North American Indians, vol.
8, California,* 1978, Smithsonian Institution,
Washington, D.C.

*The "tribal" groups and
boundaries indicated on this
map, reflecting coherent language
groups, oversimplify the varied ethnic
makeup of native California. Several tribelets,
each with its own distinct identity and territory,
typically made up a "tribal" group shown here...*

*Solid dots show the
missions founded by
Spanish franciscans,
with the years of
founding indicated.*

Tolowa, Karok, Yurok, Shasta, Modoc, Achumawi, Chilula, Hupa, Chimariko, Whilkut, Wiyot, Nongatl, Wintu, Atsugewi, Paiute, Mattole, Sinkyone, Lassik, Wailaki, Cahto, Yuki, Nomlaki, Konkow, Yana, Maidu, Pomo, Patwin, Nisenan, Lake Miwok, Wappo, Washo, Coast Miwok, Solano (1823), San Rafael (1817), San Francisco (1776), San José (1797), Miwok, Yokuts (northern valley), Santa Clara (1777), Santa Cruz (1791), Ohlone, San Juan Bautista (1797), Monache, Monterey (presidio, 1770), Carmel (1770), Soledad (1791), Esselen, Koso, San Antonio (1771), San Miguel (1797), Yokuts (southern valley), Foothill Yokuts, Tubatulabal, Salinan, PACIFIC OCEAN, Tehachapi, Chemehuevi, San Luis Obispo (1772), Kitanemuk, Mohave, Chumash, Purisima (1787), Santa Ynez (1804), Tataviam, Serrano, Halchidhoma, Santa Barbara (1786), Buenaventura (1782), Fernando (1797), San Gabriel (1771), Yuma, Los Angeles (pueblo, 1781), Gabrielino, Cahuilla, San Juan Capistrano (1776), Luiseño, San Luis (1798), Cupeño, Ipai, San Diego (1769), Tipai, Kumeyaay, BAJA CALIFORNIA

0 25 50 75 100 Miles
0 25 50 75 100 Kilometers

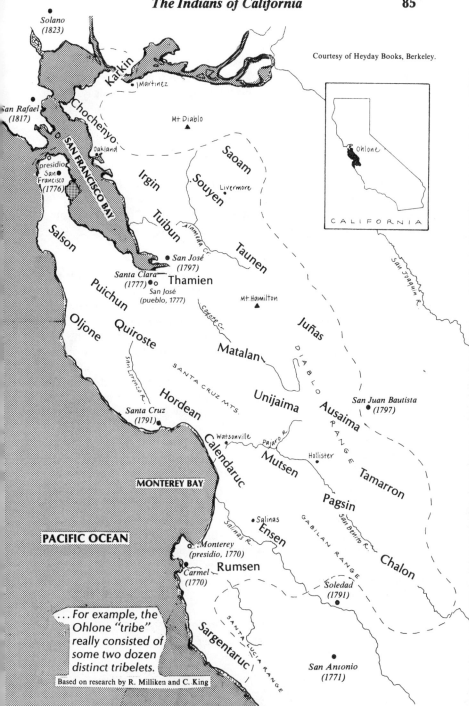

Courtesy of Heyday Books, Berkeley.

Solano
(1823)

Karkin

Martinez

Chochenyo

Mt Diablo

Saoam

San Rafael
(1817)

SAN FRANCISCO BAY

Oakland

Irgin

Souyen

Livermore

presidio
San
Francisco
(1776)

Tuibun

Salson

San José
(1797)

Taunen

Puichun

Santa Clara
(1777)

Thamien

San José
(pueblo, 1777)

Mt Hamilton

Juñas

Oljone

Quiroste

Matalan

San Lorenzo R.

SANTA CRUZ MTS.

Unijaima

Ausaima

San Juan Bautista
(1797)

Hordean

Santa Cruz
(1791)

Calendaruc

Watsonville

Pajaro R.

Mutsen

Hollister

Tamarron

MONTEREY BAY

Pagsin

GABILAN RANGE

San Benito R.

Chalon

PACIFIC OCEAN

Salinas R.

Salinas

Ensen

Monterey
(presidio, 1770)

Carmel
(1770)

Rumsen

Soledad
(1791)

SANTA LUCIA RANGE

Sargentaruc

San Antonio
(1771)

San Joaquin R.

DIABLO RANGE

Coyote Cr.

Alameda Cr.

Ohlone

CALIFORNIA

...For example, the Ohlone "tribe" really consisted of some two dozen distinct tribelets.

Based on research by R. Milliken and C. King

Between the Pacific ocean and the steep mountain ranges, California's coastal and central basin lands were far more varied and abundant in plant and animal life than they are today. Vast forests of six different species of oak trees gave way to wild grasslands, where the bunch-grasses might reach shoulder height. Marshlands saturated much of the coastal strip, nurturing a variety of reeds, fish, and mollusks. Ducks, geese, gulls, cormorants, and pelicans swarmed from sky to water and back. Extensive colonies of harbor seals and sea otters jammed the beaches. Many groups and species of whales frolicked off the coast, and dead ones often washed ashore. Grizzly bears came to scavenge from them. Herds of elk, deer and antelopes browsed on the wild grasslands. Coyotes, wolves, mountain lions, and bobcats hunted them, along with rabbits and other small animals. The native peoples adapted themselves logically into this ecosystem.

Gatherers, Fishers, Hunters

The peoples' staple food sources were wild plants and seeds they gathered—above all, acorns. In the fall, when the oak trees were bulging with acorns, a whole community would move into the forest to harvest them. Women and girls gathered the acorns in large burden baskets, with boys climbing the trees to shake them down, and men knocking acorns from the branches with poles. As the cone-shaped burden baskets were filled, the women secured them behind their backs with tumplines looped around their foreheads, and carried the acorns back to the village. The people would gather a big surplus of acorns, which they would store in special granaries built on stilts outside their huts.

The gathered acorns could not be eaten raw, or even cooked directly; they contained tannic acid, which was both poisonous and bitter to the taste. So the women had to leach them with fresh water for several hours, until the bitter poison was gone. First, having snapped the caps off the acorns, they cracked the acorns open and ground the meats into meal, pounding them between a stone pestle and a bedrock slab (often this was the task of the younger women). Sifting the meal through a fine mesh basket, they carefully laid the meal down in a basin hollowed out of the sand, or atop a special platform covered with twigs and leaves. Now it was time to leach the meal, pouring small basketfuls of water through it again and again, for as many hours as needed to make the meal sweet.

Then the women cooked the acorn meal. Most California Indian peoples, lacking pottery, had to use their watertight baskets to cook in.

*A Hupa woman, Mrs. Freddie, pouring water through acorn meal,
to leach its tannic acid into the basin she has smoothed from the sand.
Photo by Pliny Goddard, 1902.* (Lowie Museum of Anthropology, Berkeley)

Since they could not heat their cooking baskets from below without burning them, they heated them from within: The women heated large stones on a fire and, lifting them one by one on a pair of tongs made of a firm plant root looped at the far end, dropped the sizzling stones into the baskets filled with water and acorn meal. While the porridge cooked, they had to keep stirring it, keeping the stones moving so they wouldn't burn through the cooking basket. When it was done, they removed the cooking stones with the tongs. The acorn porridge could then be used as the basis for the people's daily stew, to which they added herbs, fish, mollusks, and meat. Or it could be worked up into an acorn bread. The women usually prepared several days' worth of porridge and bread at a time.

It is interesting to speculate on how the California Indians invented their technique to overcome the acorns' natural chemical defense against predation and take advantage of this very nutritious and tasty food source. The technique was by no means obvious, nor did it flow automatically from the abundance of oak trees; in other parts of North

(continued on page 90)

*Indian woman carrying her digging stick, her burden basket attached to a skullcap.
Due to their practice of digging up a variety of roots and tubers for food, the
California Indians were later scornfully nicknamed "diggers" by Yankee settlers.
That's like scorning a skilled carpenter as a "slammer."* (Bancroft Library).

Basket weaver of Sacramento valley. In the technical skill, variety, utility, and artistic beauty of their work, California Indian women were perhaps the greatest basket makers the world has ever seen.

America where oaks were also abundant, the people never discovered the secret of processing acorns.

Perhaps a clever and curious woman, having tried to eat and cook acorns but failed bitterly, discovered that waterlogged acorns she gathered after a rainstorm were sweet to the taste, and sat well with her. Then she seized on the idea of following nature's lead by leaching raw acorns with her water basket. After experimenting with leaching, shelling, pounding, and cooking the acorns, she and her sisters developed a workable production sequence, making the acorns edible and popular. Then, through outmarriage into neighboring ethnic groups, her women companions taught the new methods to the women in their adoptive villages, and so the knowledge spread through California.

Besides acorns, the women and girls gathered buckeyes, pine nuts, grass seeds, roots, herbs, and berries. As well, the women carried firewood back with them from the forest, and fetched water. In many societies, they gathered and caught mollusks and crabs. Sometimes they worked with men in communal fishing outings, driving salmon, sturgeon or other fish into nets the men held. Women and girls also caught insects and bee larvae, which the people liked to eat from time to time.[2] Both sexes participated in communal grasshopper hunts: Surrounding a wild grass field and whacking the tall grass with sticks, the people slowly drove the grasshoppers towards the center and into a deep hole the women had dug there. They piled grass atop the hole and set it afire—singeing the grasshoppers' wings. Then, they could easily gather the insects.[3]*

Hunting deer, elk, and other large game was the domain of men. Nowhere did hunting provide the people's main food supply; compared with gathering, it was an irregular activity . A man planning to hunt deer would spend several days preparing: He fasted, lived apart from his wife, went through ritual purification at the sweat lodge, and engaged the spirit of the deer in dreams and prayers. Embarking on the hunt, he placed a dead deer's head over his own as a decoy and made sly contact with a herd of deer. With patience and guile, he maneuvered to within a few feet of his target animal, and then fired his arrow. Deer might also be hunted by a group of men, some of them frightening the herd into confusion, others ambushing the fleeing animals one by one. Bringing a deer, elk or antelope carcass back to his

---

*The insects eaten by the Indians, while no doubt quite tasty, had negligible nutritional value, providing very little protein.

village brought a man prestige. But etiquette required modesty and restraint, so he often ate little or none of his own prey, sharing the food out among his family and friends.

Men and boys also hunted birds, snakes, lizards, squirrels, mice and other rodents for food, ornamentation and clothing. They employed a variety of slings, snares, deadfall traps, and animal calls to lure their prey. Communal rabbit hunts, in which women participated, were popular: The people whacked the bushes and grass bunches, or set fire to the field to drive dozens of rabbits into prepared nets. The rabbit meat was eagerly cooked and eaten, and the women worked the rabbit skins into blankets and garments; about 200 rabbit skins made a blanket.[4]

The sexual division of labor varied somewhat from one society to the next, and could flex where necessary. If a man's wife fell ill, he would take on her tasks of fetching firewood and water, cooking, and tending the children, as best he could. In many societies a menstruating woman was prohibited/relieved from cooking, so her husband did the cooking during her periods. Among the Yana, the men normally fetched fuel, made the roasting pits, and cooked the roots and tubers their wives had gathered.[5]

Domestication of animals for food production was scarcely known among the California Indians. Dogs were kept, usually for companionship and help in the hunt—less often, for meat (as among the Yokuts and Ohlones). The Chumash captured bear cubs in the wild, raised and fattened them, and then slaughtered them for their meat and skins.[6]

Often the only gardening (horticulture) done by the gatherer/fisher/hunter peoples of California was tobacco cultivation. Tobacco was smoked, chewed, and sometimes mixed with lime from burnt mollusk shells and eaten. Valued for its relaxing and stimulating qualities, it had ritual and curative uses: A shaman might blow tobacco smoke over his or her patient, and a person might ingest tobacco in search of supernatural power. Jimsonweed, a potent and dangerous hallucinogen, grew wild in many parts of California, as in Mexico. Called *datura* or *toloache* by the Spaniards (from the Nahuatl *toloatzin*), it was central to ritual and shamanic sessions among many Indian groups.[7]

The Kumeyaays of southern California raised corn and other food plants, building dams, canals, and mountainside terraces to irrigate their crops. They and neighboring peoples cultivated a variety of herbs, flowers, shrubs and trees for food, fiber, and ornaments.[8] The Yuma, Mohave and Cahuilla tribes near the Colorado river in southeast

California cultivated corn, beans, squashes and melons. The Yumas and Mohaves also differed from most other peoples of California in having a strong tribal identity which could unite all their villages over a wide area in joint actions; in their men valuing and eagerly pursuing warfare; and in travelling extensively beyond their native lands to explore, trade, and fight.[9]

Environmental Management

Unlike modern man, the Indians of California did not systematically assault the rest of nature. But neither were they passive spectators of natural process. They learned to manage their environment, especially through controlled burning. They periodically burned the thick brush to keep it from encroaching on the grasslands which nurtured and provided space for the deer, elk and antelope. Burning the brush and sections of grassland provided the intense heat for pine, grass and flower seeds of many species to germinate. By keeping the brush under control, they helped prevent unwanted fires from spreading wildly and ravaging the precious oak forests. Some groups also burned clearings within forests, so they could cultivate tobacco and wild roots used to make baskets.[10]

Restraint in taking from nature meant respect for future generations and other groups of people. The Maidu agreed that a flint miner could not take away more flint from Table Mountain than he could dislodge with one blow of his stone hammer.[11] Indian groups catching river salmon took care to let plenty of salmon pass through, so the people upstream could take their catch and the salmon population could replenish itself. Hunting was conceived as a reciprocal act, with the hunter obliged to propitiate the spirit of the hunted animal.*

---

*The native peoples of America probably developed their techniques of environmental management and conservation through bitter experience and near disasters. In particular, the sudden extinction of two-thirds of the mammalian species of the Americas, beginning about 11,300 years ago, seems to have been brought on (at least in part) by overly aggressive hunting by human groups migrating from North to South America. Most of the large mammals were wiped out, including the wooly mammoth, the giant sloth, and the horse.[12] Crude hunting methods, such as driving an entire herd of mammoths over a cliff, must have had a devastating impact on the ability of large mammal species to reproduce themselves. Some groups of people in the region of ancient Mexico also brought on environmental trauma by overzealous clearing of forests.

Property Relations

Ownership of the land and other natural resources varied between communal tribelet, village, family, and individual ownership. Most land, mines and quarries were used jointly by all the members of a village or tribelet. Ownership often rested with the lineage group, with inheritance defined by the male line. Choice oak groves, grass fields, fishing spots, and hunting areas might be allotted to families or individuals; this was especially true among the peoples of northwest California, who were more property conscious than most other California Indian groups.[13] For most tribelets, the distinction between their collective property/territory and that of their neighboring tribelets and ethnic groups, figured more prominently than internal property distinctions within the tribelet.

Most movable property was owned by the individual who produced and used it. A woman owned her baskets, cooking utensils, root harvesting sticks, and garment making tools. A man owned his bows, arrows, fishing nets, and stone and bone tools. A woman might pass her personal property down to her daughters, a man to his sons or other male relatives. But in many Indian societies, a dead person's personal effects were burned along with the dead man or woman.

Money took the form of mollusk shells bunched together on lengths of string. Measured lengths of these shell-beads became a common medium of exchange. The shell-beads were usually manufactured by men—sometimes organized into specialized artisan groups—and a man would tattoo a measuring gauge onto one forearm, to compare against actual lengths of shell-beads in money transactions. The distinction between money and personal adornment was often blurred, as the shell beads were worn as necklaces. Archeological evidence suggests that shell beads were developed as a common exchange medium around AD 1200, by the Chumash people living on the islands and coastal strip flanking the Santa Barbara channel. From the Chumash area, the use of shell beads as money spread to other cultures, and Indians farther north such as the Ohlones may only recently have begun using shell beads in this way, by the time the Spaniards arrived.[14]

People used their shell-bead money to pay for the services of professional artisans that existed in some societies, and especially to pay the shaman for curing a sick family member. Money was used to buy specialized wares brought by merchants from other tribelets and ethnic groups. But the daily activities of procuring food, clothing, tools and shelter were done directly by the people themselves, without resort to money exchange.

To speak of "private" ownership of tracts of land and natural resources among California Indian groups is misleading. In a commodity society such as capitalism, private landownership typically means ownership by people (whether individuals, or corporate or banking executives) who do not work the land themselves, or derive their personal subsistence from its products. A capitalist landowner values his land only in its ability to generate money income for him—in rents collected from tenants living on the land, through the labor of people hired to work the land, and/or through resale of the land at a higher price. California Indians owning tracts of land, forest areas, or fishing spots as individuals or families worked on their property to procure their daily food. While they did not share their resources freely with other members of their tribelet, neither did they use their property to get rich at the expense of others. Class divisions did not exist among the California Indians, except in embryo.

Kinship, Marriage, and Divorce

A village might have as few as 25 people, tribelets ranged in population from around 50 to 500 for a multi-village tribelet, and the total population of all the tribelets making up a language group ("tribe") seldom topped 3,000. Yet the peoples evolved a complex system of kinship and social relations, which provided elaborate rules and restrictions regarding marriage, hospitality, dances, and warfare.

First there were the lineage groups (clans) spanning several generations of blood relatives, demarcated by the male line. Each clan adopted a particular animal as its insignia. Several different clans made up a language group (tribe), and they crossed tribelet boundaries—so that each tribelet might contain representatives of the various clans. Each clan was, in turn, divided into the same two *moieties*. Among the Ohlones, e.g., everyone—no matter what clan he or she belonged to—was a member of either the Bear or the Deer moiety. Thus the moiety was at once a subdivision of the clan, and a *larger* grouping embracing roughly half the people of an entire language group. The crisscrossing sets of social relations that resulted, provided both rigid structure and flexibility.

Among many native groups, especially in the southern half of California, incest taboos required marriage outside both one's clan and one's moiety. This made marriage rather difficult and elaborate to arrange, as one typically had to find a partner outside one's home village. And, though in many cultures both the young man and the young woman had a good deal of free choice in selecting their marriage partner, the parents and other relatives of both bride and groom were highly interested parties to the marriage.

Bridal gifts presented by the groom's family to the bride's family, formed the key social transaction surrounding marriage. These took the form of shell beads (money), rabbit- or deer-skin blankets, and food. The initial bridal gifts might be presented upon the betrothal of the couple, with the main round of gifts presented at the wedding ceremony. Among central California peoples, the bride's family had to reciprocate by presenting gifts to the groom's family; usually these were of lesser value, though among some peoples the exchanges were nearly equal. In northern and southern California, the flow of gifts strongly favored the bride's relatives.[15]

This custom is often glibly referred to as "bride price." As with "private ownership" of natural resources among Indian groups, the term is highly misleading. The Indian societies were natural, not commodity economies. The ritual of bridal gifts did not make marriage a commodity exchange, nor did the bride thereby become the property of the groom, to dispose of as he wished. In the gatherer/ fisher/hunter societies of California, woman the gatherer, food and clothing producer was the center of human subsistence. Her labor was far more valuable to society than man's labor, so a man's family had to compensate her family when he took her in marriage.*

The newly married couple often lived and worked with the bride's family for a while (especially if the full amount of bridal gifts had not yet been paid); but eventually they would settle with the husband's clan. This meant that a woman typically had to move out of her home village after marrying and make friends with a whole new group of women,

---

*A superficial view sees "bride price" as inherently oppressive and degrading to women, whereas the later practice of a dowry passing from the bride's family to the groom's family upon marriage (supposedly to provide economic security for the wife) is seen as more humane. Actually, the reverse is true. The transition to the dowry system signals that woman and her labor have become so degraded in the eyes of (male dominated) society, that she has become a *burden* to her parents, who must therefore pay lavishly to marry her off. In India, the dowry system has become a spur to the frequent physical abuse and murder of a married woman by her husband and his parents, who often use the dowry relation and their physical power over the woman to extort more and more money from her parents. In many parts of rural Africa and the Philippines, where the opposite practice of bridal gifts still prevails, women have a good deal more autonomy (including the freedom to bring their own food and clothing products to market) than do Hindu women.

often learning a new dialect or language in the process. Her children became members of her husband's clan and moiety. There were but few exceptions to these rules of patrilocality and patrilineage among California Indians: Among some Pomo groups living north of San Francisco bay, a married couple settled permanently with the bride's kin, and descent was reckoned in the female line. Women had an unusually high status in Pomo societies, often serving as chiefs.

It is logical to infer that the matrilocal and matrilineal Pomo and Huchnom groups formed the remnants of the woman-centered ("matriarchal") societies of the past, within a region where men had overturned most of the women's communes and established their own blood lines and clan dwellings as key organizing principles for society. And the fact that the transition from mother-right (matrilineage) to father-right (patrilineage) took place among societies where private property scarcely existed, sheds light on the causal sequence involved. Frederick Engels theorized that the accumulation of private property—notably oxen, camels, horses, sheep, etc. among pastoral peoples—in the hands of men, and the men's desire to transmit this property to their sons, gave rise to the replacement of mother right by father right, and the subsequent enslavement of women to men.[16] But among California's Indians, the transition to father right took place in societies with practically no domesticated animals, no agriculture, and precious little transmission even of one's personal effects to the next generation. So the experience of California's peoples supports those feminist anthropologists who have criticized Engels for reversing the links of historical causality between private property and women's oppression: In reality, the enslavement of women through capture in warfare and forced marriage* must have *preceded* the rise of private property and enabled the overthrow of mother right; the imposition of father right,

---

*Among some California Indian peoples, it was customary for the bride to offer physical resistance to sexual intercourse with the groom, when their marriage was privately "consummated" around the time of the wedding ceremony. Among the Ohlones, e.g., the bride would vigorously scratch the groom's face before sexual intercourse.[17] This ritual was probably performed in good fun, and seldom reflected the actual emotional relationship between the young couple (who may have been clandestine lovers for some time already). Yet it might well have been a kind of reenactment of woman's response to the original institution of marriage by rape, capture, and her removal to the man's village. Among the Yokuts peoples of central California, if a man raped a virgin—with or without abduction—he was required to marry her.[18] As with a similar provision in the Mosaic law code of the old testament (Deuteronomy 22.28-9), this suggests a causal, (pre)historical link between rape, abduction, and marriage.

in turn, enabled (though did not guarantee) the rise of, and male inheritance of, private property.

Marriage was usually monogamous. But wealthier men, especially chiefs, often took two or three wives. Often the multiple wives were sisters; this had the advantage of keeping the solidarity between sisters intact, as they both (or all) moved to their husband's village and continued to cooperate in gathering and making food, baskets and clothing. This arrangement, called sororal polygyny, was reflected in the kinship terminologies of many peoples: The mother's sister was called by the same term as one's own mother.[19] The children of a man's first wife tended to have higher status than those of his subsequent wives, since his first marriage involved the most elaborate bridal gifts.

Grounds for divorce included childlessness and laziness on the part of the wife, and abuse on the part of the husband. If a man abused his wife physically and/or psychologically, she might take refuge in her parents' home. The ease with which she could get a divorce depended largely on the influence of the bridal gifts: If divorce meant that her kinsfolk had to return the bridal gifts to her husband's kin, they might be unable or reluctant to do so. Then her parents and other relatives would try and cajole her to return to her husband, and a pattern of abuse might have to repeat itself several times before they consented to divorce. If a man divorced his wife without reasonable cause, her relatives might refuse to return the bridal gifts.

So, in societies such as the Yurok and other peoples of northwest California where the bridal gifts carried great social weight, both the woman's and man's freedom to divorce was constrained by the custom of returning the bridal gifts.[20] Since the woman was the more valuable partner in the marriage and had far greater demands upon her to produce (both food and children), it was easier for the man to claim grounds for divorce, and easier to secure one. In societies where return of the bridal gifts did not apply, both the man and woman had more freedom of divorce. In the event of divorce, the children normally went with their mother, returning with her to her home village. Among the Yurok and their neighbors, however, the repayment of the bridal gifts could be reduced a certain amount for each child left with the husband.

It was common for a widow, after observing the ritual mourning period for her late husband (which might last a year), to marry one of his surviving brothers. Conversely, if a man's wife died young, he would seek a new wife among her unmarried sisters. Both customs served to disturb as little as possible the inter-kin group relation, established by the initial transfer of the bridal gifts. "Virgin" marriages with their crucial bridal gifts thus emerge as a kind of magnetic force, directing and orienting the future relations between members of the two clans involved. In this light, marriage was not so much a union between a man and a woman, as a union between two different kinship groups.

Sex Separation and Women's Autonomy

The center of men's social life was the sweat lodge. This was a large structure built into the ground, its earthen roof looking (from outside) like a shallow dome, topped by a vent to let smoke escape. The men would congregate inside, play gambling games, talk and sing about hunting, and prepare their bows and arrows for the next hunt. Several times daily, the sweating ritual would proceed: Throwing extra fuel onto the fire, the men huddled and danced round the lively blaze. Nearly scalding themselves, they soon worked up a heavy sweat, which they sustained for quite some time, using animal bone implements to rub or drain the sweat off their bodies. Finally, the men bolted out the tiny door, sprinted and plunged into the cooling waters of a nearby stream.

In most culture groups, women were excluded from the sweat lodge. Women had, in many ways, their own societies. Together they pounded and leached acorns, wove baskets, made blankets and clothing, sang, and played gambling games, in small groups of kinswomen and friends with their small children. From an early age (usually before 10), boys and girls went their separate ways. The girls stayed with their mothers and other kinswomen, learning the complex and subtle arts of plant gathering, food processing, and basket weaving. The boys joined their fathers and other kinsmen at the sweat lodge, where they learned how to make tools and weapons and prepare for hunting big animals.

The sense I get from the anthropological literature is that, in most California Indian cultures, sex separation was the rule, with social mixing of the sexes less frequent. A man spent most of his time with his fellow men at the sweat lodge, while a woman spent most of her time with her kinswomen and friends in the village, grass fields and forest. Husband and wife did not spend much time together; meal times were probably their main points of contact. In some Pomo and other Indian groups, it was customary for men to sleep overnight at the sweat lodge. If the men were preparing for war or expecting an attack on their village, they used the sweat lodge as a mobilization center, sleeping together there while posting sentries.

So how did the sweat lodge emerge historically? Gerda Lerner theorizes that, in "primitive" society, boys had a harder time developing a sense of identify and self worth than did girls—due to the central role of woman, who, as mother, seemed all-powerful. The male ego was forged through collective male action: "...Inevitably, big-game hunting bands would have led to male bonding, which must have been greatly strengthened by warfare and the preparation necessary to turn boys into warriors... The ego formation of the individual male, which must have taken place within a context of fear, awe, and possibly dread of the female, must have led men to create social institutions to bolster their egos, strengthen their self-confidence, and validate their sense of worth."[21]

The sweat lodge was such a social institution. From the scattered role they once played—marginal to women's communal, gathering society —the sweat lodge enabled men to build a parallel power, which finally eclipsed the collective power of women (without destroying women's power, as the women still remained central to subsistence). A key to the men's success was the monopoly on arms which the sweat lodge provided them. Probably they first conquered social power by overwhelming not their own kinswomen, but women of other cultures whom they captured in warfare; this would explain the replacement of matrilocal residence and mother right by patrilocal residence and father right. The actual sweating ritual, where the men danced vigorously around the blazing fire, may have reenacted their past victories in warfare, which had climaxed in the burning of an attacked village and the seizure of its women.

Sexual Relations

The data, sparse as it is, suggests a great variety of sexual relations and mores among California's Indian groups. While most adults were married, a married couple's sexual activity was probably infrequent (compared with the norm in modern bourgeois society). It was not unusual for adults to seek sexual partners outside of marriage. Homosexuality seems to have been more freely tolerated than heterosexual adultery.

Extramarital affairs were treated in a variety of ways. In some cultures they were severely frowned upon and, if discovered, could lead to violence: A man who learned that his wife was having an affair with another man might hire a shaman to work evil magic against his rival; he might fight with the rival, and even kill him. He would probably be

(continued on page 102)

A Chumash sweat lodge.

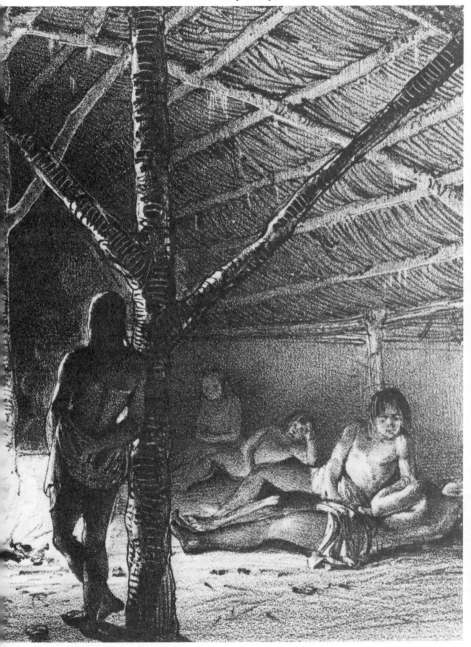

Drawing by captain W. Smyth   courtesy of Bancroft Library

less inclined to assault his unfaithful wife, especially if she were his only wife: If he killed her, her kinsfolk would refuse to return the bridal gifts, and then how would he find another wife? Unfaithfulness by either marriage partner could be grounds for divorce. Among the Yurok, if the fact of adultery were established, the offended husband would receive a payment assessed against his rival, thus averting a violent outcome.[22]

If the adultery were committed by a close kinsman of the husband, less offense was given. Among the Ohlones, this situation was often resolved by a public reprimand of the husband's rival kinsman, or of his wife.[23] Among many Chumash groups, a man could have an affair with his brother's wife, or a woman with her sister's husband, without giving offense at all. "To the Chumash the relationship between siblings, either same sex or opposite, proved so strong that nothing, not even sexual jealousy, could be allowed to harm it."[24]

Indeed the Chumash are the most sexually free culture on California's anthropological record. Sexual activity among the unmarried was openly accepted. So was homosexual activity among men. Some men dressed and worked as women, engaging in sexual relations with other men. The Spanish lieutenant Pedro Fages observed that there were two or three such men in each Chumash village he visited, men who "permit the heathen to practice the execrable, unnatural abuse of their bodies. They are called jewels, and are held in high esteem..."[25]

Evidently the transvestites who so horrified Fages were also shamans, invested with spiritual power in their people's eyes. Male transvestism was likewise practiced, accepted and cherished among most other Indian groups in California (and North America generally). Among the Yurok, one in perhaps several hundred males chose to take this road. As a youth, he revealed his preference by starting to weave baskets. Staying among the women, he adopted their manner of dress and work. Eventually he became a shaman, and was respected by the people.[26] He could marry a man and act as his "wife" in all aspects except procreation.

Lesbianism was also practiced and tolerated, and there are fragmentary references to women taking on men's roles. Fear, ignorance and prejudice against homosexuality by field anthropologists no doubt led to a gross underreportage of gay male, and especially lesbian activity. As we have seen in discussing sex separation, a man spent most of his time with his fellow men, a woman with her companion women. So there were ample opportunities for homo-sexual contact. These contacts, in many ways the easiest and most natural expressions of sexuality available, were invisible to the European observers—whereas the social institution of the male transvestite was obvious.

Reproductive Rights and Childbirth

Women largely controlled their own reproductive functions, and set the rules for childbirth. A pregnant woman was cared for by a midwife—often endowed with great spiritual power—and by her kinswomen and friends as she went into labor. She refrained from certain foods (such as meat and fish) and moved about as little as possible, to improve the chances of a healthy delivery. Her husband, while marginalized from the childbirth process, also observed the food taboos and refrained from hunting, as her pregnancy advanced.[27]

After the woman gave birth and started nursing her baby, her husband was commonly forbidden to touch her for a long period. Among some Chumash groups, the husband could not touch his wife until her child could stand alone on its feet; if he broke this taboo, he would father no more children.[28] Among the Ohlones, a woman had to finish nursing her child before her husband could again touch her and resume sexual contact. The nursing period might last two years. This taboo helped a woman space her pregnancies over time; given her burden of gathering and carrying heavy loads of seeds, roots and firewood on her back, she could not raise and carry more than one baby at a time.[29]

Abortion was commonly used to end unwanted pregnancies, especially among unmarried women. The women developed various herbal potions for this purpose. Chumash women normally tried to abort their first pregnancy, believing that if the child was born and survived, they would never bear a child again. If the abortion attempts failed, they would kill the infant upon birth.[30]

Infanticide was also used to eliminate deformed infants. (There is no evidence of sex bias in infanticide practices in California). And, among many Indian groups, a woman who bore twins would kill one of them. Among the Ipai-Tipai, however, twins were considered a blessing from the spirit world, and were both nurtured. No doubt it was the grandparents' active participation in child rearing that enabled an Ipai-Tipai woman to keep both her twins, despite her semi-nomadic life.[31]

Kindness Towards Children

The native peoples of California treated their children with great kindness and affection. There are very few reports of physical punishment of children, and in some cultures parents refrained even from scolding their children in public. So devoted were the Gabrielinos to their children that the franciscan missionaries declared, in amazement, that the children were treated like "little idols."[32]

This provides a sharp contrast to the situation in the U.S. today, where parents still have the legal right to physically punish their children, and where physical and sexual abuse of children by their elders (notably their fathers and other male relatives) has been widespread for many generations. We arrive at an irony: "Primitive" peoples treat their children with tenderness and respect, while civilized people often beat and rape their children. How can this irony be explained?

Among the California Indians, small children were raised by their mothers and other female relatives; fathers played little or no role in child rearing. At the age of perhaps six or eight, boys and girls parted ways, with the boys spending their days among their male kin and friends around the sweat lodge. Before long, both girls and boys learned a wide range of skills from their elders, and began contributing to their people's subsistence. Devotion to children in such a natural process of socialization is not hard to explain; after all, any social species that does not care for its young will soon go extinct. What is harder to explain is the frequent cruelty towards children in civilized societies.

Domestication of animals must have transformed not only human subsistence patterns, but also child rearing practices. Now fathers worked closer to home, and came into more regular contact with their young children. The practice of inflicting pain and cruel burdens on farm animals to break their free spirits and harness them to man's will, must have rubbed off on man's treatment of his own children. With urbanization, the solidarity between parents and children that had once come from engagement in common subsistence activities was more and more broken. And in today's society, the long period of economic dependence of both children and adolescents on their parents makes them extra vulnerable to domestic abuse.

Justice without Shackles

Most California Indians were strangers not only to the whip, but also to jails, prisons, police and professional armies. Since there was no antagonism between property owners and the propertyless, or between rulers and the ruled, there was no need for an apparatus of social repression.

Personal disputes were resolved in simple and direct ways. If a thief was discovered, he or she had to return the stolen object, or its equivalent. If a man assaulted another, he had to materially compensate his victim. Even murder, in some societies, was redeemed by the murderer paying a heavy fine to the victim's family. Among the Yurok and their neighbors in northwest California, who had an unusually elaborate legal system with an array of fines and redemptions, a convicted murderer might thus be impoverished for life. Another common method of redeeming murder was blood revenge—often approved of, or at least tolerated by, the chief. There were no special courts, and disputes were resolved by the chief, often in consultation with his or her council of elders.

Chiefs, Councils, and Shamans

A man might be elected chief, or inherit the position from his father, uncle or brother. While the system of choosing a chief and the amount of power vested in him varied from one culture to another, the chief was expected to embody certain qualities of moral leadership. He had to be a man of integrity, generosity and self restraint, a strong and persuasive speaker, a good dancer, and—if he was also to serve as chief in war time—an outstanding archer and fighter.

The chief was a man of wealth, although wealth in itself did not make one a candidate to become chief. In many cultures the people paid him regular tribute in food, blankets, etc., thus relieving him of the need to hunt and fish. The wealth he received from the people was not his private property, but rather a kind of public trust: He had to look after the poor, the weak and the disabled, making sure everyone had enough to eat and a place to stay. He was also expected to return his extra wealth periodically to the people, in the form of ceremonial feasts.

In tribelets that encompassed several villages, a "capital" village might serve as the trading and ceremonial center for the tribelet. The chief of this central village would then be regarded as chief of the tribelet. He entertained emissaries and merchants from other tribelets, negotiated and traded with them. He might also set the dates for feasts, dances, and seasonal migrations, and decide on questions of war and peace. But the chief almost never acted unilaterally on major questions. Indeed in many cultures, he was basically an *adviser* to the *council of elders*, a governing body of respected elder men, perhaps including women in some cases. (In a multi-village tribelet, the council of elders could take the form of the assembled leaders from each village). The council decided by consensus, and if the chief could not convince them of his point of view, he had to bow to their consensus. If the chief violated the public trust and lost the people's respect, he could be removed by his peers. In some cultures a woman could become chief[33]; if the position was hereditary and a deceased chief had left no qualified male heirs, his daughter might become chief.[34]

Women wielded more power in spiritual and curative roles than in civic ones. The *shaman* was a highly respected, and often feared, woman or man. She mediated between the world of spirits and the world of humans, and was thus thought to attain power to control the fertility of oak trees and grass fields, and the abundance of fish and wild animals. The shaman was also the native doctor: She or he employed a mixture of herbal remedies, dances, incantations, and sucking the "poison" out of a sick person's body, which ended in the sleight of hand trick of producing a small bone, stone, or lizard to show that the source of illness had been removed.

Methods of payment to shamans varied, but typically depended on the length of treatment and the success of the cure attempted; if the treatment failed and the patient died, the shaman would normally return any advance payment she or he had received from the patient's family. In some cultures the payment for treatment was set by the patient's family, and thus all could afford treatment. But in those cultures where the shaman set the payment, the cost of treatment might be so burdensome for a poor family that they preferred to let a sick kinsperson go untreated. A successful shaman could become wealthy. Among the Yurok and their neighboring tribelets, almost all shamans were women.

Being a shaman held its terrors as well as privileges. The power to heal was often considered double-edged: The same power could be used to hurt or kill a person by poisoning or sorcery. If too many patients died on a shaman, the people would turn against him or her, assuming evil intent. Then the shaman could be killed, with the chief's approval. If the shaman failed to return payments from families whose members had died under treatment, then his or her violent death was practically assured. Yet among the Yurok, Hupa and other northwest cultures where women dominated the shamanic profession, a shaman was very seldom killed[35]—probably due to those societies' well established means of litigating disputes and resolving them through fines of personal restitution.

Some cultures made a clear distinction between curing and sorcery as social functions. Among the Tubatulabal of south central California, male shamans acted both as curers and sorcerers, but women shamans only as sorcerers.[36] Among the Yurok, by contrast, women served as curers, and men as sorcerers.[37] In many cultures misfortunes—whether natural or personal—were blamed on sorcery, whose origins were often pinned on rival tribelets. So a sorcerer could win social acceptance by directing his or her destructive powers against the evil forces of a rival group. But such powers could as easily be turned against the members of one's own group, and a sorcerer might be hired to avenge a personal insult or perceived injury. Sorcerers were typically the most feared members of a community. Sometimes they engaged in dangerous contests against each other, trying to destroy each other's powers and person.

Warfare and Restraint

Conflicts over resources and territory seem to have been the prime spur to warfare among the native peoples of California. Disputes over fishing, hunting and mining rights, accusations of sorcery, or outrage over attacks upon women of a neighboring tribelet who had ranged over the boundary in their gathering activities, could erupt into war. So could inter-tribelet theft (of stored acorns, for example), or failure to reciprocate in gift giving when two tribelets engaged in ceremonial exchanges.

Most California Indian groups put little effort into making and using special weapons, armor, and other war paraphernalia, or in training their young men to fight. Warrior cults scarcely existed. With the exception of the Colorado river tribes in southeast California, it is probably false to characterize any California Indian group as warlike.

Yet the threat of attack by men of a rival tribelet was a fact of life, and when warfare did erupt, it could be swift and terrible. A war party overrunning a village would kill all the surviving men, often severing their heads or scalps as trophies. Women were subject to rape and slaughter, along with their children. Some warring groups tortured their captives before killing them. In some cases the women and children, instead of being killed, were seized and brought back to the victors' home village.[38] Captured women might then be given away or sold; less often, they were incorporated into the victors' tribelet through marriage, as among Pomo and Nisenan groups.[39] A war party, often grouped along kinship lines with an *ad hoc* war chief, would spare their own kinsfolk in a village they attacked.

Compared with peaceful trade, joint ceremonies, gift exchange and intermarriage between tribelets, warfare was no doubt infrequent. What made it so damaging was the thirst for revenge by the relatives of those killed and defeated. Revenge and counter-revenge could become the motive force sustaining feuds spanning generations, erupting now and again in violent attacks between rival tribelets—as among the Gabrielinos.[40]

But, as with their subsistence attacks on the forces of nature, most California Indian groups learned restraint in their attacks on neighboring and rival groups. Many groups ritualized warfare so as to minimize casualties and spare the noncombatant population: Hostilities would be announced beforehand by the messengers of two opposing chiefs, and the two rival teams of warriors would face off in a grass field on the agreed upon day. Hurling battle cries and insults at each other, the two lines of warriors engaged in a brief exchange of arrow fire. As soon as a warrior on either side was badly wounded or killed, the battle would end. Peace could then be restored by the "victorious" side presenting gifts of restitution to the "defeated" side. Such practices were common among Chumash, Ohlone, Wappo, Patwin and Pomo groups.[41]

The Yurok tribelets restrained warfare among themselves by an elaborate system of fines compensating war victims and their relatives for injuries, death, and property destruction. Reciprocal damages inflicted by two warring parties did not cancel out the fines; every injured party received his or her full settlement from the warrior group responsible. So a crushing victory in battle would wind up impoverishing the victorious warriors and their relatives. On the other hand, failure to pay damages assessed by the Yurok legal system seems to have been the main motive for warfare among the Yurok tribelets.[42]

The Yumas, Mohaves and their neighbors along the Colorado river were uniquely warlike. Their men rigorously practiced the arts of war, and gloried in bloody combat. The Yuman peoples, unlike most California Indian groups, had a real tribal (not merely a tribelet) organization, which could rally men from a broad expanse of villages into a united fighting force. The Mohaves, in contrast to most other Indian groups, liked to travel far and wide from their native villages, often passing through the central valley to the Pacific coast. They engaged in trade but also warfare with the settled peoples they encountered, sometimes sowing terror among them.

Life's Joys

If the fears and terrors of sorcery and warfare were a regular feature of native life, they were usually eclipsed by the joys of life. Music, rhythmic chanting, song and dance were woven together with daily activities. Women sang together and chatted exuberantly as they pounded and leached acorns, and wove baskets. Men chatted, sang and danced in the sweat lodge. Children absorbed their parents' love of rhythm and music from the cradle, along with the varied sounds of the natural world around them. Rattles, split-stick clappers, bull-roarers, wooden flutes, bone or reed whistles, drums and tambourines enlivened ceremonial dances. Their music was crude and ugly to European ears, but exciting and energizing to the people themselves.

The California Indians did not take life dead seriously. They laughed, joked and shouted during their communal fishing and small game hunting outings, and made merry feasting on their catches. They enjoyed practical jokes and deflating pompous characters. Their colorful mythology, outrageous and irreverent by judaeo-christian standards, reflects their easygoing approach to life. In many cultures a coyote-man appears as the creator of the human race. Far from being a terrible and condescending god, coyote-man is mischievous, lascivious, and sometimes half drunk and prone to fall on his face. In many peoples' cosmologies, the coyote-man and the other creators of the natural world gracefully withdraw from the scene once their creative work is done, no longer interfering in human affairs.

Games and gambling were a big part of Indian life. Shinny, the forerunner of field hockey, was enjoyed by both sexes, and played in a fiercely competitive spirit. People gambled against each other in games of chance and divination, using various implements of bone, shell and stone—the forerunners of modern dice, roulette wheel chips and playing cards. During games of shinny, athletic and acrobatic contests, spectators would offer wager against each other on the outcome. Games and gambling were played most intensely during feasts and big social gatherings; but gambling was also an everyday diversion among both men and women. Among the Ohlones, according to Malcolm Margolin, people engaged in a gambling game found release from their usual self restraint by craving each other's possessions and struggling unabashedly to win them. But once the game was over, restraint and moderation returned: The winners refrained from bragging, and the losers—no matter how much they had lost— refrained from sulking.[43]

The Communal Impulse and the Selfish Impulse

We can see two opposed trends in the social psychology of the California Indians: the selfish striving for individual gain, and the communal values of sharing and solidarity. Individual initiative was limited by the well established ways of doing things, passed down from generation to generation with little or no change, and gambling games provided a fairly harmless outlet for ego competition. The communal values were still strong enough to hold selfish impulses in check: No one could accumulate vast wealth or power at the expense of the community, and everyone—no matter how unfortunate—was provided for.

On the level of relations among tribelets, the two trends expressed themselves as a tribelet's jealous claim to its own resources and territory, *vs.* solidarity and sharing among tribelets, reinforced by intermarriage. Here the balance did not weigh nearly so heavily in favor of communal values. Inter-tribelet rivalry over resources was an ongoing source of friction and at times violent clashes; intermarriage and inter-tribelet resource sharing seldom, if ever, moved beyond the level of coalition to become an organic unity. People (or, more accurately, men) still tended to think of themselves as a group distinct from neighboring tribelets, even when those tribelets spoke the same or a similar language. So they often did not apply the same kind of humane code of ethics in dealing with other tribelets, that they applied among themselves. The communal ethic did not extend strongly beyond the boundaries of a tribelet.

Many people say that communism "would never work," because it "contradicts human nature." But human nature is itself contradictory. Class-divided society has suppressed the communal impulses that prevailed through some two million years of human life and development. Capitalism has liberated human greed from communal constraint, and liberated individual initiative from the confines of technological stasis; in so doing, it has trampled the majority of humanity underfoot, and thrust humanity as a whole into violent conflict with the rest of nature. Communism aims to liberate the oppressed majority of humanity from the confines of capitalist property interests, revive and extend the communal impulse worldwide, check the greedy impulse, rechannel individual initiative to serve the global community, and restructure technology to bring humanity into dynamic harmony with the rest of nature.

The Dead and the Historical

Many California Indian cultures, including Ipai-Tipai, Yokuts, Ohlone, and Yurok groups, imposed a strict ban against mentioning the name of a dead person.[44] It is not clear whether the dead person could still be talked about *indirectly*, without mentioning him or her by name—or whether *any* mention of the deceased, direct or indirect, was taboo. Among many nonliterate peoples, the act of naming a person is vested with great metaphysical power. Perhaps the prevailing belief was that, if you named a dead person, that would give you power over his or her soul/ghost, power which you had seized from the dead one's relatives and which you could now use malevolently.

The Yurok avoided addressing even living people by name—except sometimes in closest intimacy. They considered it horrendous manners to call a person by name, or even to mention an absent person by name in front of his or her relatives. "All sorts of circumlocution came into use..."[45] So the Yurok's taboo against mentioning the dead by name may have been a natural extension of their restrictions against mentioning the living by name.

The Yurok enforced their taboo against naming the dead by assessing fines on those who broke the taboo, to compensate a dead man's relatives or a dead woman's surviving husband. But the taboo lasted for only a year after a person's death: At the end of one year, the dead person's name was bestowed on a younger relative or child of the same sex, who thus discarded his or her previous name. In this way a person could shed several names in the course of a lifetime, each time assuming the name of a dead older relative. Alfred Kroeber thinks that many California Indian cultures besides the Yurok used this method to end the taboo a year after a person's death.[46]

What impact did this system have on the problem of blood feuds being passed down from generation to generation? If, in some cultures, there was a *permanent* taboo against mentioning a dead person—either by name or indirectly—then this might serve the social function of "wiping the slate clean" when a person died, to prevent grudges borne by that person against others from plaguing the living and future generations; if sorcery was suspected in the person's death, the hope might be to restrain the dead one's relatives and friends from seeking vengeance. If, on the other hand, the taboo was ended after one year, and the dead one's name (and, by implication, personal qualities) was transferred to a younger surviving relative, then this might help *sustain* personal grudges and even blood rivalries from one generation to the next.

At any rate, the California Indians' common use of this taboo, combined with their disregard for property inheritance, left them with precious little genealogical and historical knowledge about themselves. While a person could identify his or her distant cousin by the common lineage markings tattooed onto their faces, they probably could not trace their family tree back to their common ancestors. And the peoples had at best a very vague idea of where their distant ancestors came from.

When a society becomes widely literate and personal names a part of the written record, names become externalized from the individuals who own them. The taboo against naming the dead must then fall away. The triumph of the economic principle of property inheritance (through the male line), and of the political principle of dynastic succession, places a premium on detailed genealogies. Monotheistic religion strips individual souls of their autonomy, subsuming them under the all-powerful god/spirit. This has the advantage of stimulating an historical record and historical consciousness (however biased in favor of the people or religion elaborating it). It has the disadvantage of passing collective grudges and blood rivalries down through countless generations, indeed millennia.

Thus many Jews still resent the Egyptian people—and, by extension, the Arab peoples—because their ancestors were enslaved by the Egyptian monarchy over 3,500 years ago. Catholic, Protestant, and Russian Orthodox leaders long blamed "the Jews" for the execution of Jesus, inciting their followers to scorn and attack Jewish people for the supposed crime of a handful of their distant ancestors. And many Shiite Muslims, projecting their rivalry with Sunni Muslims back into the early history of islam, blame the Sunnis for the crushing defeat and death of Husayn, son of Ali and grandson of Muhammad, at the hands of troops sent by the Umayyad caliph in Iraq in the year 680.

A Vulnerable Balance

As we have seen, the native peoples of California were well adapted to their natural surroundings. With their varied and prudent subsistence skills, they made excellent use of the abundant food sources, and their communal values protected them against want and famine. They were well equipped to survive a range of natural disasters. They were poorly equipped to deal with an influx of Europeans bearing diseases, firearms, and an authoritarian social system.

Their great weakness was the lack of solidarity among tribelets. Early European explorers marvelled at the absence of theft between members of an Indian village, while other explorers and priests passing through native villages complained that the Indians were habitual thieves. Both sets of accounts were probably truthful: The Indians treated members of their own village, tribelet and especially kinship group with respect and restraint—but in dealing with outsiders, whether native or white, they did not feel constrained to uphold the same moral standards.

What the native peoples needed in the face of the European incursion was to transform their moral code, *extending* their communal values to encompass the entire native population. They needed bold prophets who could struggle to overcome aloofness, distrust and blood feuds between tribelets, and win the people to a new and broader vision of human identity. They needed moral and military leaders like Tecumseh, the young Shawnee chief who campaigned among tribes from Wisconsin to Florida in the early 1800's, in an effort to create a vast Indian union that could resist white encroachment. Only by uniting could the California Indians overcome their technological disadvantage in the face of the European invasion. But no such prophets or leaders emerged among them, until it was too late. Perhaps the intolerance that many of their cultures held towards misfits prevented it from happening.

In the free wheeling cosmology of the Chumash peoples, no being had the final say. Everything depended on a balance, an equilibrium of power in the natural and supernatural worlds. The fate of humanity was decided by a great gambling game.[47]

It was the misfortune of the California Indians to be thrust into a gambling game in which the invading Europeans held nearly all the trump cards.

The Missions, Culture Shock, and European Invasion

"Before baptism was administered," writes Edith Buckland Webb, "the Indians were warned that when they had become Christians they would no longer be allowed to roam through the forests, over the hills, or down to the seashore whenever they felt so inclined; they must thenceforth live at the mission..."[1]

But how could the Indians have understood that, by accepting baptism, they and their children became *perpetual vassals* of the catholic church? And how could the franciscan friars, even if they were fully honest about it, have communicated this stunning information to their first converts? After all, the friars were ignorant of the Indians' languages; even the christian Indians they had brought with them from Baja California could not, at first, understand them.

If baptized Indians (neophytes) fled the mission and tried to return to their former lives, the Spanish military authorities were obligated, under Spanish law, to track them down and bring them back to the mission. Beneath the outward trappings of voluntary conversion and fatherly love, the Spanish mission was a coercive system. And the California Indians had never before been coerced into changing their way of life.

A New Way of Life...

By baptizing children, the friars enticed their parents to come to the mission and accept baptism. By baptizing a village or tribelet chief, they encouraged the chief's people to become christians too. Each mission was typically surrounded by scattered Indian villages grouped into various tribelets. So once the friars found success in converting Indians in the fairly wide vicinity of their mission, the mission Indians faced a new living situation: Indians of different tribelets, some of them speaking different languages, now lived together on the mission premises. At mission Carmel near Monterey, Junípero Serra and his successors gathered Indian neophytes from seven Ohlone and Esselen tribelets, who fell into two language groups. At first these two groups set up separate villages attached to the mission, and were reluctant to mix with each other, either in farm work or religious services. By 1814, friar Juan Amorós could report to the Spanish government that the friars "have succeeded in making them associate together."[2] The missions concentrated the Indian population: Whereas a native village typically included between 30 and 100 people, the mission premises contained an average of 500 to 600 Indians. Mission populations of over 1,000 were common.[3]

Mission Indians and friars woke shortly after dawn every morning, at the chiming of the mission bells. They assembled at the mission church for prayers and mass, lasting an hour. Meanwhile, Indian women were boiling the breakfast meal in big iron cauldrons in the central square. Breakfast consisted of a porridge of corn, barley or wheat called *atole*, along with hot chocolate.[4] The friars or their helpers carefully ladled out the hot food to all comers.

Then the major day's work began. The men herded cattle, horses, sheep and goats, and worked with oxen in the grain fields, plowing, sowing and harvesting; during the slack seasons for agriculture, they might concentrate on making adobe bricks from soil mixed with water and straw, molding tiles from clay and firing them in the kiln, sawing logs into beams and rafters, and constructing new mission buildings with the aid of mud plaster.

The women spun and dyed yarn from wool, wove the yarn into fabric on big looms, sewed the fabrics into garments, baked bread, and cooked. They spent a lot more time indoors than the men: While the spinning wheels were light enough to be moved outdoors, the heavy looms confined their women tenders indoors in large workshops, where they had to use many candles to augment the dim natural light

116

Mission Indians, supervised by an Hispanic foreman, assembling adobe bricks to construct a new room for a mission building.

Miniature diorama from Edith Buckland Webb's *Indian Life at the Old Missions*, Univ. of Nebraska Press.

seeping in through small and high windows. Older women had to do a lot of heavy work outdoors: They fetched sand and straw for the male tile-makers, and gathered and carried wood to fuel the fires for the tile kiln, tallow and soap vats, baking oven, and porridge cauldrons.[5]

The morning work shift lasted perhaps four or five hours. At noon the bells rang for lunch, and the Indians assembled for a hot meal from the same cauldrons used at breakfast. The porridge was thicker now, containing not only grain, but also peas, beans, squash, chili, pigs' feet and perhaps beef (this stew was called *pozole*). Then came *siesta*, and work resumed at 2 o'clock. The afternoon shift lasted until 4 or 5 o'clock, and then came the evening prayers, which lasted perhaps an hour. Supper consisted of *atole* as at breakfast, perhaps containing meat. A French explorer visiting mission Carmel in 1786 estimated that the Indians had to do seven hours of work, and two hours of prayer daily. Saturday was sometimes a work day, while Sundays and holidays (of which there were many, given the catholic penchant for patron saints) were days of rest and amusement—following four or five hours of worship.[6]

The Indians were not terribly fond of the food dished out to them in the mission square, and it must have been monotonous eating similar porridge and stew three times every day. But many reports indicate that the friars were usually flexible enough to allow their neophytes to continue drawing on their traditional food sources, and even cultivate some new ones around their family huts. The French explorer La Pérouse reported that Indian women at mission Carmel kept a few chickens around their huts, giving the eggs to their children.[7] Louis Choris, an artist visiting San Francisco in 1816 as part of a Russian scientific exploration team, reported that two or three mission Indian families lived in a house, around which they kept their own gardens; they grew onions, garlic, pumpkins, cantaloupes, watermelons, and fruit trees, whose products were theirs to eat or trade.[8] Friar José Señán of mission San Buenaventura (in Chumash territory, near present day Santa Barbara) reported in the early 1800's that, in addition to their weekly beef and grain rations, his neophytes "have in their homes supplies of acorns, chia, seeds, fruits, herbs, and other various wild eatables, all of which they do not overlook, being very fond of them. They also eat fish, mussels, ducks, geese, cranes, quail, hares, squirrels, rats, and other animals which are to be had in abundance. Owing to this hodgepodge of eatables which they have in their homes, and to their being like children who eat at all hours, it is hard to determine how much they eat every day."[9]

In 1815, friar Mariano Payeras of mission La Purísima (also in Chumash territory) noted that his neophytes were out on their annual acorn gathering excursion. In 1819, friar Narciso Durán of mission San José (in Ohlone territory) informed the Spanish governor that all his neophytes were doing likewise. Durán and other friars admitted that the neophytes still preferred their native foods to the mission diet.[10] Especially during times of bad harvests or food supply problems, the friars (no doubt with a heavy heart) let their neophytes roam beyond the mission farm and pasture lands to fish and hunt. The returning neophytes often gave part of their catch to the friars, for them to share out among the mission population or present to guests.

Mission Indian girls, at the age of around eight, had to leave their mothers' home and live in the female dormitory, called the *monjerío* ("nunnery"). They were locked into their secluded sleeping quarters every night, along with widows and even married women whose husbands were on leave from the mission. During the morning, too, they were confined to the dormitory complex with its adjoining workshops and patio. The girls and women worked under the strict supervision of Indian *maestras* (instructresses), who in turn were responsible to the friars. Once the girls had finished their allotted tasks for the day, they were allowed to visit their home village on the mission premises.[11] Louis Choris reported in 1816 that the female dormitory at the San Francisco mission housed about 250 girls and women.[12] The girls had to keep living in the dormitory until they got married within the church—which they typically did at an early age, as young as 15.

The Indian boys and unmarried young men had their own dormitory, but it was much less confining: They were not locked in at night, nor were they required to stay inside during the day. The friars supervised the boys, training some of them to become bell ringers, acolytes, choir boys, violin players, pages, or servants. The boys often helped the men in their outdoor work, watching over the crops and yards of drying adobe bricks to scare birds and other animals away. Some boys came under the instruction of christian Indians from Baja California or Hispanic artisans living and working at the mission, and learned to become carpenters, masons, millers, blacksmiths, butchers, leather tanners, saddle makers, cowboys, and/or farmers.[13]

Religious instruction was generally conducted in Spanish. The Spanish monarchy decreed in 1795 that native languages in the empire should be suppressed, and all instruction given in Spanish—overturning the provision of the New Laws of the Indies (issued in 1542) that had directed missionaries to instruct neophytes in their native languages.

Yet the Spanish catholic church leaders still upheld the third provincial council of Lima in 1583, which had directed priests to give all their sermons and religious instruction in the native language, and to receive confession in the people's own languages.[14]

The franciscan friars in California, usually inclined to follow church policy in any conflict with state policy, had great difficulty mastering the many languages of their neophytes. In 1817 the catholic *comisario-prefecto*, friar Vicente de Sarría, paid a canonical visit to all the California missions and issued a critical circular to the friars. Reminding them of the language policy decreed by the third council of Lima, Sarría wrote that "it is not enough...to give instructions in Spanish and say nothing in the language which the Indians understand..."[15] Frederick Beechey, a British explorer visiting the San Francisco mission in 1826, noted that "It is greatly to be regretted that...the priests do not interest themselves a little more in the education of their converts, the first step to which would be in making themselves acquainted with the Indian language. Many of the Indians surpass their pastors in this respect, and can speak...Spanish..., while scarcely one of the padres can make themselves understood by the Indians."[16]

To bridge over their language problem, the friars chose talented Indian boys from each language group at their mission, taught them Spanish, instructed them in the ABC's of catholic doctrine and practice, and then used them as interpreters and catechists to lead the neophytes of their group in reciting the doctrine.[17] The friars often taught these exceptional boys to read and write in Spanish and Latin. But for the vast majority of the mission Indians, there was no literacy training in any language.*

---

*An 1813 questionnaire circulated to all the California missions by the Council of the Indies in Spain asked, among other questions: "Is there any inclination towards reading and writing in their [the Indians'] own languages?" The friars at mission Santa Clara replied: "We observe in the Indians no inclination towards reading or writing. Certainly some of the Indian boys learn how to read with undoubted facility. However, since we missionary fathers are interested only in teaching and explaining the christian doctrine and in having singers and musicians for church functions, we are satisfied with these efforts, taking into account on the other hand the lack of interest on the part of the Indians and the arduous labors in which we are engaged."[18] Note that the friars evaded the issue of literacy training *in the Indians' own languages,* failing to acknowledge that the limited literacy teaching they did was all in Spanish or Latin.

... and New Ways of Death

The missions became breeding grounds for the spread of European diseases among the Indians. Against a backdrop of high death rates and low birth rates at the missions, several epidemics broke out over the 60-year mission period. In 1777, a fatal respiratory disease hit the Ohlone Indians in and around mission Santa Clara, shortly after its founding. In 1802, another respiratory epidemic, probably involving pneumonia, diphtheria and/or pleurisy, ravaged the mission Indians from Carmel to San Luis Obispo. In January 1806, measles erupted at mission San Diego and spread north, reaching mission San Francisco, which was suffering crop failures, by March. At least 1,600 Indians died, including nearly all the children under age ten in some missions.[19] At mission San Francisco alone, more than 300 Indians died in 1806, and at mission Santa Clara, 226 people died of measles: 88 women, 64 men, 36 girls, and 38 boys.[20] The average child mortality rate at the California missions in 1806 was 33.5%. Other years of high child mortality were 1799 (26.5%) and 1828 (22%).[21] Overall through the sixty years of the California mission system, more than half the Indian children born at the mission died before reaching their fifth birthday.[22] In 1827-28, measles broke out at mission San Gabriel, spreading south to San Diego and north all the way to mission San Francisco Solano north of the San Francisco bay.

In the face of all the disease and death among the neophytes whom they closely supervised every day, it is remarkable how few of the friars succumbed to those same diseases, and how many of them lived into their 60's and 70's.

The franciscan missionaries were physically tough men. Most of them were born and raised in rural Spain, where infant mortality was high and deadly epidemics rather frequent. They had survived the harsh voyage to Mexico, often enduring hunger and thirst along the way. In Mexico they were exposed to malaria and other tropical diseases. By the time they arrived in California, their immune systems must have been highly developed, protecting them against a wide range of both European and American pathogens.

The California Indian men and women typically had splendid physiques, owing to their active outdoor life of work and play, and their nutritious and varied diet. But they had not been through the kind of harsh selection process that had prepared the friars so well for the conditions of life they were to establish in California. The Indians' geographical isolation had left them unexposed to many contagious diseases brought from Europe.

In the over 60 years of the California mission system—during which nearly 84,000 Indians were baptized—there was very seldom more than one Spanish or Mexican doctor in all of California. In 1773, mission president Junípero Serra wrote to the Spanish viceroy Bucareli in Mexico City, that a new doctor was badly needed in California: A supply ship had delivered a large cargo of medicines, for use both by the Spaniards and mission Indians; but Dr. Prat, who was supposed to instruct the friars on how to use the medicines, had gone insane, so the friars had nothing to go by, except a few do-it-yourself medical manuals written for missionaries.[23] The single doctor was stationed at the Monterey *presidio*, and was thus more available to the Spanish officers than to the mission Indians. Between 1824 and 1829, there was *no* doctor serving the California missions.

Medical Conditions at the Missions

To be sure, even the finest European doctors in those days were helpless in the face of most infectious diseases. In the absence of doctors to serve the mission Indians, the friars did their best to provide medical care. The college of San Fernando in Mexico City had taught them some rudiments of the healing arts.[24] They assembled the medicines they received into pharmacies, and concocted home remedies in an effort to cure their neophytes of a variety of ailments and injuries. They set up infirmaries (misleadingly called "hospitals"), staffed by male nurses they had trained, where ailing neophytes could rest and recuperate. The friars spent a good deal of time personally attending to the patients, providing them extra beef and chicken, and administering the last sacraments if they seemed to be dying.

Carrying out king Carlos 3's campaign to wipe out smallpox throughout the Spanish empire, the friars inoculated their neophytes with smallpox vaccine whenever it was available. Smallpox ravaged the Indians of Baja California through 1781. To prevent it from spreading to Alta California, the military officials and friars quarantined apparent smallpox victims. The friars and their paramedical assistants vaccinated the neophytes with smallpox pus (variolation), and later used the less dangerous cowpox pus, which was brought into medical practice in 1799.[25] Through these efforts, they may have succeeded in keeping the smallpox epidemic from reaching Alta California.*

*Rosemary Keupper Valle, in her doctoral dissertation on medicine and health in the California mission system, claims that the Indians of Alta California were saved from smallpox. Many historians and anthropologists have written that smallpox broke out among the California mission Indians; but Valle holds that the primary sources for their writings reported symptoms that correspond far better to *measles* than to smallpox.

Besides measles, syphilis was the most devastating disease suffered by the mission Indians. In 1804, the Spanish doctor based in Monterey, José María Benites, conducted a medical survey of seven missions, and reported that syphilis was the most common and serious disease there.[26] In 1815, friar Vicente de Sarría declared in a letter to governor Pablo de Solá that syphilis was destroying the poor neophytes, especially the women.[27] Infected women transmitted syphilis to their infants, an alarming number of whom were born dead, or died in their first or second year.[28] In 1817, friar Ramón Abella wrote to governor Solá that the Indians at mission San Francisco were so weak from syphilis that they were unable to work.[29] Syphilis not only killed its victims directly, but also weakened their resistance to a host of other diseases—whether chronic or epidemic—which became killers as well.*

From the devastating impact that syphilis had on the mission Indians, it is likely that most, if not all of the Indian groups brought into the missions were unexposed to syphilis at the time the Spaniards arrived. The key mode of transmission to the Indian population was the rape of Indian women by Spanish and Mexican soldiers. Then the disease spread swiftly among the mission Indian populations. The concentration of previously isolated Indian groups in the living quarters of the mission premises no doubt widened their network of sexual contacts, despite the friars' attempts to stamp out all but marital sex.

Pregnant women at the missions had practically no medical care beyond that provided by their traditional midwives—assuming the friars were tolerant enough to let the Indian midwives/shamans continue working as before. From their religious standpoint, the friars were more interested in the fetuses than in the women who carried them. In fact, they were under instructions to do everything possible to extricate a fetus from the body of a woman who died during pregnancy. In 1749, king Carlos 3 ordered that a cesarian section be performed on every woman in his empire who died in the later stages

*None of the early European explorers to California mentioned syphilis or symptoms suggesting it among the Indians. On the other hand, a study of human remains excavated at a burial ground near Bodega bay (northwest from San Francisco bay) revealed that several adult skeletons dating roughly 2000-3000 years ago showed lesions suggesting periosteal disease, which in turn might indicate syphilitic infection.[30] However, while 7 out of the 17 men's skeletons, and 2 out of the 10 women's skeletons showed such lesions, *none* of the 111 children's skeletons found at the site showed any signs of pathology. And if syphilis had been widespread among adults, it would likely have been passed congenitally to their children. So the syphilis hypothesis from this study seems doubtful.

of pregnancy, in an effort to get the fetus out alive. In his usual thoroughgoing way, king Carlos declared: "...We order that anyone who violates this pragmatic sanction [law]...whether he be a husband, a relative of the pregnant woman or any other person, who...for any reason interferes with the cesarian operation or endangers the fetus, or who maliciously promotes an abortion, be reported as a homicide and be treated as a criminal..."[31] Viceroy Bucareli introduced this policy into New Spain (Mexico) in 1772. Carlos' policy was cesarian in more ways than one, as he aimed to maximize the number of laborers, soldiers and colonial settlers for his empire. Placing the life of the fetus above the life of the pregnant woman, it meshed with the theology of the franciscans, who were zealous to procure a live birth, baptize the baby, and thus save his or her soul for eternity.

Provided with a manual written by Spanish medical authorities, the friars were instructed to perform the cesarian operation themselves, upon the death of a pregnant woman at their mission. The first such operation was performed by friars José Viader and Josef Viñals at mission Santa Clara in 1799.[32] Viader, who served at the mission from 1796 until 1833 and took a keen interest in medicines and the healing arts, proudly recorded in the mission register that the fetus had been extracted from the dead mother's womb, and survived. Only 13 more such cesarian operations were recorded during the remaining 34 years of the California mission system.[33] No doubt the horror of many friars over having to perform the operation, combined with cultural resistance from Indian groups at the missions, kept the policy from being widely carried out.

In 1820, friar Mariano Payeras, writing from mission La Purísima in Chumash territory to his religious superior in Mexico, made a stark assessment of the mission system's impact on the Indians' health: The pagan Indians, "in spite of their hunger (?), their nakedness, and their living completely outdoors almost like beasts," were admittedly healthy and robust. But the mission Indians, "as soon as they confine themselves to a sociable and christian life, become extremely feeble in their health, lose weight, sicken, and die." Payeras went on to blame the Indians themselves, for "not valuing their health as they should."[34]

Bells of Joy, Bells of Sorrow

The mission population woke daily to the chime of the main bell at sunrise, summoning the neophytes to church and the morning prayers. About an hour later, the bell chimed again for breakfast. After breakfast, the bell called the neophytes to work. The bell chimed again

Neophyte men plowing mission fields.

courtesy of Bancroft Library, Berkeley.

to announce lunch, the afternoon work shift, the evening prayers at about 5 o'clock, supper at 6 o'clock, and bedtime at 8 o'clock.[35]

In addition, many mission churches were flanked by pairs of *esquilas*, called "joyous bells" because of their lively resonance when rotated by hand, up, down and around the horizontal bars on which they were mounted. Indian boys loved to clamber up the mission church edifice and ring these special bells, and they were instructed to do so on joyous and festive occasions: the arrival of a supply ship or party of colonists, the visit of a friar from another mission, and the baptism of a baby. The joyous bells were also rung when a baby *died*: The bereaved parents were congratulated, for they now "had an angel in heaven."[36]

The mission bell was no doubt a great stimulus that helped draw the Indians towards the mission to begin with—out of wonder and curiosity over the strange new society taking shape before their eyes, and the pleasure of receiving glass beads and colorful cloth from the missionaries. But what became of that stimulus when the Indians were drawn fully into the mission, and nearly their entire daily lives were regimented by its relentless clangor? What psychological impact did it have upon them when the mission food, labor, and church services— which they may at first have found stimulating, new and exciting— calcified into monotonous and often meaningless repetition, five or six days a week, week after week, all punctuated by the monotonous chime of the bell? How did parents respond when the same joyous bells that had announced the birth and baptism of their baby also announced the child's death a few months or years later?

This brings to mind the experimental work of the Russian physiologist, Ivan Pavlov. In his most famous experiment, Pavlov trained (conditioned) a dog to salivate by presenting food, while simultaneously ringing a bell; when the bell was rung with no accompanying food reward, the dog salivated as before. Through further experiments, Pavlov found that multiple repetition of the old stimulus without the reward once coupled with it, caused the stimulus not only to lose its positive effect, but to become an "inhibitory agent."[37]

Pavlov distinguished between two basic types of animal and human response: *excitation* and *inhibition*. In modern psychological terms, excitation carried to an extreme is mania, while inhibition carried to an extreme is depression. Pavlov defined the healthy personality as one expressing an equilibrium between excitation and inhibition. In another experiment, he presented his dogs with two stimuli that were at once similar and different: One stimulus (agitating the skin of a dog) was coupled with a food reward, while the other stimulus (also agitating the dog's skin, but only half as fast) had no reward coupled with it. By alternating these two stimuli one after the other, Pavlov found that several of his dogs quickly became ill, suffering what might be called nervous breakdowns. The dogs of an excitable temperament became manic, and those of an inhibited temperament became depressed. Only those dogs with a personality solidly balanced between excitation and inhibition remained healthy through the capricious and conflictive treatment.[38]

While the franciscan friars were compassionate men who saw their mission as one of advancing the spiritual and material welfare of their Indian neophytes, the actual system of social conditioning they imposed upon the neophytes was, in many ways, crueler than any experiment that Pavlov and his disciples subjected their dogs to. For the friars, the dawn bell waking the mission population and summoning the neophytes to church was a positive stimulus: It brought, if not immediate pleasure and reward, at least the challenge of converting the Indians to the catholic faith; and the friars had been conditioned, through their long years of missionary training, to seek long term, indeed eternal rewards. For most of the mission Indians, the same bell meant confinement inside a building, listening to and repeating monotonous phrases in a foreign language, pledging obedience to a strange and terrible god. Then the same bell rang again, calling them to breakfast.

The psychological impact of this conflictive conditioning must have been profound. Those neophytes who grew irritable, manic or rebellious soon fell under the physical discipline of the soldiers and friars. So the main response among the neophytes became one of depression. This explains the frequent reports of explorers visiting the missions that the Indians were sullen, listless, and dull: They had lost the vitality, joy and initiative they had once expressed in their own societies.

Chronic depression must have impacted the overall physical health of the mission Indians. As we have seen on page 117, once the missions got established as food production units, the food available to the neophytes was normally abundant and varied—so that malnutrition is hardly a likely cause of the high mortality rates.* But depression

*Sherburne Cook, on the basis of a thorough survey of Spanish records of food provisions to the California missions, calculated that the average neophyte ate only about 2300 calories' worth of food daily—which he judged as probably
(continued at bottom of next page)

probably played a big role in reducing the Indians' resistance to disease. Many friars lamented that, despite their efforts to care for and heal their sick neophytes, the neophytes seemed to lack the will to live. To be sure, it sometimes happened among California Indians in their native state that a person, convinced that he or she had fallen under a deadly sorcerer's spell, pined away and died, even though no symptoms of illness had appeared before. But under the mission system, a self defeating attitude towards life often became widespread.

Moreover, the rigid labor system imposed at the mission was a culture shock for the Indians. The work routine of perhaps seven hours a day, five or six days a week, was not very burdensome by the capitalist standards of the day (or even of today, for that matter). But the Indian men were not used to working every day, and none of the Indians were used to working by the clock, under the strict supervision of others. While native women had shouldered the daily burden of food gathering and preparation, the entire native community had worked hard only on specific tasks that occurred seasonally—such as the annual acorn gathering and salmon fishing. Indian men were used to getting quick results and gratification from their work. They built their huts and boats out of wild reeds and grasses, and could dispose of them easily. When an Ohlone reed hut became rotten or thoroughly infested with insects, for example, the owners would burn it down and quickly build a new one.

The christian Indian men now had to do systematic work for long term construction projects, in whose design they had no say. They had to dig up soil, mix it with water and binding materials (shards of straw or glass), tread on the mixture with their bare feet to get an even consistency, pour it into molds, and wait several days for the resulting forms to dry into adobe bricks, which weighed about 60 pounds each.[39] It took years, sometimes decades, to complete construction on a mission church. And the church was more a place of confinement, confusion and boredom for many neophytes than a source of pleasure.

---

inadequate to sustain good health. (*The Conflict Between the California Indian and White Civilization*, pp. 39-48). Facile critics of the mission system have accepted Cook's estimates as the last word in scientific analysis of the mission food regimen. However, Cook clearly underestimated the mission Indians' ongoing access to their traditional food sources—allowing only 200 calories per person per day from these sources (p. 47). The friars' responses to the 1813 questionnaire, after some 40 years of mission-building, indicated that their neophytes kept ample supplies of acorns, grass seeds, and small and big game meat in their huts on the mission premises. And the friars would have had no motive to exaggerate this "primitivist" tendency among their neophytes; indeed they would have had an interest in downplaying it, since it was a source of dismay and embarrassment to them.

Mission Indian women had to spend long hours manufacturing woolen clothing, which did not protect them as well against the winter cold as did their traditional rabbit- and otter-skin garments.

The French explorer LaPérouse made a striking, if superficial observation upon touring mission Carmel in 1786: "The color of these Indians, which is that of blacks; the house of the monks; their storehouses, which are built of brick and plastered; the threshing floor on which they tread out the corn; the cattle; the horses, in short, everything we observed, presented the appearance of a plantation in Santo Domingo [Haiti, then a French colony employing African slave labor], or any other colony. The men and women are also assembled by the sound of a bell, and a monk leads them to work, to church, and to all their employments. We declare with pain, that the resemblance is so exact, that we saw both men and women loaded with irons, while others had a log of wood on their legs..."[40]

The Whip and the Cross

As Junípero Serra and his comrades had done in the Sierra Gorda mission in Mexico (see page 44), the franciscans in California relied on bold visual dramatizations of catholic doctrine to spur the neophytes to assimilate the faith. The ritual of Jesus' death march was performed not only every year at Easter time: It was performed *every week*, and the neophytes were expected to participate. At every one of the stations of the cross, the friar leading the procession would stop and deliver a prayer to his flock, urging them to engage in holy meditation. Inside the mission church, the walls flanking the congregation often depicted contrasting scenes: One wall showed the joys and bliss of heaven, while the other showed the terrors and torments of hell. No doubt the friars used these murals as graphic points of reference in their daily sermons.

> *The ancient Mayas celebrated life, elevated its most diverse aspects to divine categories. Today the Holy Week processions produce sad exhibitions of collective masochism: They drag heavy crosses, participate in the flagellation of Jesus step by step on the interminable ascent to Golgotha; with dolorous wails they convert his death and burial into a cult of their own death and burial. (The Indians' Holy Week ends without a resurrection). When victory is talked about in the language of the conquistador's culture, the Indians celebrate their own defeat. To know this, it is enough to see their dances or listen to that rancorous silence which replaces the songs they no longer sing.*
>
> —Eduardo Galeano, *Guatemala: Occupied Country*
> (New York: Monthly Review Press, 1967)

Even so, it is doubtful whether the friars ever won more than a minority of their neophytes to embrace christianity with a passion. Louis Choris reported on the Sunday and holiday service at mission San Francisco in 1816 as follows:

> All the Indians of both sexes, without regard to age, are obliged to go to church and worship. Children brought up by the superior [friar], 50 of whom are stationed around him, assist him during the service which they also accompany with the sound of musical instruments. These are chiefly drums, trumpets, tabors, [etc.]. It is by means of their noise that they endeavor to stir the imagination of the Indians... It is, indeed, the only means of producing an effect upon them. When the drums begin to beat they fall to the ground as if they were half dead. None dares to move, all remain stretched upon the ground without making the slightest movement until the end of the service and, even then, it is necessary to tell them several times that the mass is finished. Armed soldiers are stationed at each corner of the church. After the mass, the superior delivers a sermon in Latin to his flock.[41]

Ten years later, Frederick Beechey reported on a service in the same mission church:

> The congregation was arranged on both sides of the building, separated by a wide aisle passing along the center, in which were stationed several bailiffs with whips, canes, and goads, to preserve silence and maintain order, and, what seemed more difficult than either, to keep the congregation in their kneeling posture. The goads were better adapted to this purpose than the whips, as they would reach a long way, and inflict a sharp puncture without making any noise. The end of the church was occupied by a guard of soldiers under arms, with fixed bayonets...[42]

Neophytes judged "delinquent" in their worship, labor, or personal behavior were punished by whipping them on the bare back with a rope, lariat, or a flexible reed or cane. Bruising or drawing blood in the course of the whipping was to be avoided, according to Fermín de Lasuén, Junípero Serra's successor as California mission president. The maximum number of strokes delivered usually ranged between 21 and 25, and in unusual cases reached 50.[43] For an offense judged especially heinous, such as physically assaulting his friar, a neophyte might get 25 lashes daily for nine days, plus a whipping every Sunday for nine Sundays. The man who delivered the flogging was typically an Hispanic soldier or an Indian bailiff, elected by the neophytes from a list of candidates approved by the friars, and subservient to the friars. It was common for an Indian awaiting punishment to ask forgiveness — in which case the force, but not the number of whip strokes was decreased.[44]

Indian men were thus whipped in the public mission square. "Delinquent" Indian women, on the other hand, were whipped "in a secret place, and at a distance, in order, perhaps, to prevent their cries exciting too lively a compassion, and thereby stimulating the men to revolt—whereas the men are exposed before all their fellow citizens, that their punishment may serve as an example..."[45] The "secret place" where women were flogged was the female dormitory, and the whip there was wielded by a woman supervisor (*maestra*).[46]

The humiliation of being whipped in front of one's peers must have been appalling—especially when one recalls that the Indians in their own societies did not physically punish one another, and seldom punished or even publicly scolded their own children.* And what was it like for an Indian woman neophyte to be whipped by another Indian woman? How could they reconcile this cruelty with the image of the all-loving, all-forgiving virgin Mary brought by the friars?

Francis Florian Guest, a contemporary franciscan historian, points out that public floggings of convicted delinquents and criminals were common in Spain and elsewhere in western Europe in those days, as was the flogging of rebellious school children (which was not banned in Spain until 1834). A man convicted of theft or escape from prison typically received 200 lashes in Spain.[48] Physical punishment within the Spanish military was mild compared with the dreaded cat-o'-nine-tails used by the British navy, which helped provoke the famous mutiny on the British cargo ship *Bounty* in 1789. And physical punishment

---

*Jacob Baegert, a German jesuit missionary who served in Baja California from about 1750 till 1767, reported: "Nothing causes the [native] Californians less trouble and care than the raising of their children, which is merely confined to a short period, and ceases as soon as the latter are capable of making a living for themselves—i.e., to catch mice and to kill snakes... Nothing is done... in the way of admonition or instruction, nor do they set an example worthy to be imitated by their offspring. The children do what they please, without fearing reprimand or punishment, however disorderly and wicked their conduct may be. It would be well if the parents did not grow angry when their children are now and then slightly chastised for gross misdemeanor by order of the missionary; but, instead of bearing with patience such wholesome correction of their little sons and daughters, they take great offense and become enraged, especially the mothers, who scream like furies, tear out their hair, beat their naked breasts with a stone, and lacerate their heads with a piece of wood or bone till the blood flows, as I have frequently witnessed on such occasions."[47]

imposed by the franciscans in California was not much harsher than that used within the Spanish military.

But for the California Indians, the comparison between their treatment and the norms of punishment prevailing in various European institutions was meaningless. What counted for them was that their punitive treatment at the missions ruptured the freedom and dignity they had once enjoyed. Guest also points out that many friars were accustomed to whipping *themselves* much harder and more often than their neophytes had to endure the whip.[49] But self flagellation, however absurd and unnatural, is a voluntary act—whereas instituting a system that inflicts physical pain on others is a basic violation of human trust.

A Setback for Women

Vital statistics derived from the friars' thorough recording of baptisms and burials at their missions show that deaths exceeded births, usually by a wide margin, throughout the mission period. And the birth rate among the mission Indians declined, from an average of 45 births per thousand neophytes in 1780, to 40 births (per thousand people) in 1800, to 35 births in 1820, to 32 births in 1830.[50] Sherburne Cook estimates that the average birth rate among nonmission Indians, by contrast, was about 45 to 50 births per thousand people per year.[51]

The declining birth rate among the mission Indian *total population* may not have been due to a declining birth rate among the mission Indian *women*. Cook, who did the most comprehensive statistical studies of the California mission system, rather infers that the decline in the *crude* birth rate among the mission Indians was due more to the sharply *decreasing ratio of females to males* among the mission Indians: While the mission Indian population was about 50% female in 1770-80, by the end of the mission period in 1834 it was only 42.6% female. Since the sex ratio for mission Indian children under age ten remained steady at about 50/50, a *higher death rate among female adolescents and women* than among males of comparable ages probably played the key role in tipping the numerical scales against women, and therefore against children, and therefore against the Indian people as a whole.[52]

The friars defined *adults* as those ten years of age and older—and by that age, girls were confined in the female dormitory. Among the Ohlone mission Indians, the *adult* female/male sex ratio fell, over the course of the mission period, to 41.2% female.[53] At mission Santa Clara, the adult population shifted from 44.4% female in 1782, to only 37.9% female in 1832.[54] Among the Salinan mission Indians, the adult

Declining percentage of women among mission Indians, 1774-1833

Percentage of women among adults

equal sex ratio

Data from Sherburne Cook, The Conflict Between the California Indian and White Civilization, 1976, p. 427.

population was 44.4% female by 1830. This trend of a relative decrease in the number of mission Indian females aged ten and older took off around 1800, notably at the missions of central and northern California; at the southern California missions, however, the sex ratios remained nearly equal between males and females.[55]

Aside from child mortality, the high rate of female mortality was concentrated among adolescents and young women. At mission Santa Clara, 64% of the female deaths occurred before age 25, and 27% occurred between the ages of 10 and 25. Among males, 58% of the deaths occurred before age 25.[56] The strikingly high female mortality among younger women and adolescents brings us back to the female dormitory.

The Spaniards had designed the female dormitory to protect the girls and young women from rape, and to preserve their virginity prior to marriage. But in many ways the female dormitory and workshops came to concentrate the medical, cultural, and psychological stresses of the mission system upon the girls and women confined in them.

The enclosure of dozens, in some cases hundreds of girls and women in common sleeping quarters must have promoted infectious diseases, including the dreaded measles. Sanitary facilities were crude, and the water piped into the dormitory could easily be contaminated— so gastro-intestinal diseases were probably common. Spinning wool into yarn (indoors, at least during the cold winters) and weaving the yarn into cloth, inside poorly ventilated workshops, saturated the air with dust; dust borne pathogens must have spread respiratory infections. Skin diseases, and especially itching, were also common among women and children. The friars, after initial resistance, often allowed neophyte men to build sweat lodges at the missions, and the regular sweating ritual combined with bathing kept the men fairly free from skin ailments; but the women lacked access to the sweat lodges, and the girls and women confined at the dormitory lacked ready access to river bathing.[57]

Given the cramped living quarters, the unhealthy conditions, and the strict regimentation, many girls must have desired to escape. But where could they escape to? They were no longer permitted to sleep in their mothers' huts. If they tried to escape from the mission and were caught, they were liable to be whipped; repeat offenses might get them confined in irons or in "the log," a hinged contraption binding their legs and preventing them from standing up.

The only other escape from life in the dormitory was marriage. According to Spanish catholic law, girls could marry at 12, and boys at 14—and the mission records show that it was common for females to take marriage vows at around age 15. But marriage often brought with it the dreaded syphilis; since the friars did not repress the sex lives of teenage boys nearly as tightly as those of teenage girls, a young groom was more likely to be carrying syphilis than his young bride. In 1815, friar Sarría wrote that, owing to the syphilis epidemic, in some missions "to marry is to die."[58]

Moreover, life in the female dormitory and at the mission generally disrupted Indian women's control of their reproductive power, and the social status that had once flowed from it. In native societies, a girl's first menstruation marked her rite of passage into womanhood. She went into seclusion—often in a separate hut built just for the occasion— fasted, bathed, and received visits from mature women of the village, who instructed her in the secrets of female power. Given the lack of privacy and the strict supervision in the female dormitory, it must have been very hard, if not impossible, to sustain this crucial rite. So a young woman now lacked the self confidence and sense of connection with her female elders that her mother and grandmothers had enjoyed.

When she married, she was no longer free to choose when and whether she would bear a child. To be sure, many mission Indian women defied the catholic ban on abortion and infanticide. In 1795, mission president Lasuén declared: "The failure of the mission Indians to show a greater increase [in population] may be attributed to their great incontinence [i.e., promiscuity] and the inhumanity of the mothers who, in order not to become old and unattractive to their husbands, manage to abort or strangle their newly born children. Little by little these grave evils are being corrected."[59] Five years later, Lasuén denounced "...the inhuman cruelty to which the Indian women are too much addicted...to abort and strangle their children. To remedy this all means are being employed..."[60]—including, presumably, whipping the guilty women and placing them under confinement.

Lasuén's explanation that the Indian women were concerned "not to become old and unattractive to their husbands" seems rather contrived and male centered. If they now feared growing old, it was more likely due to the sharp loss of status suffered by older women—as the friars now usurped the powers of shamans, and even of midwives.

There is no way to determine whether abortion and infanticide were practiced more frequently at the missions than among the native Indian societies. Lasuén failed to consider the possibility that the Indian women might abort or kill their newborn children because they simply could not raise more than one child at once, especially now that widows were confined in the female dormitory—or that they could not tolerate bearing children into a forced labor system.

According to Victoria, an Indian girl raised at mission San Gabriel, an Indian woman who had a miscarriage there was accused of infanticide. She was punished by having her head shaved, being whipped daily for 15 days, having her feet bound in irons for three months, and "having to appear every Sunday in church, on the steps leading up to the altar, with a hideous painted wooden child in her arms." The mission was ruled at the time by friar José María Zalvidea, an unusually harsh disciplinarian. He often whipped himself and wore punishing undergarments, in the fashion of Junípero Serra. Zalvidea later suffered a nervous breakdown.[61]

The growing excess of men over women (in the central and northern coastal missions) must have intensified sexual rivalries among the mission Indian men; and the friars' banning of homosexuality, polygamy and divorce,* and their disruption of the bridal gifts system that had regulated relations between kinship groups, made it harder to resolve such conflicts peacefully. Two cases help illustrate the point:

---

*The Spanish catholic system, while banning divorce, did not deprive a married woman of all her rights: The married woman retained her own family name, and her own legal identity. She had the right to manage her own property and enter into contracts. She also was to share equally in all profits earned by the married couple, and her husband could not sell their land without her consent. A woman married under the Spanish system thus had more legal and property rights than a woman married according to English common law.[62] However, since mission Indian couples did not live on independent homesteads, these rights probably meant little to mission Indian women—except those who married Spanish or Mexican soldiers.

1) Aurelio, a married neophyte at mission San Juan Capistrano (near present-day Anaheim), was himself promiscuous. But, angrily accusing his wife of adultery, he beat her to death in 1797. Confessing his sins and crime, he insisted that he had not intended to kill his wife—but only to beat her. The San Diego presidio commander who ruled on the case judged Aurelio's crime "accidental," and recommended release without punishment. But the viceroy intervened and sentenced Aurelio to four years' hard labor on public works.[63] (And the Spanish authorities' frequent use of hard labor as a punishment for convicted criminals no doubt strengthened the Indian men's aversion to the mission labor system).

2) Primo, a neophyte at mission San Antonio (in Salinan territory), had a secret love affair with Eulalia, a married woman. With the help of a friend named Ventura, and apparently with Eulalia's connivance, Primo murdered Eulalia's husband. The two Indian men were sentenced to death by hanging; since there was no hangman in California, they were shot, in 1802.[64] This was a rare instance of the death penalty being carried out under the Spanish mission system.

The male agricultural system imposed by the missions dislodged women as the main food producers. Their gathering of acorns, roots and grass seeds now became supplementary, instead of central to the mission Indians' diet. The male head of each mission household received the weekly rations of grains and meat from the friars, delivering them to his hut or house. So the more the missions prospered, the more status Indian women lost.

Even after a woman married, her freedom of movement was more severely restricted than that of her husband. She could no longer simply step out into her natural surroundings and start gathering her food and basketry materials: The mission was surrounded by farm and pasture lands, male dominated territory. If she wanted to gather grass seeds, she had to compete with the longhorn cattle, horses and sheep. She had far less opportunity to leave the mission than her husband, who might go on occasional hunting and fishing excursions, go off to work for a time at the presidio or nearby colonial settlement, or join expeditions to capture runaway neophytes. And when he left the mission without her, she was confined, along with the adolescent girls, young women and widows, to the female dormitory. According to Louis Choris' observation of mission San Francisco in 1816, the Indian men requested the friars, out of jealousy, to lock their wives up in the dormitory whenever they went on leave from the mission.[65] Such confinement was inconceivable in the Indians' native societies, where both men and women enjoyed basic personal freedoms.

Indian Resistance and Rebellion

Flight from the missions was the most common form of resistance. The Indians' longing to return to their native villages and their unfettered ways of life was their key motive for escape. The friars, unable to suppress this longing either by persuasion or coercion, had to flex and accommodate it: They let the neophytes visit relatives and friends in their home villages, for a total of perhaps ten or twelve weeks each year. While this policy provided new opportunities for escape, the friars saw it as a necessary safety valve. Mission president Fermín Lasuén, Junípero Serra's successor at Carmel, observed that if the neophytes were strictly banned from visiting their pagan relatives in the mountains, the missions would face the danger of a riot.[66]

In 1780, the franciscans founded two missions among the Yuma Indians on the California (west) side of the Colorado river. Contrary to Serra and his colleagues' careful policy of separating the presidio by some distance from the mission and discouraging colonial settlement near the mission lands, here the mission, presidio, and colonial pueblo were combined into a single establishment, to cut costs. Friars Juan Díaz and Francisco Garcés, who was keenly attuned to Indian cultures and famous for trekking thousands of miles across desert and mountains to contact Indian groups, assured the Spanish commander general that this novel approach would succeed. But Francisco Palóu, learning of the experiment, scornfully dubbed it a "new mode of conquest."[67]

The settlers' livestock intruded on the Yumas' gardens, and land disputes between Indians and Spaniards soon erupted. Captain Fernando de Rivera, heading south for Sonora (today a state of northwest Mexico) with a party of soldiers and their families, aggravated the situation by setting up camp on the east bank of the Colorado river in July 1781. The visitors let their horses graze on Yuma fields near the missions, and their cattle destroyed part of the Yumas' mesquite bean crop. Rivera and his soldiers seemed oblivious to the social conflict brewing at the missions, to the Yumas' combat prowess, and to their tribal solidarity.

On 17 July, Yuma warriors led by chief Salvador Palma destroyed both missions, killing two of their four friars. The next morning, they crossed the Colorado river and attacked the unwelcome visitors. The soldiers, surprised and overwhelmed, fought to the last man, inflicting heavy casualties on the Yuma archers. In the end, all the Hispanic soldiers, including Rivera, lay dead. The Yuma warriors then captured the survivors, most of them women and children. On 19 July, they caught up with friars Francisco Garcés and Juan Barrenche, who had fled from the assault on pueblo Concepción two days earlier. Both friars were killed, despite efforts by some of their neophytes to save them.

In September, lieutenant Pedro Fages led a punitive expedition against the Yuma villages, and freed 61 Hispanic captives by paying a ransom of flannel, beads and tobacco. The Yuma people suffered heavy casualties, but the Spaniards failed to subdue their warriors.[68] The Yuma revolt severed the Spaniards' route across the Colorado river, breaking a key link between New Spain/Mexico and the California mission chain.

Toypurina the Sorceress and the San Gabriel Uprising

On the night of 25 October 1785, a group of painted Indian warriors from nearby villages, led by the neophyte Nicolás José, silently scaled the parapet surrounding mission San Gabriel's inner quadrangle. The men, armed with bows and arrows, slipped into the friars' sleeping quarters, eager to confirm a prophesy: The young Indian sorceress Toypurina had convinced them to attack the mission by promising to kill both friars with her magic spell, clearing the way for them to kill the soldiers guarding the mission.[69] And, sure enough, as the warriors entered the friars' quarters, they found both friars laid out in coffins.

But suddenly, the two "dead friars" leapt out of their coffins. As the warriors shrieked in terror, armed Spanish soldiers appeared from hiding, raising their war cry, *"Santiago!"* In the ensuing melee, ten Indian warriors, including their leaders, were captured—without a bullet or arrow being fired. The remaining Indian warriors fled. Toypurina was soon arrested as well.

It turned out that the Indians' plot had been overheard by a soldier of the mission guard who understood their language. He had informed his superior, corporal José María Verdugo. With the approval of the friars, Verdugo had planned a bold counterplot, asking two of his soldiers to dress in friars' garb and play dead.

The key figures arrested were the neophyte Nicolás José, two chiefs from nonchristian villages, and Toypurina. The remaining warriors arrested—most of them neophytes—were given a public whipping of 20 lashes, and released from jail. Their punishment was designed to show the Indians "that the sorceries and incantations of the woman Toypurina are powerless in the face of the True Faith," in the words of California's military governor, Pedro Fages.[70] Then began the military trial of the four accused leaders of the revolt, presided over by Fages.

Nicolás José, under interrogation, admitted that, six years earlier, he had plotted to kill a fellow neophyte—indeed, his baptismal sponsor (*padrino*)—for laying covetous eyes on his bride to be. He had also plotted earlier to kill the priests and soldiers; the plot had been discovered, and he had then been let off leniently. Now he declared he led the recent revolt because the friars had refused to allow him and his fellow neophytes to stage their native dances at the mission.

Nicolás José further testified he had approached Toypurina, respected and feared as the most powerful sorceress among the Indians of the region. He had paid her glass beads and colorful ribbons, to incite her fellow nonchristian Indians to revolt; he was to organize the plot among the mission Indians. Under Toypurina's influence, five villages from the mountain, three from the valley, and others still more distant had joined forces to form the attacking war party.

The 24-year-old Toypurina now took the stand, facing down the Spanish military officers and speaking defiantly in her native language. She admitted having ordered chief Tomasajaquichi (one of her fellow defendants) to go to the mission Indian village and persuade the neophytes not to believe another word of the friars, but to trust only in her. "I commanded him to do so," declared Toypurina, "for I hate the *padres* and all of you, for trespassing upon the land of my forefathers..."[71] This was her real reason for rallying the warriors to attack—not the trinkets Nicolás José had paid her.

In January 1786, governor Fages ordered Nicolás José and the two chiefs sent in irons to the presidio. Nicolás José was later sentenced to six years' imprisonment at half rations in the most distant, northern presidio, to be followed by transfer to a similarly distant mission and a ban on ever rejoining his family. The two chiefs, after two years in prison, were released and allowed to return home, but were kept under surveillance.

Toypurina, while in detention after her trial, informed one of the friars that she wanted to become a christian. This was really the only option open to her: If she were released back to her home village, she would surely be murdered by the defeated warriors, who were furious over her false prophesy and the humiliation they had suffered at the Spaniards' hands. On 8 March 1787, Toypurina was baptized at the mission San Gabriel she had plotted to destroy. She proceeded to cast off her husband, who refused to become a christian. Exiled north to mission Carmel, she married a soldier from the Monterey presidio on 26 July 1789. She bore four children in less than ten years. On 22 May 1799, after having received all the final sacraments of the church, Toypurina died, at the age of about 39.

If this account is true, it shows the extraordinary importance which the Spanish friars and military officials gave to psychological warfare in their struggle to convert the Indians. The sorceress Toypurina was engaged in mortal combat with the San Gabriel friars for moral and spiritual power over the Indians, whether christian or nonchristian. It is significant that she did not order the warriors to attack the mission soldiers straight away—but insisted on first killing the friars (through her spell): Once the friars were gone, their spiritual power to protect the soldiers and the whole mission establishment would also disappear. The Spaniards, for their part, would not have taken the trouble and risks of hatching their dramatic counterplot, had it not been for the psychological value of shocking and terrorizing the Indian warriors, debunking Toypurina's prophesy, and presenting the friars as invulnerable and the soldiers as invincible in the eyes of the Indians.

Soldiers/Colonists vs. Indians

In 1794, California's military governor began allowing retired soldiers to establish ranches near the various presidios. In the Salinas valley east of Monterey/Carmel, several retired soldiers quickly set up their estates. The friars protested this policy as an infringement on Indian land rights. In 1795, Indians burned the fledgling ranches. The Spanish military took reprisals against the Indian "bandits," and the colonists soon got their ranches started again, with official support from the Spanish royal hierarchy.[72]

Here we see the roots of the social conflict that was to spell the end of the California mission system some 40 years later. Once the Spanish and Mexican soldiers and colonists took hold of their landed estates, they needed Indian labor to run them profitably. The only source of training and discipline of the Indians in European style labor were the missions. So the ranch owners had to draw on the mission Indians for their labor supply. But the friars tried to protect their neophytes from private exploitation, and were dedicated to "eventually" turning over all the mission lands to the christian Indians, who would then work the land as independent family farmers. The Hispanic ranching system and Indian land rights could not coexist for long. The big question was whether the mission Indians could make an alliance with their "wild" Indian cousins to destroy the ranching system, before the ranch owners and soldiers destroyed what was left of Indian freedom.

Persistence of Indian Customs and Beliefs

"The majority of our neophytes have not yet acquired much love for our way of life," lamented mission president Fermín de Lasuén in 1797. "And they see and meet their pagan relatives in the forest, fat and robust and enjoying complete liberty."[73] Lasuén concluded that, were it not for the restraining force of the military guard at the mission, most of the neophytes would return permanently to their home villages. This was after more than 25 years of mission building and evangelizing in California.

As it was, perhaps one in every ten mission Indians tried to escape, and perhaps one in twenty-four managed to elude the soldiers and make his or her escape permanent.[74] In September 1796, some 200 neophytes fled mission San Francisco and paddled across the bay. Their grievances were overwork, harsh punishment, inadequate food rations (they had not been getting three hot meals per day, as was standard at other missions), and a recent epidemic that had claimed many children's lives. Many of those who fled later returned to the mission, either through capture by the soldiers or their own choice.[75] Those who returned voluntarily were probably influenced more by a desire to live with their captured relatives and friends, than by any preference for the mission over their native villages. The captured fugitives were punished, whereas those returning voluntarily were spared punishment.

At mission Santa Barbara in 1801, in the midst of an epidemic of pneumonia and pleurisy, a Chumash christian woman, under treatment by a native shaman, had a vision stimulated by the hallucinogen datura: She met Chupu, the Chumash earth goddess, who told her that all baptized Indians would die; only those mission Indians would be spared who annulled their baptism by bathing in the "tears of the sun." News of her vision spread to the outlying villages, and Chumash people from the offshore islands and inland areas came to see this woman and worship Chupu. The ferment lasted three days before the friars got wind of it and squelched it, probably by forcing the woman to renounce her vision. Still, the cult of Chupu persisted clandestinely at the missions in Chumash territory; the friars' policy of transferring neophytes to nearby missions according to labor requirements actually helped spread the cult.[76]

The franciscans' policy towards Indian shamans seems to have varied from mission to mission. Many neophytes continued to honor their traditional shamans and seek treatment from them. Shamans—men and women—were the friars' main rivals for moral and spiritual power over the neophytes. At those missions where the friars felt insecure in their power, they exerted themselves to squelch all shamanic activity among their neophytes, physically punishing those who practiced "witchcraft" and "devil worship." Other friars, sensing the inadequacy of their own efforts to provide medical care, allowed shamans to continue their healing practices at the missions. But the shamans, like the Spanish doctor and friars, were overwhelmed by the epidemics that swept the neophyte population. This must have shattered the moral authority of many shamans in the eyes of the neophytes, undermining a key aspect of the native belief structures.[77] But rather than strengthening their catholic faith, it only added to their melancholy and despair.

Despite a 1782 order banning all dancing among christian Indians, many friars found it necessary to give ground and allow their neophytes to keep engaging in one of their major pleasures. Lasuén lamented the influence of pagan Indians on his Carmel neophytes in the dancing arena: "...They [the nonchristian Indians living near the mission] put on a heathen and abominable dance or *fiesta*; if the christian who is present refuses to participate in that vile diversion, they mock him and laugh at him and persecute him until he gives in."[78] Louis Choris observed at mission San Francisco in 1816:

> On Sunday, when the [church] service is ended, the Indians gather in the cemetery, which is in front of the mission house, and dance. Half of the men adorn themselves with feathers and with girdles ornamented with feathers...or they paint their bodies with regular lines of black, red, and white... The men commonly dance six or eight together, all making the same movements and all armed with spears. Their music consists of clapping the hands, singing, and the sound made by striking split sticks together... This is finally followed by a horrible yell...along with a whistling noise. The women dance among themselves, but without making violent movements.[79]

Since the neophytes had trouble assimilating the franciscans' contempt for sensual pleasure and contempt for their own flesh, they likewise had trouble accepting the friars' restrained dress code. In 1814, friar Juan Amorós of mission Carmel, responding to a questionnaire from Spain, wrote that, thanks to the use of woolen and cotton garments, the neophytes "...all are clothed somewhat decently... If all valued wearing apparel much more would be given them, and in a short time we would have them going about as civilized beings. But they (i.e., the men) are not concerned whether they go about with or without clothing, inasmuch as they gamble away their wearing apparel;

(continued on page 147)

Gambling games at mission San Francisco, 1816. Painting by Louis Choris.

Sunday afternoon dance by Indians at mission San Francisco, 1816.

Painting by Franquelin, based on Louis Choris' original.   Courtesy of Bancroft Library

Indians dancing on the land of mission San José, 1806. Painting by Wilhelm von Tilenau.

nothing is worn from that which is given them; it is sold, exchanged, gambled or given away, then another garment older or newer is sought. They do, however, enter the church and *padres'* dwelling decently apparelled, because otherwise they would be reprimanded..."[80]

The same questionnaire asked, "Do they [the Indians] retain any superstitions? What means can be used to destroy these superstitions?" To this, the friars of mission Santa Clara replied:

> The Indians are very superstitious. They worship the devils, offering them seeds, and they fast and dance in their honor, in order to placate them... By using certain herbs, roots, feathers and other items, they believe they can free themselves from their enemies and from illness. They practice witchcraft by means of herbs, thorns, and other enchantments by means of which they attempt to injure others and obtain revenge. Finally, they believe in all they dream about. To destroy such an accumulation of evil, we know of no methods more opportune than frequent preaching and instruction, time, and patience.[81]

Turn of the Century, Turn for the Worse

As the 1800's began, many of the missions were prospering as farming, ranching and food production centers. Indian labor was the backbone of the missions' productive success. But far from spurring the cultural development of the mission Indians, this prosperity thrust them into bitter, at times violent conflict with nonchristian Indian groups, and with Hispanic land and ranch owners.

As the missions multiplied (five new ones were founded in 1797-8, bringing the total in California to 18) and their farm and pasture lands expanded, their large herds of cattle and horses became choice targets for nearby Indian groups. The Hispanic soldiers were hard pressed to prevent the mission cattle and horses from being driven off by nonchristian Indians, who used the horses sometimes for meat, sometimes for their own transport. Punitive expeditions against "wild" Indians accused of stealing mission animals, attacking the missions, or sheltering runaway neophytes became more bitter and systematic. The official Spanish rationale for these aggressive campaigns was *escarmentar a los gentiles,* to teach the pagans a painful lesson.

Whereas, in the late 1770's, the soldiers under governor Neve had refused to cooperate with the friars in capturing runaway neophytes (see page 72), now they hounded and captured the runaways with zeal.

In their drive to punish nonchristian Indians for sheltering runaways and for other alleged crimes against the missions, the Spanish military forces sometimes arrested an entire Indian village, confining the men at the presidio and the women and children at the mission.*

Indian labor, which the friars had proved productive, was at a premium, and the soldiers badly needed to control it. Not only were the mission Indians producing meat, milk, grains and fruits for the presidios, but the presidios were directly exploiting Indian labor—often under slavelike conditions and over the friars' objections—to maintain their own premises and serve the officers' families. Since the soldiers hoped for comfortable retirements as ranch owners commanding Indian laborers, they had a strong self interest in keeping both christian and nonchristian Indians under the taskmaster's whip.

*This is where the dispute over the Spaniards' *forced conversion* of California Indians to catholicism arises. Sherburne Cook wrote that "By 1810 extensive expeditions in search of fugitives were established policy...As time went on, the friction between wild Indians and whites increased, until toward the end of the mission period all pretense of voluntary conversion was discarded and expeditions to the interior were frankly for the purpose of military subjugation and forced conversion."[82] Cook's claim that forced conversion became Spanish policy in California has been uncritically accepted by many writers on the mission system during the 1800's.

Francis Florian Guest, a franciscan historian and biographer of Lasuén, disputes Cook's thesis of forced conversion. Guest shows how Cook, in the course of reading forced conversion into the Spanish punitive campaigns, mistranslated some key Spanish terms and misestimated the force of Spanish imperial law upon the soldiers. Guest, to be sure, documents several cases of wholesale military arrests of Indian villages, and admits that the soldiers did incalculable harm to the Indians in discharging their role as frontier police for the Spanish empire. But he explains: "...The reasons why the Spanish captured and imprisoned whole [villages], or the remains thereof, were judicial and military... The Indians were brought to the Spanish settlements... for the purposes of punishment, not necessarily for conversion. Now then, it is evident from Spanish documentation that many Indians who had been captured and imprisoned or were for other reasons fearful of Spanish military power had a tendency to ask for baptism, often, it would seem, as a means of appeasing their conquerors... [But] the fact that Indian men were forced into a presidio, and Indian women and children into a mission, does not prove that either were compelled to accept conversion..."[83] Guest stresses that Spanish imperial law, while requiring converted Indians to live at the mission, also required that all conversions be voluntary.

As in the case of the defeated rebel sorceress Toypurina (see page 139)—when Indian men, women and children found themselves detained at the presidio or mission after a traumatic clash, the line between voluntary and forced conversion became blurred. And, while Guest's criticisms of Cook's thesis are well taken in many respects, I think that Guest's own analysis is too legalistic, underestimating the Spaniards' drive to exploit Indian labor.

The outbreak of the Mexican revolution and independence struggle in 1810 broke most of the remaining links between the California mission system and the Spanish imperial regime in Mexico. The modest annual salary of 400 pesos issued by the Spanish viceroy to each missionary was terminated, and the soldiers as well stopped getting paid. Now the missions emerged as more crucial than ever to the material wellbeing of Spanish California. The government, still commanded by military interests, imposed taxes on and requisitioned supplies from the missions, to keep the presidios going.

Forced to support themselves and the entire military establishment, the missions became more commercial. Defying Spain's protectionist laws, they sold cattle hides and tallow (beef fat, used to make soap and candles) to English and Yankee sea merchants. The Anglo merchants made easy fortunes from this trade, taking advantage of the friars' ignorance of real world prices of the goods produced by their neophytes. The mission work routine was molded more and more in the service of the hide and tallow trade. To keep up with the surges in demand, the mission Indians had to slaughter far more cattle than they could possibly eat at one time, and a great deal of meat went to waste.

The Hispanic farmers and ranchers traded with the missions and foreign merchants for the foodstuffs and manufactured goods they lacked. As early as 1790, they widely conscripted nonchristian Indians to work their estates. Among themselves, the colonists of pueblos San José and Los Angeles were roughly equal in status during the early years of settlement; but later, they stratified into rich and poor. The poor farmer worked a small plot, and owned a few head of cattle. The rich colonist—often a retired military officer or his heir—received a big land grant from the government, and commanded a large labor force of Indians to till his crops and tend his herds.[84] The total non-Indian population of California grew from about 1,000 in 1800 (mainly concentrated in three pueblos) to about 3,000 by 1821—more through natural increase than through fresh colonization.[85]

The missions, still suffering higher death rates than birth rates, continued to depend on recruitment and conversion of "wild" Indians for their numerical growth. At several missions, after 20 years of evangelizing, virtually the entire Indian population in the area had been brought into the mission and baptized; those Indians who rejected the lure of christianity had fled into the interior, beyond the soldiers' reach. The friars had to found new missions in pagan territory, and begin the process anew. But now the pagan Indians were far wiser about what baptism and mission life meant, and could not be so easily lured by trinkets and sweet songs into accepting baptism. On the other hand, the friars had cultivated a group of loyal Indian catholics, whom they used both to evangelize the pagans and to search out and help the soldiers capture runaway neophytes.

The delay in founding a mission on the eastern shores of San Francisco bay led the friars and their helpers to range more widely in their search for fresh converts. In the 1790's, converts from east bay Ohlone tribelets were brought across the bay into mission San Francisco. Their dismay over being confined so far from their native homes was no doubt a big factor in the September 1796 mass escape from the mission. In 1797, the friars sent a party of neophytes headed by a man named Raimundo across to the east bay in search of runaways and new converts. The party was massacred by east bay Indians.[86]

In other cases, neophytes collaborated with Hispanic soldiers in launching bloody reprisals against pagan villages dubbed rebellious or accused of harboring runaways. Under the pressure of evangelizing campaigns, armed searches for runaways, and ruthless attacks against villages defying the Spanish authorities, the nonchristian Indians faced a stark choice: either full cooperation with the mission system (leading eventually to their own conversion), or armed rebellion, or flight into the interior.

Frederick Beechey observed of San Francisco in 1826:

It does not often happen that a voluntary convert succeeds in his attempt to escape, as the wild Indians have a great contempt and dislike for those who have entered the missions, and they will frequently not only refuse to re-admit them to their tribe, but will sometimes even [betray] their retreat to their pursuers... The [mission] Indians, besides, from political motives, are, I fear, frequently encouraged in a contemptuous feeling towards their unconverted countrymen by hearing them constantly held up to them in the degrading light of *bestias* [beasts]...[87]

By recruiting Indians from (and sometimes all the members of) several tribelets into a given mission, and convincing them to live and work together, the friars succeeded in suppressing traditional warfare between those tribelets. But at the same time, they created a new cultural cleavage among the California Indians, between neophytes and pagans. The reciprocal distrust and misunderstanding that festered between neophyte and pagan Indians erupted, at times, into violence—as neophytes identified pagans as thieves of their (mission) animals, and pagans identified neophytes with Hispanic encroachment against their land, resources, and labor.

The mission Indians, who remained "neophytes" through virtually the entire 60 years of the mission system, scarcely had a chance to develop the political and intellectual skills needed to overcome this fateful cleavage. The 1813 questionnaire from Spain to the missionaries asked, among other things: "What virtues are the most eminent among them [the Indians]?. . .." The Santa Clara friars replied: "Without doubt, their dominant virtues are their love for their relatives and members of their household, docility, respect, and obedience towards the Spaniards or *gente de razón* [artisans, overseers and colonists from Mexico], and particularly towards the missionary fathers."[88] This was 36 years after the founding of mission Santa Clara, and 26 years after Indian self government was formally required by Spanish law. It is not clear to what extent the friars' response reflected the actual behavior of their neophytes, or rather the friars' ideal of how the neophytes *should* behave. But in either case, it shows the paternalistic mentality that continued to pervade the missions.

The Mission Indians under Mexican Rule

In 1821, Mexico cast off the Spanish colonial yoke, becoming an independent monarchy and then, three years later, an independent republic. California now became a province of Mexico. The new Mexican government in 1821 granted citizenship to Indians, declaring protection of their person and property, and the republican constitution of 1824 granted Indians the right to vote and hold office. But in California, the relationship between Indians, friars, military officers and colonial landowners continued much as before. Indeed the expropriation of Indian lands was spurred on by Mexican policy favoring colonial settlement in California. Individuals could now get land grants of up to 50,000 acres (about 20,250 hectares).

The sons and grandsons of Spanish military officers who had carved out the first private estates now rose to economic prominence. Culturally insecure, they developed a racial caste consciousness and tried to separate their family lines from the peoples of colors they exploited. They married "white" and presented themselves as Spanish, renouncing Mexico and its *mestizo* culture.[89] These new aristocrats relocated entire Indian villages onto their estates to employ the Indians as full time laborers; where they needed only part time labor, they let the Indians continue living in their home villages, conscripting them for the harvests and other seasonal tasks. The Indian laborers received food, clothing, and some utensils from their masters. They were subject to physical punishment for even petty violations of the work rules.

A growing number of California Indians thus fell victim to feudal exploitation. In many respects, they were worse off than the mission Indians. The friars failed to teach more than a few of their neophytes to read; the big landowners, often illiterate themselves, were even more negligent about educating their laborers. Nor did the owners concern themselves with the medical conditions of their Indians, who were subject to the same diseases that ravaged the mission Indians.

The Chumash Uprising of 1824

In 1818, the California coast was threatened with invasion by the seafaring band of Hippolyte de Bouchard, a privateer from Buenos Aires. Friars at the missions in Chumash territory responded by training their neophytes for combat. At mission Santa Barbara, friar Antonio Ripoll placed 180 Indian men under arms: 100 archers made up the infantry, 50 more men carried machetes, and 30 mounted lancers made up the cavalry. The Indians got to choose their own corporals and sergeants, though their entire unit was led by the presidio commander. At mission La Purísima, friar Mariano Payeras organized a similar Indian fighting force, and wrote to governor Pablo Solá: "It would cause me joy if you could see the preparation and enthusiasm of these Indians."[90]

As it turned out, Bouchard's band invaded Monterey, failed to destroy the provincial government, and had no impact on Chumash territory. But the arming and large unit drilling of the Chumash neophytes took on a momentum of its own, more powerful than the threat it was designed to check. The friars did not foresee that European martial arts, in the hands of the Indians, could be turned against the mission system.

Continuing to worship their goddess Chupu, Chumash neophytes secretly built little shrines of sticks and brush adorned with pieces of cloth and feathers. The friars harshly punished any neophyte caught practicing such "idolatry."[91] Persistent and resourceful, the Chumash used every social organization available to them, including even the military drill units, to communicate with one another and preserve as much as they could of their traditional customs and beliefs.

After 1820, the friars launched a systematic campaign to root out the old Chumash ways. Friar José Señán designed a line of questioning (*confesionario*), largely in the Indians' own language, to be used at the annual Lenten confession of each neophyte. The neophytes were asked a series of specific questions about their kinship relations, marital status, sexual practices (including homosexuality and bestiality), use of the ritual hallucinogen datura and tobacco, and resort to shamans for healing. Señán and his colleagues might have done some fine anthropological research with their *confesionario*, if they weren't so intent on undermining the customs they asked their neophytes about. As it was, coming at the time of greatest stress and guilt imposed upon a practicing catholic, the *confesionario* provoked the Chumash into cultural, and soon physical resistance.[92]

Added to the cultural and psychological pressure from the friars was rough treatment from the soldiers who, not receiving their salaries, requisitioned foodstuffs, clothing, and other goods produced by the mission Indians. As Lent and the annual interrogation approached in February 1824, the atmosphere at the Chumash missions grew tense. The death of friar Señán the summer before, and the appearance of a large comet in the southern California sky beginning December 1823, probably convinced the shamans and their followers that the time was ripe for a sudden change, a bold return to the old ways. When a Mexican corporal ordered the flogging of a Purísima neophyte who had come to visit a relative imprisoned at mission Santa Ynez, he triggered the revolt.

On Saturday afternoon, 21 February, Indians from both missions showered arrows upon the soldiers at Santa Ynez, burned a building, and besieged the soldiers and a friar. When Mexican reinforcements arrived, the Indian warriors—having lost two men in combat—retreated to mission La Purísima, where their comrades had driven out the soldiers and taken over. Fortifying the mission quadrangle by erecting palisades, they cut ammunition slits through the church walls, awaiting a Mexican counterattack.

The rebels sent messengers to the Indian mayors at missions Santa Barbara and San Buenaventura, demanding that they join the insurrection. At San Buenaventura the mayor turned the rebel messenger over to the soldiers for imprisonment. But at Santa Barbara, Chumash mayor Andrés armed his fellow neophytes and nearby pagan Indians to confront the soldiers. After a skirmish costing three Indian lives, the rebels briefly took over the mission, but then fled to the hills. The returning soldiers took revenge by killing five more neophytes at Santa Barbara. Friar Antonio Ripoll, caught in the middle of this conflict, tried to maintain contact with the rebels and arrange their peaceful return to the mission. But the distrustful rebels fled further inland, to the tule marshlands in the southern San Joaquín valley.[93]

On 16 March, the Mexican counterattack against the La Purísima rebels finally rolled into motion. The 109 Mexican soldiers were well equipped with cavalry and artillery. The Indian rebels had massed a

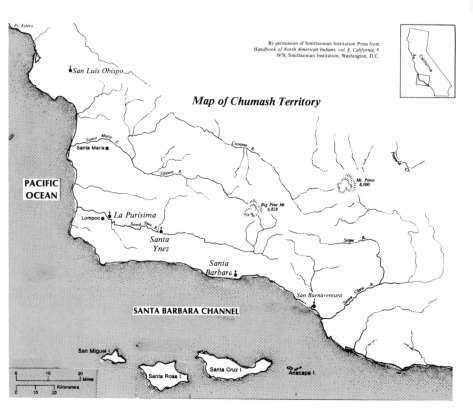

Map of Chumash Territory

Pt. Estero

San Luis Obispo

PACIFIC
OCEAN

Santa Maria R.

Santa Maria

Cuyama R.

Sisquoc R.

Mt. Pinos
8,000

Big Pine Mt.
6,828

Lompoc ▪ La Purísima

Santa Ynez R.

Santa
Ynez

Sespe R.

Santa
Barbara

Santa Clara R.

San Buenaventura

SANTA BARBARA CHANNEL

San Miguel I.

Santa Rosa I.

Santa Cruz I.

Anacapa I.

California

0   10   20
Miles

0   10   20
Kilometers

defending force of over 400—including nonmission Indians, some of
them Yokuts. They met the attackers with arrows, musket fire, and
volleys from the mission's small ceremonial cannons. But the Mexicans'
heavy artillery carried the day. Unable to break the siege, the Indians
asked friar Antonio Rodríguez—who had remained with them since
they took over La Purísima—to negotiate their surrender. Sixteen
Indians, and one Mexican soldier lay dead. In July, the Mexican
authorities tried 19 rebel leaders for murder: Seven Indians were
condemned to death; four were sentenced to permanent exile and ten
years of presidio labor; and eight were sentenced to eight years each of
presidio labor.

The Chumash rebels from Santa Barbara wanted to create a new life
for themselves in the valley marshlands. Released from the inhibitions
of catholic worship and social mores, they spent a lot of time gambling,
and engaged in free wheeling sexual activity, without respect for
marriage bonds. Yet they planned to use the technical skills they had
learned at the mission to build the community they desired. "We shall
maintain ourselves with what god provides us in the open country,"

they replied to friar Ripoll's request for them to return. "Moreover, we are soldiers, stone masons, carpenters, etc., and we will provide for ourselves by our work."[94]

But the Mexican authorities could not let the missions unravel to the benefit of Indian freedom. In June, they mounted an expedition of some 130 troops equipped with heavy artillery, to capture the runaways. Mission president Vicente de Sarría and friar Ripoll accompanied the expedition, bearing a pardon from the governor to convince the rebels to return to mission Santa Barbara. The friars thus negotiated the surrender of many of the rebels. But many more fled deeper inland, some of them entering Yokuts territory. Nearly half the Indian population of Santa Barbara at the time of the revolt, numbering several hundred, escaped the military campaign and retained their freedom. They cultivated corn, pumpkins, melons and other crops they had learned to grow at the mission, and integrated the golden images and other ritual objects they had taken from the Santa Barbara church into their traditional modes of worship.

The 1824 Chumash uprising was directed mainly against the soldiers as enforcers of mission discipline. The kind treatment which the neophytes gave the friars even at the height of their revolt showed that, while they hated the mission system, they still respected the friars—viewing them as friendly, or at least neutral, in their conflict with the soldiers. In the wake of the revolt, the Mexican authorities ordered the friars at each mission to surrender all machetes, lances and firearms to the nearest presidio. The rebel neophytes who returned were not only disarmed, but also broken spiritually. The shamans among them faded from prominence, their old kinship bonds broke down, and the annual Lenten confession came to mean submitting humbly to the priest's authority.[95]

Farther north in the San Joaquín valley, groups of "wild" Indians launched protracted armed resistance against the private ranches that kept intruding upon their ancestral lands and food sources. Becoming skilled horsemen, the Indians rustled cattle and horses from the ranches with speed and flair. They made their societies more mobile, and developed guerrilla tactics to fend off the private and official armed parties sent to punish them. A Miwok Indian named Estanislao (after the Polish saint Stanislaus) became one of several brilliant guerrilla leaders among the valley Indians. After routing several Mexican attacking parties, Estanislao and his warriors had, in 1829, to face an invasion force of a hundred soldiers supported by heavy artillery and led by lieutenant Mariano Vallejo. The Mexican attackers with their Indian auxiliaries killed many Miwoks, but failed to defeat Estanislao's forces.

Secularization and Dispersal

The mission Indians continued to suffer low morale and high mortality. "I am weary of all this sickness and dying," lamented friar Narciso Durán in a note in the death register he kept at mission San José. "These Indians are more fragile than glass."[96] Friar José Viader, a 34-year veteran of mission Santa Clara who had made strenuous efforts to provide medical care for his neophytes, wrote in 1830: "There are many deaths and few births. Sickness is always with us, and I fear it is the end of the Indian race. What can we do?"[97] Over the next three years, a malaria epidemic devastated the Indians of California's central valley, including the free Chumash people who had fled from mission Santa Barbara in 1824.

Friar Durán, in a letter to the president of Mexico in 1830, denounced the "invincible repugnance they [the Indians] have for becoming civilized and for relinquishing their heathen preferences and prejudices." Durán shifted the blame for the failings of the mission system onto the Indians' shoulders: "They are children of a vicious upbringing, of an immemorial and eternal tradition, of absolute liberty exempt from all bonds of excellence and law. It is from this, in spite of the elaborate efforts of the missionaries, that there follows the tendency or inclination, also insuperable, toward the savage life in which they were brought up and which, because of their communication with neighboring nonchristian Indians, they always keep in mind..."[98]

In 1833, the Mexican government passed a law secularizing California's 21 missions. The governor of California, José Figueroa, did not implement the law until the following year, when he issued his own secularization decree: The friars had to stop running the affairs of the missions, and were to perform only religious duties until being replaced by parish priests. The missions were to become pueblos, with their lands parcelled out among the neophytes. Each head of a family or adult male over 20 years of age was to get 33 acres (about 13 hectares) of land. Half the missions' livestock, tools, and seeds were also to be distributed to the neophyte men. All the remaining lands, livestock and other property were to come under the missions' new administrators, appointed by the governor. And the government reserved the right to force neophytes to work on these state owned fields and orchards. The Indians could not sell or mortgage their new property; if a head of family died without a legal heir, his landholding would revert to the state.[99]

Most of the neophytes, spurning the offer of land ownership, declared their freedom and fled the missions—sometimes leaving their elders behind. For those who stayed, the legal right to own land was no great blessing: Under the friars' regime, neophyte families had been able to keep their own gardens and a few fruit trees, disposing of the products as they wished. Now they had few cattle to plow and graze on the lands they owned; the friars, fearing for their own sustenance as secularization approached, had directed the mass slaughter of cattle, placing the revenues from sale of their hides into the Pious Fund.[100]

Moreover, Figueroa's handpicked administrators soon took advantage of the forced labor clause to enrich themselves and their families at the Indians' expense. The "emancipated" Indians now had to labor in the fields and private homes to support the administrator, the soldiers, and the governor. Many of the administrators were so greedy and corrupt that, within a few years, they drove the mission Indians into poverty.

Meanwhile, many poor Hispanic settlers were allowed to borrow cattle from the mission herds to get a start at extending their own farms and ranches. Few of these cattle were returned to the missions, and many of the Hispanics, calling themselves *Californios*, prospered and grew rich. The fertile mission lands, instead of becoming a source of Indian industry and happiness as the early missionaries had dreamed, became a source of Indian peonage. The newly rich landowners contented themselves with exporting rawhide and beef tallow, buying all the finished products they needed from merchant ships. The mission soap, candle, shoe, saddle, blanket, pottery, and wine industries disappeared, and the Indians skilled in them had no place to continue their work.

Many of the Indians fleeing the missions in the wake of secularization wandered into the pueblos such as Los Angeles and San José, living through casual labor and begging. Deprived of their traditional food sources, they faced starvation, and often resorted to theft and scavenging for food discarded by the Californio townspeople. Demoralized, the men spent a lot of time drinking and gambling.

Other former neophytes fled inland into free Indian territory. In southern California, Cahuilla and Kumeyaay Indians fought the Hispanics and raided their ranches and settlements along the coast, maintaining their own freedom among the inland mountains. At Pleasanton east of San Francisco bay, plains Miwoks, coastal Miwoks, northern valley Yokuts, Chochenyo and Patwin Indians who had been brought together at the missions founded a new, multi-ethnic community. Other such communities, crossing old tribelet and language barriers, were created in the regions around the northern missions.[101]

But most of the mission Indians wound up working as farm hands, ranch hands, and domestic servants for the big Californio land owners. The carving up of the rich mission lands left the growing class of big landlords in the saddle. During the period of Spanish rule from 1769 to 1821, only 20 private land grants had been made in California; under Mexican rule from 1821 to 1846, about 500 landed estates were authorized.[102] A few mission Indian men received land grants of their own. But the vast majority of mission Indians were dispossessed, despite their legal land rights. For years they tried to hang on to the legal papers they had received, entitling them to their shares of land. But most of those papers were eventually stolen, or burned along with the Indians' houses when the dwellers were absent.[103]

The Indian laborers, while free in theory, were really bound to their estate owner for as long as he wanted their services. The owners and their foremen trapped the Indians in a net of debt obligations, pulling the net ever tighter. They used physical punishment to keep their Indians in line. The Indians were banned from moving from one place to another, without a discharge signed by their last employer proving they were not in debt to him.[104] Bitter, smallscale fighting raged back and forth between the landlords' forces and "wild" Indians of the central valley, who resisted the expanding estates by raiding their horses and cattle. The Californios now had a dual aim in their bloody raids against free Indian groups: punishing stock thieves and capturing laborers for their estates.

Starting in October 1845, the California missions, already gutted by their administrators and the newly rich landowners, were placed on the auction block by governor Pío Pico. An order from Mexico prohibiting their sale was ignored. In 1846, a group of Yankee mercenaries overran the feeble Mexican government forces and declared California an independent republic. In February 1848, the U.S. military victory over Mexico made California a U.S. possession.

The Gold Rush and Yankee Invasion

The Yankees' discovery of vast gold deposits later that year was to prove even more devastating to the California Indians than the Spaniards' discovery of Aztec, Mayan and Incan gold had been to the

Indians of Middle and South America. Through the sixty years of the Spanish mission system, the California Indians—especially those living near the Pacific coast, where the missions were established—had suffered terrible losses in population, due mostly to diseases and demoralization. Their total population may have been reduced by half, from roughly 300,000 in 1769 to roughly 150,000 by 1845. Yet most of their cultures and languages survived, and they still formed a large majority of the California population. They seemed to have a fighting chance to reassert their cultures and regain their numbers.

But the gold rush was, for the Indians, an overwhelming invasion of white, fortune-seeking scoundrels. These invaders, far from wanting to save Indian souls, were intent on uprooting all Indian obstacles to their lust for quick wealth. Within a few years, the California Indians were a besieged minority in a land that was once their own.

At first, many Indians labored for white Californians to dig and pan for gold. Other Indians became independent prospectors, and their basketry skills came in handy for sifting gold from the mountain stream silt; they traded their gold to white merchants, who typically took advantage of their commercial naiveté to pay them way below the market value of their finds. As competition for prospecting claims sharpened, whites violently drove Indians out of the goldfields. Murder of Indians, and rape of Indian women became commonplace.

California's constitutional convention of September 1849, dominated by white male Yankees, extended the right to vote only to white male citizens. A California state law of 1850 barred Indians and Blacks from testifying in court, either "in favor of, or against a white man." In 1854, California's chief justice declared that Chinese men—who, as wage-working goldminers employed by big companies, were being lynched by frustrated white losers—were legally Indians. Another 1850 law, deceptively titled the "act for the government and protection of Indians," subjected able bodied Indians to arrest "on the complaint of any resident" if they could not support themselves, or were found loitering or "leading an immoral or profligate course of life." An Indian judged vagrant could be hired out within 24 hours to the highest bidder, for a labor term up to four months. This law opened the way for the conversion of California's Indians to chattel slaves. It also provided that an Indian convicted of any offense punished by a fine could be bailed out by any white person willing to pay the fine; the Indian then had to work for the white man until he had discharged the amount of the fine.

The gold rush dealt a body blow to many Indian groups in eastern California who had escaped recruitment into the missions and landed estates. After rich gold deposits were found in the mountain streams and valleys of the Sierra Nevada and Cascades of eastern California and central Oregon, aggressive whites flooded in. The pile-up of dirt and silt from their mining activities blocked salmon from swimming up the rivers to spawn. In the central California valley as well as the coast, gold and mass immigration spurred a feverish expansion of private farming and logging. The conversion of grasslands and river bottoms to plowed fields and orchards deprived the Indians of vast seed and fish food sources. The draining of swamps and marshlands drove away the wild birds and the reeds which the Indians used for basketry and building. The farmers' cattle and hogs gobbled grass seeds, clover, and acorns.[105] By 1850, the total Indian population of California had been reduced to about 100,000. By 1855, it was down to about 50,000.[106]

In the 1850's, the Californios' (Hispanics') feudal estates came under the ax of the Yankee legal system. Land hungry Yankees contested the Californios' land titles, and dragged them through long court battles. Even when a Californio won the case, he often had to sell his estate to pay his attorney's fees. The big feudal landholdings were carved up into a multitude of small subsistence farms, and the land came under much more intense cultivation. The wage labor market was now glutted with white ex-miners and Chinese workers, so Indians were no longer much needed to work on the farms, except as domestic servants. Released from the feudal yoke, they were now fully vulnerable to murder of their men, rape, and enslavement of their women and children.

Indian Slavery in the Free Republic

The 1850 California law "for the government and protection of Indians" also set up a system of Indian "apprenticeship": Any white person wanting to employ an Indian child could come before a judge with the child's "parents or friends"; if the judge decided that the child had been obtained without coercion, he would issue the white person a certificate giving him "the care, custody, control, and earnings of such minor, until he or she obtains the age of majority," which was 18 for Indian boys, and 15 for Indian girls. The white master was legally required to feed and clothe his Indian wards, and treat them humanely. But if he failed to meet these requirements, his maximum penalty was a $10 fine and reassignment of the abused youth to another master. An 1860 amendment extended the terms of "apprenticeship" by several years: An Indian boy could be held until he was 25, a girl until 21; an

Indian first "apprenticed" while a teenager could be held until 30 if male, and until 25 if female.

According to Robert Heizer, up to 10,000 Indians became indentured servants under the laws of 1850 and 1860. Judges made few or no efforts to enforce even the minimal protections for Indians specified in the laws. Outright kidnapping and enslavement of Indian children became common; often the kidnappers murdered the children's parents, after raping their mother. They then held the children under threat of death, shooting them if they tried to escape. Young Indian women "apprentices" often became concubines of their masters. Yet California was supposedly a free state, its constitution having banned slavery and involuntary servitude.[107]

The Indian acts of 1850 and 1860 were repealed by the California legislature in 1863. But the kidnapping and selling of Indian children, and the private enslavement of Indian adults, continued until at least 1867. Between 1852 and 1867, perhaps 3,000 to 4,000 Indian children were kidnapped and enslaved, with northern California natives suffering the heaviest assaults.[108] In the summer of 1865, the *California Police Gazette* demanded an investigation of the treatment of Indians in the state: "Slavery exists in California in precisely the same condition that it did until lately in the southern states... Here *in almost every county* Indians are unlawfully held as chattels... Many of them have fallen into cruel hands and the barbarities inflicted upon them by inhuman masters would put to blush the most unfeeling wretch that ever lorded it over a gang on a Southern plantation."[109]

Yankee Genocide

Killing off "wild" Indians to clear the way for mining, lumbering and farming became a matter both of private passion and state policy. In the 1850's, the California government issued over a million dollars in state bonds to pay local volunteers for their armed campaigns against Indians. Governor Peter Burnet declared to the legislature that a "war of extermination will continue to be waged between the races until the Indian race becomes extinct."[110] The federal government in Washington, at first reluctant, reimbursed the state for most of the blood money it paid to its white citizens. In 1855, Shasta City in northern California offered $5 for each Indian head delivered to the city center. In 1863, the citizens of Honey Lake paid 25¢ for each Indian scalp turned in.[111]

The Yahi (Yana) Indians of north central California, living on hilly land covered with oak trees, tried to avoid all contact with white society. But white gold seekers, and later white farmers and ranchers, hunted them

Ishi, one of the last Yahi Indians. Found scavenging for food in a slaughterhouse in 1911, Ishi was romanticized as "the last Yahi" and became a living anthropology museum display. This photo of him was taken by Alfred Kroeber in 1914, two years before Ishi's death. According to Native American writers Rupert and Jeannette Henry Costo, Ishi had actually been ostracized by his own people, for stealing. Although Ishi's sister survived him, the Yahi people have now died out.
(Lowie Museum of Anthropology, University of California, Berkeley)

down like wild animals. In 1871 a rancher found one of his steers wounded, and blamed the local Yahi Indians. Trailing a group of Yahis with dogs, he drove them into a cave, and shot about 30 of them to death there; he shot the adults with his hunting rifle, the children with his revolver.[112] And by that time, the Yahis were nearly extinct.

By the 1870's, the total number of California Indians was less than 30,000—a reduction by about 80% since 1845. Nearly all the surviving Indian groups of northern and central California had been herded onto government reservations. About 60% of the Indian deaths were caused by disease, 30% by malnutrition and starvation, and 10% by private and official murder by armed whites. By 1900, the California Indian population was less than 16,000.[113]

As we have seen, the California Indians suffered genocide, the near total destruction of their populations and cultures, between the years 1845 and 1870. The main culprits were the invading Yankee gold seekers, farmers, ranchers and loggers, along with the U.S. federal army. Once Indian labor was no longer very useful to the white man, extermination of the native peoples became a goal openly embraced by the aggressive vanguard of the new white majority, with official state backing. The Indians "must fade away before the Saxon race as the cloud in the west before the light and heat of a greater power," declared the *San Francisco Alta California* newspaper in 1851.[114]

Was Serra a Racist?

The racism of the Yankee invaders was flagrant. But what about Junípero Serra and the Spanish franciscan friars? Were they likewise racist towards the California Indians?

The Spanish mission system did not aim to destroy the Indian race, but rather to convert the California Indians into catholic citizens of the Spanish empire. The franciscan friars, through their long training in catholic dogma and missionary techniques, were imbued with contempt for the culture of native peoples who worshipped a bewildering variety of goddesses, gods, animals, and spirits. They underestimated the power of the belief systems of those peoples who ignored the True Religion of the Lord Jesus Christ, and studied their beliefs only superficially, and then only to undermine them.

Yet the Spanish friars did not consider the Indians inherently inferior beings. The Indians had souls worth saving, just like all other human beings (with the exception of infidels and those who knowingly consorted with the devil). Junípero Serra, in particular, seems to have held more respect for the California Indians' intellectual capacities, than did most of his franciscan colleagues. Towards the end of his life, Serra objected, with mild sarcasm, to the official distinction between *gente de razón* ("people of reason") and Indians; he suggested that the Indians too were people of reason (see page 73). By contrast, his successor, Fermín de Lasuén, described the Indians as "a nation that is barbarous, ferocious and ignorant..."[115]

Serra also encouraged intermarriage between Spanish soldiers (including white Catalonians) and christian Indian women, and several such marriages took place under his regime. The Spanish empire was extremely race conscious, employing a detailed list of ethnic categories—including *"color quebrado"* ("softened color") for people of a multiracial mix—in gathering census data on its subjects. Yet the

Spaniards and Mexicans, with a long history of racial mixing behind them, were generally far more relaxed and matter-of-fact about interracial marriage than were the Yankee boneheads who later invaded California. In 1860, the *Humboldt Times* of northern California, reflecting popular white sentiments, declared: "It is as impossible for the white man and the wild Indian to live together as it is to unite oil and water."[116] The Yankee invaders viewed the Indians as a contemptible and inferior race, even while they held Indian women as concubines and fathered children by them.

Serra, to be sure, was no less paternalistic towards the Indians than were the rest of the franciscan missionaries. "... They are our children (*hijos*)," he wrote of the Indians, "for no one else has begotten them in Christ. For this reason, it is our duty to regard them highly, which indeed we do in a paternal way."[117]

If the franciscan friars were not overtly racist towards the Indians, they were culturally chauvinistic. Their attitude was: 'We will love and respect you, *if* you give up your primitive ways, stop speaking your strange languages, and become like us.' In this sense, the franciscans' approach to the indigenous peoples was—ironically enough—similar to the stance of enlightenment liberals and vulgar marxists.

An Apprenticeship for Feudalism

The franciscans' paternalism proved disastrous for the Indians of California. By teaching them farming and ranching without allowing them to govern their own lives and labor, the friars made the Indians exploitable by private landowners. By teaching them mechanical trades without the scientific and engineering principles behind those trades, they guaranteed that the Indians' new skills would be lost once the missions were dismantled. By teaching them catholic dogma in Spanish and Latin, de-emphasizing literacy and failing to give the Indian languages written forms, the friars hastened the disappearance of the Indian languages and left the Indians without resources to claim the formal rights they had under Mexican law. By confining women and downgrading their social status, the friars broke their independent spirits, making them exploitable as domestic servants and concubines.

The objective, historical impact of the Spanish mission system was to train the California Indians for feudal exploitation by Hispanic landlords, to be followed by capitalist enslavement, assault and genocide at the hands of the Yankee invaders. The Spanish mission system was not, in itself, genocidal. But it softened the Indians up for genocide.

Chapter 4

The Vatican *vs.* the People's Movements:
Reconciliation or Liberation?

The catholic church today—whether the Vatican likes it or not—is a pluralistic institution. It includes those who preach spiritual communion with the Lord Jesus Christ as humanity's prime goal—and those who preach that the people should struggle to end injustice and oppression in the material world. It includes archbishops who support fascist military dictatorships in their countries—and priests who have joined the workers' and peasants' movements against those dictatorships. As in the early years of the christian movement, catholics of various races and colors have recast god, Mary, and Jesus in their own images, breaking the monopoly of the white god, blonde Mary and blue-eyed Jesus: The brown virgins Mary remain influential in Latin America and the Philippines, while black catholics in the U.S. south worship a god, Mary, and Jesus of their own color. Traditional church doctrine that woman must submit unconditionally to the rule of man is being challenged by catholic women demanding equal rights in the church and in society. While top church officials denounce homosexuality as a sin against nature and god, openly gay and lesbian catholics struggle to find acceptance and grace within the church. In California, the church includes franciscan priests who embrace Junípero Serra as a saint—and Native American catholics who accuse Serra of having committed crimes of genocide against the Indians of California.

During the church's years of greatest power and greatest insecurity between about 1200 and 1700, such lively differences and disputes were often resolved through the torture rack, strangulation, burnings at the stake, and confiscation of the property of the weak by the strong men of the church. In today's world, the Vatican must resort to more nuanced means to safeguard the purity of its doctrine and the security of its command structure.

Catholic Democracy, Liberation Theology

Ironically, it was the Vatican itself, under pope John 23 and his colleagues, that gave the key impulse for the lively pluralism that now tears at the traditional fiber of the church. Pope John denounced the exploitation of the third world by the rich countries of the north, championing the rights of the poor and the hungry. His social encyclicals inspired the second Vatican council of 1962-65, which decentralized church power down towards national bishops' conferences and the active laity.

Vatican 2 instructed every catholic religious community to assemble all its members, hold free discussions, and revise its constitution on the basis of democratic consensus. An experimental period of 12 years was allowed, during which religious communities could explore new modes of organization and activity—so long as they stopped short of overturning the church's traditional structure.[1] Nuns emerged from their traditional cloistered lives into the wider world, actively serving the catholic laity—and especially poorer women—in a variety of social settings. The barriers between religious and lay catholics began breaking down.

In upholding the rights of the poor while stimulating democratic ferment among its own lower ranks and laity, Vatican 2 openly contrasted its methods with those of "totalitarian communism." In the Soviet Union, to be sure, marxism-leninism had long since turned into its opposite: from a liberating theory and practice to overthrow all forms of social oppression, into a conservative rationale for the bureaucratic *status quo* that entrenched a privileged minority in power. But in several third world countries, *revolutionary* marxism-leninism was making headway, rallying broad masses of peasants and workers in struggle against the big landowners, local ruling cliques, and imperialist armed forces (as with the U.S. in Indochina and Latin America).

The catholic grassroots communities that sprouted among the rural poor and shantytown dwellers in Latin America and the Philippines were viewed, by the liberal catholic hierarchy, as an alternative to marxism. These communities often stepped into a vacuum of popular leadership, building peasant cooperatives and farmworkers' unions and training local people's leaders in areas where marxist-leninist groups had failed to gain a foothold, or had suffered defeat due to their tactical blunders or insensitivity to the local peoples' cultures. As the catholic people's movements came under violent repression by the landowners and military cliques, their leaders had to grapple with the problem of how to continue the movement.

The Latin American bishops' conference in Medellín, Colombia in 1968 offered some guidance by declaring that, in the face of unjust social systems driving masses of people into poverty and despair, armed resistance by the people was not immoral. But christian teachings could hardly be a source of practical inspiration for a people's movement struggling against repressive terror; for this, the theories and practice of Lenin and Mao were a much surer guide. By the time Vatican 2's 12-year period of community experimentation expired in 1977, catholic grassroots community movements had helped train a new generation of revolutionary activists in Nicaragua, El Salvador, Guatemala, and the Philippines. The following year, the Polish traditionalist Karol Wojtyla became pope John Paul 2.

John Paul 2's Counter-Reformation

One of John Paul 2's first big political tasks was to clamp the lid on the radical and revolutionary catholic currents in Latin America. At the Latin American bishops' conference he convened in Puebla, Mexico in February 1979, the pope rejected the concept of a "church born of the people," a concept embraced by the catholic grassroots communities. While denouncing political repression, the pope and his conservative Latin American colleagues firmly denounced class struggle and marxism.[2]

The pope's efforts failed to prevent the victory of the Nicaraguan revolution five months later, or the outbreak of civil war in El Salvador within two years of the Puebla conference. Yet his counter reformation-ist agenda is by no means confined to Latin America. In Italy, the pope has given his public blessing to "Communion and Liberation," a catholic fundamentalist movement founded in 1954. Based among younger Italians in their 20's and early 30's, Communion and Liberation opposes premarital sex, contraception, abortion and divorce, defends the church's hierarchical structure, and denounces all dissent within the church as "creeping protestantism." It aims to impose its social dogma as state policy in Italy, and about a thousand members of its political arm have won election to city councils. In 1986, the movement's magazine gave a rave review to the film "Rambo," embracing Sylvester Stallone as "a new David."³*

Italy's catholic bishops, most of whom find Communion and Liberation too extreme in its rightwing politics, have declared their support for Catholic Action, an apolitical lay organization.⁴ But the pope insists on supporting Communion and Liberation, which has spread its movement into some 20 other countries—notably in Africa and Latin America. In the U.S., the movement's main supporter in the catholic hierarchy is New York's archbishop John O'Connor, who served as a U.S. navy commander during the Vietnam war and later became a rear admiral.

Latin America is the world's most catholic continent by far: Some 350 million of the world's 870 million catholics live in Latin America, where they make up over 90% of the population. Political struggles within the church take on their sharpest form there. These struggles reflect the class conflict polarizing Latin American societies between the ruling landowning and financial oligarchies on the one side, and the workers and peasants on the other.

As with Latin America's fragile middle classes, which vacillate politically between the big bourgeoisie and the working people, the liberal and moderate bishops are weak and vacillating. The key dispute in the Latin American church is between the top hierarchy—which in most countries supports the ruling class—and the radical priests, nuns and layworkers who side with the working people in their struggles to overthrow tyranny and achieve social justice.

The grassroots activists of the *people's church* have long held a set of religious and social/political ideas to guide their practice: *liberation theology*, as outlined by Vatican 2 and the Medellín conference and elaborated by the Peruvian priest Gustavo Gutiérrez, the Brazilian franciscans Clodovis and Leonardo Boff, and other radical theologians. The bishops and cardinals who support the ruling classes have relied, for

---

*It must be admitted that the comparison between Stallone and king David is rather apt. King David, like Rambo, was a racist mass murderer. According to the old testament account, after conquering the city of Rabbah and plundering its riches, David had its inhabitants slaughtered in various sadistic ways—"and thus did he unto all the cities of the children of Ammon." (2 Samuel 12.31). To be sure, David would have been a lightweight boxer compared with Stallone, while Stallone's mass murder has been confined to the movies.

their part, on traditional catholic doctrine. A group of these conservatives, headed by Colombia's cardinal Alfonso López Trujillo and supported by Nicaragua's cardinal Miguel Obando y Bravo, have proposed a "reconciliation theology" to combat liberation theology.[5] This proposal will not require much innovation: "Reconciliation theology," which urges slaves to be reconciled with their masters and hope for a happy afterlife, is as old as the holy Roman empire. The pope made reconciliation his key slogan during his visit to South America in the spring of 1987.

The Pope in Chile and Argentina

"Reconciliation as proposed by the church is a genuine road of christian liberation, without recourse to hate, to class struggle, to reprisals, to the inhuman dialectic that does not see others as brothers but as enemies to combat..." declared the pope to the assembled throng at a park in Santiago, Chile on 3 April 1987. "Violence is no road to solving the real difficulties of individuals or peoples."[6]

But the pope's sermon was interrupted by a violent clash sparked by youths in the crowd. They hurled rocks and sticks at the press section of the assembly, injuring journalists, priests, and others in the area. Riot police swarmed into the park, showering the people with water cannons and tear gas. The gas wafted up to the holy dais, where the pope and his colleagues tried to continue the mass, the pope often squeezing his eyes shut as the tear gas took its effect. Priests among the people—including Mariano Puga, himself bleeding from a rock wound—tried to defuse the clash between youths and police.

Ronaldo Muñoz, a priest and liberation theologian, was not pleased with the pope's performance: "For us, the action against the police vans—aggressive, violent—is a scandal, but not so big a scandal. For us, the scandal is that the pope speaks to us against violence while he is protected by these violent people," referring to the police and "security" forces of general Augusto Pinochet, who gave a cordial welcome to pope John Paul 2. "Young people don't believe him when he is protected by the same guns that hurt them... Jesus had no military protection. You cannot bear witness in a violent situation without sharing the risks in which the people live—or you have no authority."[7]

The police finally ended the struggle by firing bullets into the crowd, and the wounded at day's end numbered over 300 civilians, and over 100 police. It was not clear whether the youths who started the conflict were freelance radicals, or agents of the dictatorship who provocatively assaulted sections of the peaceful crowd so as to allow the police to

Santiago, Chile—1 April 1987:
General Pinochet welcomes
pope John Paul 2 to Chile.

appear as protectors of the people against "terrorists" and insolent atheists. In any event, Pinochet's police forces, again using tear gas, water cannons and bullets, crushed four groups of poor Chileans who had seized the occasion of the pope's visit to occupy vacant lands— resulting in one dead and many wounded.

So the political breathing space that the pope's visit seemed to provide the people's movement was quickly smothered, and the pope refused to take the side of the poor. Yet he was shrewd enough not to side overtly with general Pinochet. He denounced torture and violence several times, clearly chiding the dictatorship's forces in the southern town of Punta Arenas, heavily populated by military personnel and a site of concentration camps for political opponents of Pinochet in the early years of his reign.

Chile's conservative cardinal Juan Francisco Fresno, who had received a medal from Pinochet, was roundly booed by the people wherever he went during the pope's visit. Archbishop Angelo Sodano, the *papal nuncio* (Vatican representative) in Chile since 1978, censored statements submitted by the people for public reading by the pope, softening their denunciation of the dictatorship. Chile's radical priests and lay theologians, complaining that Sodano has intervened to appoint more and more conservatives to the church hierarchy, have launched a campaign for his recall to Rome. In the wake of the pope's visit, cardinal Fresno was whisked to Antarctica in an airforce plane to give a televised communion to general Humberto Gordon, head of the army and former head of Pinochet's dreaded secret police.[8]

The pope moved on to Argentina, where his watchword of reconciliation took on special poignancy. It bolstered the strident campaign by the military hierarchy for amnesty for the many officers guilty of kidnapping, torturing and murdering thousands during the military dictatorships of 1976-83. Just two days after the pope left Argentina, a military revolt broke out in Córdoba, resulting in president Alfonsín's capitulation to the officers' demand for a swift halt to further prosecutions of military criminals.

Córdoba was where the pope had chosen to denounce a bill granting Argentinians the right to divorce, which had already swept parliament and awaited ratification by the senate. Bombastically referring to himself as "bishop of Rome and the successor of saint Peter," the pope thundered against divorce as a harbinger of public immorality and decay of the social order.[9] He might have added that he is also a successor of saint Paul, who exhorted women to "submit yourselves unto your own husbands as unto the Lord" (Ephesians 5.22), forbade women to teach (1 Timothy 2.11-12), ordered women to remain silent in church (1 Corinthians 14.34-5), and urged slaves to "obey them that have the rule over you, and submit yourselves..." (Hebrews 13.17). Even so, the senate went on to ratify the divorce bill.

On 8 April 1987, the pope, outfitted in colorful native dress, spoke before a crowd of Argentine Indians. He criticized the "weaknesses and errors" of the church's treatment of Indians during the Spanish conquest of America, and urged his audience to "love your own cultures, and make them blossom."[10] The pope can afford such liberality in Argentina, where the Indians have been exterminated by European invaders to the point of numbering only about 100,000 out of a total population of 28 million. But in Peru and Guatemala, where Indians number in the millions and form the core of armed revolutionary movements, the pope is far less enthusiastic about promoting Indian culture.

The upshot of the pope's visit to Chile and Argentina was to weaken the people's liberation movements, strengthen the reactionary church hierarchies, and encourage the armed forces of the ruling classes. But in so doing, the pope avoided a head-on collision with liberation theology. Indeed in April 1986, after three years of Vatican polemics against liberation theology and a ten-month order banning Leonardo Boff from teaching, writing, and preaching his liberating gospel to the people of Brazil, the pope gave ground before the people's church movement in Latin America. In a letter to Brazil's bishops (the most vigorous defenders of liberation theology among national bishops' groups), he declared that "liberation theology is not only opportune, but useful and necessary."[11] Note that the pope did not call liberation theology *true*, or *just*: He weighed every word carefully, hedging against the day when liberation theology will no longer be "opportune, useful and necessary" for his purposes.

Even so, this was an interesting turnabout, in light of the fact that the pope's righthand man at the Vatican, cardinal Joseph Ratzinger, had earlier denounced liberation theology as "the heresy of our time." Pope John Paul 2 is a clever political tactician. He realizes that if he pushes too hard against the people's church and liberation theology, he might provoke an open rebellion among the ranks of his church, from Chile up through Mexico and Haiti. He would like, if possible, to gut liberation theology of its radical content, redefining liberation in purely "spiritual," christological terms. And besides, by arranging a temporary truce with liberation theology, he can concentrate his heavy guns against liberal and radical currents in the North American church.

The Struggle within the North American Church

On 7 October 1984, at the height of the U.S. presidential campaign, a full-page advertisement appeared in the Sunday *New York Times*, titled: "A Diversity of Opinions Regarding Abortion Exists Among Catholics." The $30,000 ad, sponsored by the 5,000-member Catholics for a Free Choice, came in response to New York archbishop John O'Connor's anti-abortion political agitation. O'Connor was pressuring Democratic vice presidential candidate Geraldine Ferraro and New York state's governor Mario Cuomo to renounce their pro-choice positions, and submit to official church doctrine banning abortion. The text of the ad began: "Statements of recent Popes and of the Catholic hierarchy have condemned the direct termination of pre-natal life as morally wrong in all instances. There is the mistaken belief in American society that this is the only legitimate Catholic position. In fact, a diversity of opinions regarding abortion exists among committed Catholics."[12]

Without coming out positively for a woman's right to abortion, the dissenters urged "that the Catholic community encourage candid and respectful discussion on this diversity of opinion within the Church, and that Catholic youth and families be educated on the complexity of the issues of responsible sexuality and human reproduction.

"Further, Catholics—especially priests, religious, theologians, and legislators—who publicly dissent from hierarchical statements and explore areas of moral and legal freedom on the abortion question should not be penalized by their religious superiors, church employers, or bishops..." The ad/statement was signed by 97 catholics, the majority of them women, including 24 nuns.

Catholic Women Advocates against the Vatican

The Vatican reacted by demanding that the 24 nuns, two monks and one priest who had signed the statement make a public retraction, or face expulsion from their religious communities. The U.S. national bishops' conference endorsed the Vatican position, pointing out that it was based on canon law, and urged the signers to retract for the sake of reconciliation. The franciscan priest who had signed the statement, Jerry Kaelin of Cincinnati, soon retracted, as did the two monks. But the nuns held firm. Their religious superiors now came under heavy pressure to expel these 24 women, who had served the church for a total of some 500 woman-years.

Rosemary Radford Ruether, theology professor at Garrett-Evangelical Theological Seminary in Illinois and a prominent lay signatory of the ad/statement, read the women signers' collective response to the Vatican attack: The Vatican "seeks to stifle freedom of speech... in the Roman Catholic church and create the appearance of consensus where none exists." The women criticized the Vatican's efforts "to silence public discussion in the church, whether voiced by theologians of the First or Third Worlds, bishops, clergy and religious holding public office, especially women in the church." They charged that the hierarchy had violated the spirit and teaching of Vatican 2 by requiring women "to comply with the directives of a patriarchal system in which they have no real voice or power."[13] Maureen Fiedler, one of the six Sisters of Loretto who had signed the statement, concluded: "The male clerics are not only trying to control our bodies, but also our minds."[14]

Chicago cardinal Joseph Bernardin lamented that the 24 dissenting nuns had created "a real problem," since they "directly challenged the church's constant teaching about the immorality of abortion." Disciplinary action, including expulsion from their religious orders, might be necessary, said Bernardin, to uphold the church's "integrity and unity."[15] Bernardin, while "deploring" the destruction of abortion clinics by anti-abortion terrorists, added slyly that "violence begets violence." He is the author of the "seamless garment" doctrine, which holds that absolute opposition to abortion is the logical extension of a catholic's concern for the sanctity of human life, as expressed in catholic opposition to war, capital punishment, and human rights abuses.

Feminist theologian Rosemary Radford Ruether exposed the true motives behind the hierarchy's anti-abortion and anti-contraception dogma, and its boomerang effect in practice:

> ... Central to patriarchal power from its foundations is the control over women's reproductive capacities... If women are autonomous decision-makers about reproduction, then they, not men, hold the key to life...
>
> Contrary to popular rhetoric, such banning of abortion [as the church leaders demand] does not actually reduce the number of abortions. It simply criminalizes it and kills women, as well. But the deaths of women in botched abortions are no concern to 'pro-life' advocates. On the contrary, in their view, such women 'deserve' to die. The net effect of such repression of reproductive freedom of women is, in fact, a very high abortion rate, particularly among Catholic women... Polish women have an estimated 300,000

abortions a year, a fact the pope chooses to ignore when he goes to Poland.[16]*

...When the effort to ban abortion takes place in a cultural context in which contraception is also made illegal or discouraged, the result is, in fact, to assure that abortion will be the primary way that women make reproductive choices. This is the reason Catholic women have more abortions than Protestant women in the United States, and Catholic countries such as Poland and Italy have the highest abortion rates in Europe.[18]

Jeannine Gramick, a School Sister of Notre Dame since 1960 and a signer of the Catholics for a Free Choice ad/statement, was no stranger to controversy. In 1977, she co-founded the New Ways Ministry, to serve gay and lesbian catholics. Her innovative pastoral work invoked the wrath of Washington DC archbishop James Hickey. In 1984, at Hickey's request, the Vatican ordered Gramick to leave New Ways. But she continues to work with gay and lesbian catholics around the country. In early 1985, as the 24 dissenting nuns continued to resist Vatican pressure, she wrote: "Because of the imminent threat of dismissal from my congregation and other indignities I have suffered from authoritarian bishops and Vatican officials because of my ministry, I feel like a battered woman in the Roman Catholic church. Innumerable times in the past, uncompromising attitudes have prevented the Catholic church's male hierarchy from humbly sitting down at the table of trusting dialogue and healing reconciliation with the women who have faithfully served the church. This is a blatant scandal that women religious hope will be rectified. We must refuse to be battered any longer."[19]

A year and a half later, on 1 July 1986, under the stress of the unresolved conflict, Margaret Ellen Traxler, also of the School Sisters of Notre Dame, suffered a mild stroke. Traxler, who ministers to women prisoners in Chicago, had also signed the ad/statement on abortion. She and Gramick learned that nearly all their superiors were willing to go ahead with their dismissals—"all other options failing."[20]

In April-May 1985, the Vatican elevated archbishop O'Connor to the position of cardinal—punctuating its support to the man who had

Official Polish government figures show over 300,000 abortions performed each year. But this statistic includes only those abortions carried out in state hospitals. Many more abortions, perhaps up to 600,000 per year, go unreported. Effective contraceptive devices are hard to obtain in Poland—a problem aggravated by the church's aggressive campaign against birth control as well as abortion. A chronic housing shortage facing young adults also contributes to Poland's very high abortion rate.[17]

Jeannine Gramick, of the School Sisters of Notre Dame. A co-founder of the New Ways Ministry for lesbian and gay catholics, she was one of 24 nuns who signed the 1984 New York Times ad/statement urging a free discussion of the abortion question within the church.

provoked the public catholic debate over abortion in the first place. Around the same time, the Vatican retreated slightly from its insistence that the 24 nuns publicly recant: Each nun now had to write a letter to her superior, saying that she did not, in signing the ad/statement, support abortion.[21] The six Sisters of Loretto in Denver who had signed the ad/statement took this route some ten months later, and their case was closed.[22] On 21 July 1986, the Vatican issued a triumphant press release, announcing that all of the nuns who signed the 1984 ad had now retracted their statement.

But 11 of the nuns, accusing the Vatican of deceit, firmly denied that they ever publicly submitted to official church doctrine on abortion. Notre Dame de Namur nuns Barbara Ferraro and Patricia Hussey, under threat of expulsion, refused to take the loyalty oath demanded of them. Ferraro and Hussey, who codirect a day shelter for the homeless in Charleston, West Virginia, cited Vatican 2's declaration of religious freedom in their defense. Hussey denounced the paternalism of the church officials from Rome who, under the guise of dialogue, were treating the mature and steadfast nuns like errant girls. "We no longer have burnings at the stake," she observed, "but we have burnings of careers and of psyches."[23]

Many of the dissenting nuns felt the recent death of their dominican sister, Marjorie Tuite, was related to the stressful accusations she had endured since signing the 1984 ad/statement on abortion. Tuite, who had made several trips to the war zones of Nicaragua in a campaign to stop the U.S.-backed *contra* aggression, died of cancer on 28 June 1986, at the age of 63. Before dying, she requested that her ashes be buried in Nicaragua.[24]

Maryknoll sister Rose Dominic Trapasso has served as a missionary in Peru for 32 years. Living in a shantytown in Lima, she works with women on a variety of human rights and social issues. She laments the church hierarchy's total opposition to birth control information and techniques, which drives poor women frequently to abortion. In Peru, where abortion is illegal, a poor woman who chooses abortion has to face not only the dangers of an amateur job under unhygienic conditions, but also the threat of being betrayed to the police by her husband or boyfriend, and thrown into jail. Trapasso signed the 1984 *New York Times* ad/statement on abortion. In the summer of 1986, she was notified that the Vatican expected her to retract her position.[25]

By September 1987, there still remained two dissenting nuns who had yet to settle the three-year-old dispute with their order and get clearance from the Vatican: Barbara Ferraro and Patricia Hussey.

The Case of Archbishop Hunthausen

On 30 September 1985, cardinal Joseph Ratzinger sent a stern letter from the Vatican's Congregation of the Doctrine of the Faith to Seattle's archbishop Raymond Hunthausen. Ratzinger ruled out divorce and contraceptive sterilization among practicing catholics, and stressed the subordinate role of women in the church. He also rebuffed Hunthausen for his solidarity with gay catholics: "The archdiocese [of the state of Washington] should withdraw all support from any group which does not unequivocally accept the teaching of the magisterium [the Vatican theologians] concerning the intrinsic evil of homosexual activity. The ill-advised welcome of a pro-homosexual group to your cathedral [has] served to make the church's position appear to be ambiguous on this delicate but important issue..."[26]

Hunthausen had welcomed Dignity, the U.S. gay catholic group, to Seattle on the occasion of its national meeting in 1983. He also allowed women to conduct mass in his archdiocese. The Vatican was now secretly investigating his activities. So were the FBI and U.S. Naval Intelligence, which has kept a file on the archbishop since June 1982, when he participated in demonstrations against Trident nuclear submarines stationed in Puget Sound.[27] Denouncing the nuclear arms race as blasphemous, Hunthausen refused to pay 50% of his federal income tax in 1982, and called on the people of Washington state to consider joining his tax protest.

In September 1986, Hunthausen announced that the Vatican had transferred his authority in five key areas to auxiliary bishop Donald Wuerl. Wuerl, assigned to Seattle from his base in Rome in 1985 to keep tabs on Hunthausen, had been ordained bishop by the pope in January 1986. In March, Hunthausen and Wuerl had clashed over the archdiocese's position on a local ordinance proposed to protect minorities, including gays, from job discrimination. Hunthausen supported the legislation, but Wuerl opposed it, and insisted that he had the final say in determining the archdiocese's position. In June, the Vatican confirmed that Wuerl had the final authority.[28]

The U.S. bishops were thrown into turmoil. The staunch conservatives among them liked the idea of neutralizing Hunthausen, and even moderates and liberals found his radical anti-militarism and support for women's and gay rights hard to defend. But progressive priests, nuns, and catholic laypeople across the country pressured the hierarchy to defend Hunthausen. And the Vatican's crude intervention against their colleague was an affront to the U.S. bishops' national and professional pride. So they lobbied at the Vatican on Hunthausen's behalf.

Hunthausen defended himself by humbly objecting to the irregular *procedures* used to discipline him. He did not take a stand against the Vatican on the social and political issues which were at the heart of the dispute. In May 1987, the Vatican restored Hunthausen to his full authority as archbishop. Wuerl was removed from Seattle, and replaced by liberal bishop Thomas Murphy from Montana, a friend of Hunthausen. By insisting on appointing a new "coadjutor"—even if a friendly one—to work with Hunthausen, the Vatican showed that it still distrusts him, and wants to restrict his progressive political action. By softpedalling his social and political convictions when his church career was on the line, Hunthausen showed a willingness to give ground on the key issues.

The Gay Question

"... It is only in the marital relationship that the use of the sexual faculty can be morally good. A person engaging in homosexual behavior therefore acts immorally," declared cardinal Joseph Ratzinger in the "Letter to the Bishops of the Catholic Church on the Pastoral Care of Homosexual Persons," approved by the pope and issued by the Vatican's Congregation for the Doctrine of the Faith on 30 October 1986. "... Although the particular inclination of the homosexual person is not a sin, it is a more or less strong tendency ordered toward an intrinsic moral evil, and thus the inclination itself must be seen as an objective disorder."[29]

"It's a horrible statement," responded Daniel Berrigan, a jesuit priest imprisoned for several years for his militant opposition to the Vietnam war, who now counsels AIDS patients in New York City. "Can you imagine a catholic dying of AIDS and hearing something like this?" Carl Meirose, a priest who directs the AIDS Pastoral Care Network in Chicago, noted: "This is the first major statement from any church that doesn't promote reconciliation and call for an end to fear and prejudice." He added that AIDS ministers in Chicago will "continue to promote reconciliation between AIDS patients and their religious traditions, despite the Vatican document..."[30]

Indeed, the Vatican seemed to have discarded its "reconciliation theology" in favor of traditional bigotry. Ratzinger's letter was an explicit reaction against the movements for gay and lesbian rights within and without the church: "... Increasing numbers of people today, even within the church, are bringing enormous pressure to bear on the church to accept the homosexual condition as though it were not disordered and to condone homosexual activity. Those within the church who argue in this fashion often have close ties with those with similar views outside it. These latter groups are guided by a vision opposed to the truth about the human person, which is fully disclosed in the mystery of Christ..."[31] How the *"mystery"* of christ can *"disclose"* anything (especially since Jesus himself did not claim to be the christ), is a mystery known only to Ratzinger and the pope.

More from the Vatican's 'Letter to the Bishops of the Catholic Church on the Pastoral Care of Homosexual Persons'

There is an effort in some countries to manipulate the church by gaining the often well-intentioned support of her pastors with a view to changing civil statutes and laws. This is done in order to conform to these pressure groups' concept that homosexuality is at least a completely harmless, if not an entirely good, thing. Even when the practice of homosexuality may seriously threaten the lives and well-being of a large number of people, its advocates remain undeterred and refuse to consider the magnitude of the risks involved.

... It is deplorable that homosexual persons have been and are the object of violent malice in speech or in action. Such treatment deserves condemnation from the church's pastors wherever it occurs...

But the proper reaction to crimes committed against homosexual persons should not be to claim that the homosexual condition is not disordered. When such a claim is made and when homosexual activity is consequently condoned, or when civil legislation is introduced to protect behavior to which no one has any conceivable right, neither the church nor society at large should be surprised when other distorted notions and practices gain ground and irrational and violent reactions increase.

'I Cannot Continue to be Silent...'

John McNeil, a jesuit priest and openly gay psychotherapist in New York City, published *The Church and the Homosexual* in 1976. His book, subsequently published in several foreign languages, was the first systematic attempt to reconcile homosexuality with the judaeo-christian tradition. In 1977, the Vatican ordered McNeil to be silent on sexual ethics, and not publish anything further in the field. He obeyed the ban for nine years, while continuing to serve gays as priest and psychotherapist.

On 19 October 1986, eleven days before cardinal Ratzinger's letter was to be publicly released, McNeil received an order from his jesuit superiors: He was banned from ministering to gays or commenting

John J. McNeil, the gay liberationist priest and theologian, expelled from the jesuit order for criticizing the Vatican's 1986 statement on homosexuality.
—Donna Binder/Impact Visuals

publicly about homosexuality. "...As a jesuit priest, as a moral theologian, as a psychotherapist, as a person who is himself gay, I cannot obey the order in conscience," declared McNeil. The order had been imposed by Ratzinger himself.[32] The jesuit leaders now began proceedings to expel the 61-year-old McNeil, who had been a jesuit for 40 years.

McNeil denounced the letter by Ratzinger and his Vatican colleagues: "When they assert that homosexual orientation is an 'objective disorder' without taking into account all the scientific evidence that calls that judgment into question, when they accuse all of us who have sought civil justice for gay people as being 'callous' to the risk of the lives of our gay brothers and sisters because of the AIDS crisis, and, finally, when they lay the blame for the 'irrational and violent reactions' of homophobes on the victims of that violence because they have had the effrontery to speak for justice and their civil rights, the Vatican betrays a mean and cruel spirit that is in conflict with both the spirit and the letter of the gospels. I cannot continue to be silent in the face of this evil."[33]

Responding to conservative catholic leaders who preach that same-sex love is tolerable only as long as it stops short of sexual expression, McNeil asserted: "...I was aware that most catholic gays trying to live out a life of total chastity for a lifetime ended up destroying themselves either with alcohol, drugs, [or] promiscuous sexuality, and very few seem to receive the grace to be chaste in a happy and healthy way."

Minnesota priest William Dorn, Jr., is also openly gay. After publishing a piece in his diocesan newspaper criticizing traditional catholic sexual dogma and calling on the church to minister to gay catholics, Dorn was fired from his position as co-pastor of Christ Church Newman Center in St. Cloud. In the wake of the Vatican letter, he was suspended indefinitely from the priesthood by bishop Victor Balke. Dorn declared he will continue to speak out for gay rights, and counsel gays and their families.[34]

The Vatican now moved full speed ahead with its assault against Dignity, the gay catholic organization founded in southern California in 1969 during the rise of the secular gay pride movement. Decreeing that all gay catholics must become celibate, the Vatican pressured the North American bishops to oust Dignity chapters for refusing to chasten themselves out of existence. By the summer of 1987, Dignity—which has a total membership of about 5,000—had seen 13 of its 108 chapters in the U.S. and Canada banned from church property. The New York City chapter, falling within the diocese of the homophobic cardinal

O'Connor, was the most prominent Dignity group expelled. Joseph Novak, head of New York's jesuit community, barred his priests from offering mass for Dignity members, and from participating in the annual gay pride parade in June 1987. While many bishops elsewhere in North America have resisted the pressure to expel Dignity, so far not a single one has publicly defended Dignity against the Vatican.[35]

Hoping to lobby the bishops to accept gay expression within the church, Dignity had previously avoided championing homosexual activity: Its original statement of purpose called ambiguously for sexual expression to be "consonant with Christ's teaching." Now, abandoned by its hoped-for allies among the bishops, Dignity rallied and radicalized its sexual politics. "We affirm that gay and lesbian people can express their sexuality physically in a unitive manner that is loving, life-giving and affirming," reads the new Dignity statement of purpose, adopted in the summer of 1987. The statement also calls for a reexamination of official church teaching on homosexuality. Nate Gruel, Dignity's regional director from Indiana, observed: "Some people [in Dignity] still have trouble with this statement. But in the long run, psychologically, it's got to be better for everybody. We're overcoming anger and fear and saying who we are."[36] Ironically, Dignity's membership has been *increasing* since Ratzinger issued his anti-gay letter.

When Dignity was banned from church property in Norfolk, Virginia in March 1987 by liberal bishop Walter Sullivan, Vincent Connery, a 37-year-old diocesan priest, resigned in protest. Sullivan, a vocal critic of the arms race, had been investigated by the Vatican three years earlier, after conservative catholics had accused him of being too lenient towards homosexuals.[37] Now he evidently caved in to Vatican pressure, and he in turn pressured Vincent Connery to resign from the priesthood.

Connery, during his youth, had been active against the Vietnam war, registering as a conscientious objector. In 1983, he called for the ordination of women to the catholic priesthood, suggesting that sympathetic priests go on strike to press the issue. He believed that gay as well as heterosexual catholics should be included within his ministry, and treated with equal respect.

"Rome wants to continue giving orders," said Jack Kane, a parishioner at Sacred Heart church, where Connery had ministered. "They don't understand that we are the church. Vince Connery is a grounded priest. He's the most gifted priest in this diocese. He works where the tire meets the road. Rome knows little and cares less about

Chapter 4

where American Catholics are. They're going to find themselves like the British generals at Yorktown. They will give orders and discover that they don't have an army."[38]

In Toronto, Canada, 11-year-old Sandra Bernier wanted to become an altar girl at her Sacre Coeur church. Since girls had already been serving at the altar in some parts of the archdiocese, she thought she had the right to do so. But in June 1987, Toronto's cardinal G. Emmet Carter,* apparently bowing to Vatican pressure, issued an order forbidding Sandra to attend the altar. "You have no guts, Carter," shouted a man in a protest demonstration outside Sacre Coeur as the cardinal entered the church for its nationally televised hundredth anniversary celebration. "Give the women a chance! Shame, shame on the church!"[39]

He Who Pays Peter's Pence Doesn't Call the Tune

In March 1987, the Vatican announced a $63 million budget deficit—owing to its rising labor costs,** swelling bureaucracy, and financial mismanagement, as well as the pope's frequent and extravagant trips abroad. Faithful catholics were urged to double their contributions to the pious fund, called "Peter's Pence." About 60% of the pious fund has come from donations by U.S. catholics.

Already over the past 25 years, U.S. catholics have mutely expressed their dismay with Vatican policy by reducing their donations to the pious fund. According to a sociological study done by priest Andrew Greeley, in 1960, U.S. catholics donated an average of 2.2% of their personal income to the church; but by 1984, the average was down to 1.2%. Greeley traces the decline directly to lay catholics' disagreement with the Vatican's ban on contraception, and its unresponsive and hierarchical leadership.[41]

In April 1987, cardinal Giuseppe Caprio publicly declared, for the first time in history, the financial worth of the Vatican's global estate: He estimated the total worth of the Vatican's investments and landholdings at $570 million—but quickly added that less than half of that

(continued on page 186)

---

*Cardinal Carter is known for his "pro-life" activism. In February 1985, he backed an anti-abortion group's calls for mass picketing to close the abortion clinic headed by Dr. Henry Morgenthaler.

**To be sure, the Vatican's lay employees have been grossly underpaid. As of 1985, a middle-level Vatican lay employee in Rome made around $7,000 a year. Workers such as cleaners and gardeners employed on the Vatican premises sometimes joke wryly that the Vatican has imposed birth control upon them: "On this pay we can't afford to have children."[40]

On the Ordination of Women

A It's cruel and ironic that the Vatican refuses to allow women to become priests.

B Cruel, certainly, But ironic?

A Absolutely. Jesus' most faithful followers were women. When he was arrested and placed on trial for his life, his vaunted male disciples abandoned him in terror and confusion. Only his female disciples—Mary Magdalene, Mary the mother of James, Salome, and other women—accompanied Jesus to the end, bearing witness to his anguish and death.

B So the male clergy have some nerve denying women equal status!

A In fact, were justice to be done, *all* the male priests, bishops, archbishops, cardinals and pope would be stripped of their authority, and the *entire* church leadership handed over to women—until the men have done adequate historical repentance.

B ...for having monopolized the clergy and subordinated christian women in the first place...

A ...and for depriving woman of the right to divorce, while enshrining her husband as lord and master over her...

B ...and for repressing woman's control of her own reproductive functions, banning contraception and abortion and thus dooming many desperate women to mutilation or death, for lack of access to safe abortion by a midwife or doctor...

A ...and for denouncing, torturing, and executing hundreds of thousands of women during the inquisition and 'witch' persecutions...

B ...and for elevating and adoring the virgin Mary, while degrading and scorning real life women.

A Then, once the men have made thorough and sincere repentance for their own and their forefathers' sins against women, they can be selectively readmitted to the clergy by the self governing women's leadership body, and so gain equal status.

B But then, they'll find that the whole clergy has been radically transformed: no more rigid, self serving hierarchy. No more claims to infallible authority, and no more intimidation and suppression of dissent. Democracy will reign supreme in the church.

A I see you like the idea. So do I!

B In fact, catholic women will probably have to make such a radical demand for sweeping change—to shake up the mule-headed male hierarchy, and pressure them into ordaining women into the existing clergy as a compromise solution.

A ...which goes to show the wisdom of that old anarchist motto:
'Be realistic—Demand the impossible!'

amount produces income. "I hope the good faithful will now realize that the appeal by the cardinals and the pope is truly necessary and corresponds to the facts," pleaded Caprio.[42]

Like a true dogmatist, cardinal Caprio declared the financial disclosures *over* when, in reality, the investigation has barely begun. Some journalists have estimated the Vatican's total worth at over $10 billion. The Vatican has yet to make an honest public accounting of its involvement in the Banco Ambrosiano scandal, nor does it bother to inform U.S. catholics how their donations are being spent. "The string of scandals at the Vatican bank suggests that Americans have good cause to balk at Roman centralization of church finances," wrote the *National Catholic Reporter*.[43]

Serra vs. Liberation Theology

How would Junípero Serra have lined up on today's social and political disputes within the catholic church? Serra, as we saw in chapter 1, was an apostle of the counter reformationist church, and a zealous missionary of the Spanish empire. He became an official of the inquisition during its waning years. While he often wrangled with the military officials he had to deal with in California, he stressed unconditional obedience to his church superiors and the pope. While he was a pioneer in the sense of opening up a vast new territory of spiritual conquest for the church and crown, he was never a pioneer in terms of his social policy towards the Indians he converted. Even for his day, Serra was a staunch catholic traditionalist.

Serra's theology was the polar opposite to the bold new theology proclaimed by the priest Miguel Hidalgo in Mexico in 1784, the year of Serra's death. Hidalgo's concept, that the church should take the side of the poor and the oppressed in their struggle against the rich and powerful, has been further developed in Latin America in recent decades, and dubbed liberation theology.

Serra preached salvation for the people *in heaven* through their "happy death" in the arms of the church. Liberation theology preaches salvation for the poor *on earth*, through mass struggle against unjust social systems. Serra and his franciscan colleagues, underestimating the mental capacity of their Indian converts, generally refused to teach them how to read and write. The apostles of liberation theology today teach humble peasants and farmworkers literacy, as well as paramedical skills. Serra and his colleagues, paternalistic to the end, deprived the mission Indians of nearly all initiative and dignity, and failed to prepare them for self government.

The grassroots leaders of the catholic communities today in Latin America and the Philippines promote democratic decision making among community members, helping prepare them for conscious social struggle and social revolution.

Around the year 1570, three Indians from the new world were brought to France for a visit. They found that French society, like their own, was divided into two halves or *moieties*, as with the Bear and Deer moieties of the Ohlones of California. But the moieties in Europe were strangely skewed, as if the entire society had been wrenched out of its natural equilibrium. In the words of the essayist Michel de Montaigne, some 250 years before the birth of Marx and Engels, these American Indians delivered their pithy verdict on European civilization:

> ...They had observed that there were, among us, men full and crammed with all sorts of good things, while others were begging at their doors, emaciated with hunger and poverty. And they thought it strange that these needy ones could endure such an injustice, and that they did not take the others by the throat, or set fire to their houses...[44]

Reference Notes

Introduction

1. "Vatican Surprise on Serra," *San Francisco Examiner*, 9 August 1987, p. B-4. For information on the Tekakwitha Conference, see *National Catholic Reporter*, Kansas City, 19 June 1987, p. 18.
2. Don Lattin, "Pope Hails Serra Record on Indians." *San Francisco Examiner*, 15 September 1987, p. A-4.
3. *San Francisco Chronicle*, 18 September 1987, p. A19.
4. Thomas Sheehan. *The First Coming: How the Kingdom of God Became Christianity*. New York: Random House, 1986, pp. 53-4.
5. *Ibid.*, p. 57.
6. *Ibid.*, p. 86. For Sheehan's debunking of overblown interpretations of Jesus' use of the term "son of man," see pages 82 and 187.
7. Edward Scobie, "African Popes." Ivan van Sertima, editor. *African Presence in Early Europe*. New Brunswick, New Jersey: Transaction Books, 1985, pp. 96-107.
8. Danita Redd. "Black Madonnas of Europe: Diffusion of the African Isis." *African Presence in Early Europe*, op. cit., p. 108.
9. *Ibid.*, pp. 110-12.
10. Runoko Rashidi. "African Goddesses: Mothers of Civilization." *Black Women in Antiquity*. New Brunswick: *Journal of African Civilizations*, 1984, p. 86.
11. Danita Redd, *op. cit.*, pp. 124, 126.
12. Wayne Chandler. "The Moor: Light of Europe's Dark Age." *African Presence in Early Europe*, op. cit., pp. 154.
13. *Encyclopedia Britannica: Macropaedia*, 15th edition, 1977, vol. 17, pp. 406-7, 414.
14. Chandler, *op. cit.*, pp. 154-5.
15. *Encyclopedia Britannica: Macropaedia*, op. cit., p. 414.
16. Chandler, *op. cit.*, pp. 157, 159.
17. George Cox. *African Empires and Civilizations*. New York: African Heritage Studies Publishers, 1974, p. 144.
18. *Encyclopedia Britannica: Macropaedia*, op. cit., pp. 407, 410.
19. *Ibid.*, p. 416.
20. Chandler, *op. cit.*, pp. 164-8.

21. Edward Scobie. "African Women in Early Europe." *African Presence in Early Europe, op. cit.*, p. 203.

22. *Encyclopedia Britannica: Macropaedia, op. cit.*, p. 423.

23. Jacques Soustelle. *Daily Life of the Aztecs on the Eve of the Spanish Conquest.* Translated from the French by Patrick O'Brian. Stanford University Press, 1961, p. 214.

24. Manuel Giménez Fernández. "Fray Bartolomé de las Casas: A Biographical Sketch." *Bartolomé de las Casas in History: Toward an Understanding of the Man and His Work*, edited by Juan Friede and Benjamin Keen. Dekalb: Northern Illinois University Press, 1971, p. 67.

25. *Enciclopedia Universal Ilustrada.* Madrid, 1916, vol. 29, p. 909.

26. *Encyclopedia Americana:* International Edition. Article by Neill Macaulay. Danbury, Conn.: Grolier Inc., 1986, vol. 16, p. 770.

27. *Encyclopedia Britannica*, 11th edition. New York: Cambridge University Press, 1911, vol. 16, p. 232.

28. *Enciclopedia Universal Ilustrada, op. cit.*, p. 910 (my translation).

29. *Ibid.*

30. *Ibid.*, p. 911.

31. *Ibid.*, citing Las Casas' *Historia de las Indias* (Mexico, 1951, vol. 3, pp. 117, 275). See also *Bartolomé de las Casas in History*, edited by Juan Friede and Benjamin Keen, Dekalb: Northern Illinois University Press, 1971, pp. 505-6.

32. *Ibid.*, p. 912.

33. *Diccionario Enciclopédico* U.T.E.H.A. Mexico: Unión Tipográfica Editorial Hispano Americana, 1951, vol 4, p. 621.

34. Manuel Giménez Fernández. "Fray Bartolomé de las Casas: A Biographical Sketch," *op. cit.*, p. 88.

35. *San Francisco Examiner*, 15 September 1987, p. A-4.

36. *Enciclopedia Universal Ilustrada, op. cit.*, p. 912.

37. *Encyclopedia Britannica*, 15th edition, 1985, vol. 7, pp. 168-9.

38. Lewis Hanke. *All Mankind is One: A Study of the Disputation between Bartolomé de las Casas and Juan Ginés de Sepúlveda in 1550 on the Religious and Intellectual Capacity of the American Indians.* Dekalb: Northern Illinois University Press, 1974, pp. 74-5.

39. *Ibid.*, p. 76.

40. Angel Losada. "The Controversy between Sepúlveda and Las Casas in the Junta of Valladolid." *Bartolomé de las Casas in History, op. cit.*, p. 294.

41. *Ibid.*, p. 297.

42. Lewis Hanke, *op. cit.*, p. 76.

43. *Encyclopedia Britannica.*, 1985, vol. 7., p. 168.

44. *Ibid.*, p. 169.

45. *New Catholic Encyclopedia.* Washington DC: Catholic University of America, McGraw-Hill, 1967, vol. 12, p. 849.

46. T. R. Fehrenbach. *Fire and Blood: A History of Mexico*. New York: Collier Books, 1973, p. 243.

47. Jacques Soustelle, *op. cit.*, p. xix.

48. Hugh Hamill, Jr. *The Hidalgo Revolt: Prelude to Mexican Independence*. Gainesville: University of Florida Press, 1966, pp. 61-2.

49. *Ibid.*, pp. 62-3.

50. Fehrenbach, *op. cit.*, p. 316.

51. Hugh Hamill, *op. cit.*, p. 119.

52. Fehrenbach, *op. cit.*, p. 322.

53. *New Catholic Encyclopedia, op. cit.*, vol. 6, pp. 821-2.

54. *Enciclopedia Universal Ilustrada, op. cit.*, vol. 27, p. 1385.

55. Fehrenbach, *op. cit.*, p. 323.

56. *Enciclopedia Universal Ilustrada, op. cit.*, vol. 27.

57. Fehrenbach, *op. cit.*, p. 328.

58. *Ibid.*

59. *Diccionario Enciclopédico* U.T.E.H.A. Mexico: Unión Tipográfica Editorial Hispano Americana, 1951, vol. 5, p. 1218.

60. Fehrenbach, *op. cit.*, p. 332.

61. Eric O'Brien, O.F.M. "The Life of Padre Serra." *Writings of Junípero Serra*. Antonine Tibesar, O.F.M., editor. Washington, DC: Academy of American Franciscan History, 1955, vol. 1, p. xxix.

62. Ronald Wright, Canadian anthropologist, CBC radio broadcast, 1986.

63. Jacques Soustelle, *op. cit.*, p. 170.

64. *Ibid.*, pp. 55-6.

65. *Ibid.*, p. 104.

66. *Ibid.*, p. 98. Also George P. Murdock, *Our Primitive Contemporaries*, New York: Macmillan Co., 1934, pp. 395-6).

67. *American Heritage Book of Indians*. Narrative by William Brandon. Editor in charge, Alvin Josephy, Jr. American Heritage Publishing Co., 1961, pp. 118-19.

68. David J. Weber, editor. *New Spain's Far Northern Frontier: Essays on Spain in the American West, 1540-1821*. Albuquerque: University of New Mexico Press, 1979, p. ix.

69. *American Heritage Book of Indians, , op. cit.*, pp. 120, 134.

70. *Ibid.*, p. 120.

71. *Ibid.*, pp. 214-15.

72. *Ibid.*, p. 193.

Chapter 1: Junípero Serra & California Missions

1. Maynard Geiger, O.F.M. *The Life and Times of Fray Junípero Serra, O.F.M.: The Man Who Never Turned Back (1713-1784).* Washington DC: Academy of American Franciscan History, 1959, vol. 1, p. 6.

2. Don DeNevi and Noel Francis Moholy. *Junípero Serra: The Illustrated Story of the Franciscan Founder of California's Missions.* San Francisco: Harper & Row, 1985, p. 15.

3. Geiger, *op. cit.*, vol. 2, p. 375.

4. Junípero Serra, letter to Francesch Serra, Cádiz, 20 August 1749. *Writings of Junípero Serra.* Antonine Tibesar, O.F.M., editor. Washington, DC: Academy of American Franciscan History, 1955, vol. 1, p. 5.

5. Eric O'Brien, O.F.M. "The Life of Padre Serra." *Writings of Junípero Serra, op. cit.*, p. xxxii.

6. DeNevi and Moholy, *op. cit.*, pp. 49-50.

7. *Ibid.*, pp. 50-1.

8. Geiger, *op. cit.*, vol. 1, pp. 116-17.

9. DeNevi and Moholy, *op. cit.*, p. 52.

10. *Ibid.*, pp. 55-6.

11. Geiger, *op. cit.*, vol. 1, p. 115.

12. "Report to the Inquisition of Mexico City." Xalpan, 1 September 1752. *Writings of Junípero Serra, op. cit.*, pp. 19-21.

13. *Writings of Junípero Serra, op. cit.*, vol. 1, p. 410 (reference note).

14. Geiger, *op. cit.*, vol. 1, p. 149. Also, DeNevi and Moholy, *op. cit.*, p. 56.

15. DeNevi and Moholy, *op. cit.*, p. 55.

16. Geiger, *op. cit.*, vol. 1, pp. 146-7.

17. *Ibid.*, pp. 171-2 (drawing on Francisco Palóu's account).

18. *Ibid.*, p. 172.

19. *Ibid.*, pp. 172-3.

20. James J. Rawls and Walter Bean. *California: An Interpretive History.* New York: McGraw-Hill, 1983, p. 22.

21. DeNevi and Moholy, *op. cit.*, p. 7.

22. Manfred Barthel. *The Jesuits: History and Legend of the Society of Jesus.* Translated from the German by Mark Howson. New York: William Morrow and Co., 1984, pp. 222-3.

23. DeNevi and Moholy, *op. cit.*, p. 66.

24. Francisco Palóu, 24 November 1769 report to the guardian of the college of San Fernando. MM 1847, f 273, Bancroft Library, Berkeley.

25. Manuel Patricio Servín. "California's Hispanic Heritage: A View into the Spanish Myth." Reprinted in *New Spain's Far Northern Frontier: Essays on Spain in the American West, 1540-1821.* Edited by David Weber. Albuquerque: University of New Mexico Press, 1979, p. 120.

26. DeNevi and Moholy, *op. cit.*, pp. 74-6.

27. Eric O'Brien, "The Life of Padre Serra," *op. cit.*, p. xxxvii.

28. James Rawls and Walter Bean, *op. cit.*, p. 24.

29. DeNevi and Moholy, *op. cit.*, pp. 93-4.

30. Maynard Geiger, *op. cit.*, vol. 1, p. 235.

31. *Writings of Junípero Serra, op. cit.*, vol. 2, p. 476 (reference note).

32. DeNevi and Moholy, *op. cit.*, p. 11.

33. Edith Buckland Webb. *Life at the Old Missions.* Lincoln: University of Nebraska Press, 1952, p. 104.

34. James A. Sandos. "Levantamiento! The 1824 Chumash Uprising Reconsidered." *Southern California Quarterly*, Historical Society of Southern California, vol. 67, no. 2, summer 1985, p. 114.

35. Edith Buckland Webb, *op. cit.*, p. 84.

36. Maynard Geiger, *op. cit.*, vol. 1, pp. 302-3. Based on Palóu's account.

37. Serra, letter to father Rafael Verger, Monterey, 8 August 1772. *Writings of Junípero Serra, op. cit.*, vol. 1, pp. 257-9. See also Serra's letter to viceroy Bucareli, Mexico City, 21 May 1773, pp. 361, 363.

38. Geiger, *op. cit.*, vol. 1, p. 308.

39. James Rawls and Walter Bean, *op. cit.*, p. 30.

40. Report of corporal Periquez to captain Callis, undated. *Writings of Junípero Serra, op. cit.*, vol. 1, p. 403.

41. *Ibid.*, p. 405.

42. Maynard Geiger, *op. cit.*, vol. 1, p. 253.

43. Maynard Geiger. "Fray Junípero Serra: Organizer and Administrator of the Upper California Missions, 1769-1784." *The California Historical Quarterly*, vol. 42, no. 3, Sept. 1963, pp. 201-2. Also, Serra, letter to viceroy Bucareli, Mexico City, 11 June 1773, *Writings of Junípero Serra, op. cit.*, vol. 1, p. 383.

44. Serra, letter to viceroy Bucareli, Mexico City, 22 April 1773. *Writings of Junípero Serra, op. cit.*, vol. 1, p. 341. The Spanish original of this excerpt from Serra's letter reads: "El continuo tránsito de unas requas tras de otras, por medio de más de trecientas leguas de gentilidad y de tantos arrieros, gente (por lo común) desastrada, *de mal color*, y de ningunas obligaciones, qué no ocasionaría de disturbios, sin sabores e inquietudes en los miserables, y humildes gentiles? La codicia de sus coras, bateas y otras curiosidades verdaderamente apetecibles, haría, sin duda...que si los gentiles no se las davan o de valde o por algún frívolo cambalache, ellos se las quitarían..."

"Lo agradable de tanto mugerío, havía de ser gran milagro y muchos milagros, el que no hiziesse romper en tanta y tal gente en los desórdenes, que lamentamos en todas las missiones cada día más apestadas de luxuria..." (p. 340, emphasis added).

The franciscan translator rendered Serra's phrase, "gente... desastrada, de mal color, y de ningunas obligaciones," quite freely, as "men... from the dregs of society, bereft of high principles and conscience." But, in view of the highly race-conscious Spanish officialdom, "de mal color" may well have referred to the skin color of the "Spanish" soldiers and mule drivers in California — many, if not most of whom, were men of color from Mexico.

45. DeNevi and Moholy, *op. cit.*, pp. 133.

46. *Ibid.*, p. 141.

47. Serra, letter to Francisco Pangua, guardian of the college of San Fernando in Mexico City: Monterey, 24 July 1775. *Writings of Junípero Serra, op. cit.*, vol. 2, p. 295.

48. Maynard Geiger, *The Life and Times of Fray Junípero Serra, op. cit.*, vol. 2, p. 341.

49. Florence Connolly Shipek. "Saints or Oppressors: The Franciscan Missionaries of California." *The Missions of California: A Legacy of Genocide*, Rupert Costo and Jeannette Henry Costo, editors, San Francisco: Indian Historian Press, 1987, pp. 34-6.

50. Luis Jayme, letter to Francisco Palóu, 22 August 1772. See DeNevi and Moholy, *op. cit.*, pp. 149-50.

51. Luis Jayme, letter to guardian of the college of San Fernando, 1 October 1772. Translated by Maynard Geiger. San Diego: Dawson's Book Shop, 1970. Cited in *The Missions of California: A Legacy of Genocide, op. cit.*, p. 55.

52. Sherburne F. Cook. *The Conflict Between the California Indian and White Civilization.* Berkeley: University of California Press, 1976, p. 66.

53. DeNevi and Moholy, *op. cit.*, pp. 148-9.

54. Maynard Geiger, *op. cit.*, p. 60.

55. Vicente Fuster to Junípero Serra, San Diego, 28 November 1775. *Writings of Junípero Serra, op. cit.*, vol. 2, p. 457.

56. DeNevi and Moholy, *op. cit.*, p. 158.

57. *Ibid.*, pp. 161-2.

58. Serra, letter to viceroy Bucareli: Monterey, 15 December 1775. *Writings of Junípero Serra, op. cit.*, vol. 2, p. 407.

59. Maynard Geiger, *The Life and Times of Fray Junípero Serra, op. cit.*, vol. 2, p. 73.

60. Serra, letter to commander Rivera, San Diego, 5 October 1776. *Writings of Junípero Serra, op. cit.*, vol. 3, p. 37.

61. Serra, letter to commander general Teodoro de Croix, Monterey, 22 August 1778. *Writings of Junípero Serra*, vol. 3, p. 253.

62. Serra, letter to Fermín de Lasuén, Monterey, 12 January 1780. *Writings of Junípero Serra*, vol. 3, p. 423-5. The Spanish original reads: "... Es posible que teniéndoles bastante tiempo presos, explicándoles por intérpretes la otra vida, y la eternidad de ella, y encomendándoles a Dios, no se havía de lograr su arrepentimiento, y enmienda. Haziéndoles cargo de que viven, porque nosostros lo quisimos, y diligenciamos, mereciendo ellos por lo pasado, una muerte cruel, y los liberamos por Dios para que fuesen buenos etc..." (pp. 422-4).

63. Maynard Geiger, *op. cit.*, vol. 2, p. 300.

64. *Ibid.*, pp. 166-7.

65. Eric O'Brien, "The Life of Padre Serra," *op. cit.*, p. xli.

66. DeNevi and Moholy, *op. cit.*, p. 154.

67. *Ibid.*, p. 189.

68. *Writings of Junípero Serra*, vol. 2, p. 470 (note).

69. Francis Florian Guest, O.F.M. "Cultural Perspectives on California Mission Life." *Southern California Quarterly*, Historical Society of Southern California, spring 1983, p. 31.

70. Serra, letter to viceroy Antonio María de Bucareli: Monterey, 8 January 1775. *Writings of Junípero Serra*, vol. 2, p. 199.

71. Serra, letter to commander Rivera: Monterey, 6 July 1775. *Writings of Junípero Serra*, vol. 2, p. 421.

72. Serra, letter to Francisco Pangua, guardian of the college of San Fernando: Monterey, 26 February 1777. *Writings of Junípero Serra*, vol. 3, p. 89.

73. Manuel Patricio Servín. "California's Hispanic Heritage: A View into the Spanish Myth." Reprinted in *New Spain's Far Northern Frontier: Essays on Spain in the American West, 1540-1821*. Edited by David Weber. Albuquerque: University of New Mexico Press, 1979, p. 124.

74. Serra, letter to Francisco Pangua: Monterey, 8 December 1782. *Writings of Junípero Serra*, vol. 4, pp. 167-9. The Spanish original reads: "El Señor Governador... determinó fundar un pueblo de gentes que llaman de razón (como si no lo fueran los indios)..."

75. Joseph Antonio Murguía and Thomás de la Peña, letter to Junípero Serra: Santa Clara, 2 November 1782. *Writings of Junípero Serra*, vol. 4, p. 400.

76. Maynard Geiger, *op. cit.*, vol. 2, pp. 191-200.

77. *Ibid.*, pp. 172-83.

78. Serra, letter to governor Felipe de Neve: Monterey, 18 April 1780. *Writings of Junípero Serra*, vol. 3, p. 437.

79. Maynard Geiger, *op. cit.*, vol. 2, p. 306.

80. James Rawls and Walter Bean, *op. cit.*, pp. 18-19.

81. Randy Milliken. "Ethnohistory of the Rumsen" (plastic-comb-bound monograph). *Papers in Northern California Anthropology*, No. 2, April 1987, Northern California Anthropological Group, Berkeley, p. 28.

82. Serra, letter to governor Neve, Monterey, 7 January 1780. *Writings of Junípero Serra*, vol. 3, pp. 413-15.

83. Finbar Kenneally, O.F.M., and Mathias Kiemen, O.F.M., introduction to *Writings of Junípero Serra*, vol. 4, *op. cit.*, p. xvi.

84. Serra, letter to Francisco Pangua, guardian of the college of San Fernando: Monterey, 24 July 1775. *Writings of Junípero Serra*, vol. 2, p. 297. The Spanish original reads: "... Y en San Antonio están con dos consechas a un tiempo, que es la del trigo, y la de una plaga de muchachitos que se les van muriendo..." (p. 296).

85. Francisco Palóu. *Life of Junípero Serra*. Translated from the Spanish by C. S. Williams. Pasadena: G. W. James, 1913, p. 213.

86. Serra, letter to Juan Sancho, San Gabriel, 27 October 1783. *Writings of Junípero Serra*, vol. 4, p. 193.

87. Maynard Geiger, *op. cit.*, vol. 2, p. 373.

88. *Ibid.*, p. 355.

89. *Ibid.*, p. 374.

Chapter 2: The Indians of California

1. The oft-repeated claim, attributed to Robert Heizer, that 70% of the California Indians' over 100 languages were as mutually unintelligible as English and Chinese is, according to Randy Milliken, an exaggeration. To be sure, linguistic research in this area poses great difficulties, since few of the California Indians' languages ever attained written form, and most of them are no longer spoken.

2. Edith Wallace. "Sexual Status and Role Differences." *Handbook of North American Indians*, volume 8, edited by Robert Heizer. Washington, DC: Smithsonian Institution, 1978, p. 683.

3. Malcolm Margolin. *The Ohlone Way: Indian Life in the San Francisco-Monterey Bay Area*. Berkeley: Heyday Books, 1978, pp. 48-9.

4. *Ibid.*, p. 25.

5. Edith Wallace, *op. cit.*.

6. Pedro Fages. *A Historical, Political, and Natural Description of California by Pedro Fages, Soldier of Spain*. Herbert Priestley, editor. Berkeley: University of California Press, 1937.

7. Sylvia Brakke Vane & Lowell J. Bean. "Cults and their Transformations." *Handbook of North American Indians*, *op. cit.*, p. 667.

8. Florence Connolly Shipek. "Saints or Oppressors: The Franciscan Missionaries of California." *The Missions of California: A Legacy of Genocide*, edited by Rupert Costo and Jeannette Henry Costo, San Francisco: Indian Historian Press, 1987, pp. 34-5.

9. James J. Rawls. *Indians of California: The Changing Image.* Norman, Oklahoma: University of Oklahoma Press, 1984, p. 12.

10. Martin Baumhoff. "Environmental Background." *Handbook of North American Indians, op. cit.*, pp. 22-4.

11. R. F. Heizer and A. E. Treganza. "Mines and Quarries of the Indians of California." *The California Indians: A Source Book*, edited by R. F. Heizer and M. A. Whipple. Berkeley: University of California Press, 1962, p. 300.

12. Nigel Calder. *Timescale: An Atlas of the Fourth Dimension.* New York: Viking Press, 1983, pp. 162, 240.

13. Edith Wallace, *op. cit.*, pp. 686-7.

14. Randy Milliken, personal conversation, 2 August 1987.

15. Edith Wallace, *op. cit.*, p. 685.

16. Frederick Engels. *The Origin of the Family, Private Property, and the State.* Marx and Engels, *Selected Works*, New York: International Publishers (New World Paperbacks), 1968, pp. 493-6.

17. Margolin, *op. cit.*, p. 81.

18. Pedro Fages, *op. cit.*, pp. 73-4.

19. Lowell John Bean. "Social Organization." *Handbook of North American Indians*, vol. 8, *op. cit.*, p. 677.

20. Alfred L. Kroeber. "Yurok Law and Custom." *The California Indians: A Source Book*, edited by R. F. Heizer and M. A. Whipple. Berkeley: University of California Press, 1962, p. 346.

21. Gerda Lerner. *The Creation of Patriarchy.* New York: Oxford University Press, 1986, p. 45.

22. Alfred Kroeber, *op. cit.*, p. 348.

23. Margolin, *op. cit.*, p. 83.

24. James A. Sandos. "Levantamiento! The 1824 Chumash Uprising Reconsidered." *Southern California Quarterly*, Historical Society of Southern California, vol. 67, no. 2, summer 1985, pp. 110-11.

25. Pedro Fages, *op. cit.*.

26. Alfred Kroeber, *op. cit.*, p. 362.

27. Alfred L. Kroeber. "Elements of Culture in Native California," 1922. *The California Indians: A Source Book*, compiled and edited by R. F. Heizer and M. A. Whipple. Berkeley: University of California Press, 1962, p. 35. Also, Malcolm Margolin, *op. cit.*, p. 67.

28. Zephyrin Engelhardt. "San Buenaventura Mission: The Mission by the Sea." Mission Santa Barbara, California, 1930, p. 34.

29. Margolin, *op. cit.*, pp. 71, 85.

30. James Sandos, *op. cit.*, p. 111. Also, José Longinos Martínez, "Journal: Notes and Observations of the Naturalist of the Botanical Expedition in Old and New California and the South Coast, 1791-2," translated by Lesley Simpson, San Francisco: John Howell, 1961, p. 56.

31. Katharine Luomala. "Ipai-Tipai." *Handbook of North American Indians*, vol. 8, *op. cit.*, p. 602.

32. Bernice Johnston. "California's Gabrielino Indians." Los Angeles: Southwest Museum, 1962.

33. *Handbook of North American Indians.* Volume 8: *California*, edited by Robert Heizer: Washington, DC: Smithsonian Institution, 1978, pages 259 ("Wappo," by Jesse Sawyer), 487 ("Costanoan," by Richard Levy), and 687 (central Miwok, mentioned in article by Edith Wallace).

34. Malcolm Margolin, *op. cit.*, p. 105.

35. Alfred Kroeber, "Elements of Culture in Native California," *op. cit.*, p. 43.

36. Charles R. Smith. "Tubatulabal". *Handbook of North American Indians.* Volume 8, *op. cit.*, p. 441.

37. Robert Spott and Alfred L. Kroeber. "Yurok Shamanism." *The California Indians: A Source Book*, edited by R. F. Heizer and M.A. Whipple. Berkeley: University of California Press, 1962, p. 450.

38. Alfred Kroeber, "Elements of Culture in Native California," *op. cit.*, p. 39

39. Thomas McCorkle. "Intergroup Conflict." *Handbook of North American Indians*, volume 8, *op. cit.*, p. 699.

40. Lowell John Bean and Charles R. Smith. "Gabrielino." *Handbook of North American Indians*, volume 8, *op. cit.*, p. 547.

41. Campbell Grant, "Eastern Coastal Chumash," *Handbook of North American Indians*, volume 8, *op. cit.*, p. 513; Patti Johnson, "Patwin," same volume, pp. 352-3; Thomas McCorkle, "Intergroup Conflict," *op. cit.* (same volume), p. 697; Malcolm Margolin, *The Ohlone Way*, *op. cit.*, pp. 110-12.

42. Thomas McCorkle, *op. cit.*, p. 696.

43. Malcolm Margolin, *op. cit.*, p. 93.

44. *Ibid.* (for Ohlones), pp. 18, 58, 148; Katharine Luomala, "Tipai-Ipai," *Handbook of North American Indians*, volume 8, *op. cit.*, p. 603; William Wallace, "Southern Valley Yokuts," same volume, p. 455; Robert Spier, "Foothill Yokuts," same volume, p. 479.

45. Alfred Kroeber, "Yurok Law and Custom," *op. cit.*, pp. 363-4.

46. *Ibid.*, pp. 355, 365.

47. "Stories from the Spirit World: December's Child." KQED radio, San Francisco, 21 June 1987.

Chapter 3: Missions, Culture Shock, & Invasion

1. Edith Buckland Webb. *Life at the Old Missions.* Lincoln: University of Nebraska Press, 1952, p. 27.

2. Randy Milliken. "Ethnohistory of the Rumsen." *Papers in Northern California Anthropology*, Northern California Anthropological Group, No. 2, April 1987, Berkeley (plastic comb-bound monograph), pp. 31, 33.

3. Sherburne F. Cook. *The Conflict Between the California Indian and White Civilization.* Berkeley: University of California Press, 1976, p. 86.

4. Jean Francois de Galoup de La Pérouse. *The Voyage of La Pérouse Round the World in the Years 1785-88.* Translated from the French. London: John Stockdale, 1798, vol. 1, p. 210. Also, Sherburne Cook, *op. cit.,* p. 52.

5. Edith Buckland Webb, *op. cit.,* pp. 108, 200, 211-12.

6. La Pérouse, *op. cit.,* p. 211. Also, Francis J. Weber, "The Structure of Daily Life at the California Missions," *The Pacific Historian,* vol. 15, no. 1, spring 1971, p. 14.

7. La Pérouse, *op. cit.,* p. 212.

8. Louis Choris. *San Francisco 100 Years Ago.* Translated from the French by Porter Garnett. San Francisco: A. M. Robertson, 1913, p. 4.

9. Edith Buckland Webb, *op. cit.,* p. 40.

10. Francis Florian Guest, O.F.M. "Cultural Perspectives on California Mission Life." *Southern California Quarterly,* Historical Society of Southern California, spring 1983, p. 53.

11. Edith Buckland Webb, *op. cit.,* pp. 27-8.

12. Louis Choris, *op. cit.,* pp. 6-7.

13. Edith Buckland Webb, *op. cit.,* p. 29.

14. James A. Sandos. "Levantamiento! The 1824 Chumash Uprising." *The Californians,* San Francisco, vol. 5, no. 1, Jan./Feb. 1987, p. 12.

15. Edith Buckland Webb, *op. cit.,* p. 48.

16. Frederick W. Beechey. *Narrative of a Voyage to the Pacific and Beering's Strait in 1825-28.* London: Henry Colburn and Richard Bentley, 1831, vol. 2, pp. 21-2.

17. Francis Florian Guest, *op. cit.,* p. 35.

18. 1813 *Interrogatorio,* translated by Maynard Geiger. Presented in Rosemary Keupper Valle, "Medicine and Health in the Alta California Missions, 1769-1833, as exemplified by a study of mission Santa Clara de Asís." Doctoral dissertation (unpublished), University of California at San Francisco, History of the Health Sciences, 1976, p. 212.

19. Sherburne Cook, *op. cit.,* pp. 13-22.

20. Rosemary Keupper Valle, "Medicine and Health in the Alta California Missions," *op. cit.,* p. 75

21. Sherburne Cook, *op. cit.,* p. 424.

22. James J. Rawls and Walter Bean. *California: An Interpretive History.* New York: McGraw-Hill, 1983, p. 38.

23. Junípero Serra, report to viceroy Antonio María Bucareli, Mexico City, 13 March 1773. *Writings of Junípero Serra.* Antonine Tibesar, O.F.M., editor. Washington, DC: Academy of American Franciscan History, 1955, vol. 1, p. 323.

24. Rosemary Keupper Valle, *op. cit.,* p. 81.

25. *Ibid.*, p. 89. Background information from Dr. Günter Risse.

26. California Mission Documents, no. 671, Santa Barbara Mission Archives.

27. Taylor Papers, no. 441, Archbishop's Archives, San Francisco.

28. Sherburne F. Cook, *op. cit.*, p. 26.

29. Taylor Papers, *op. cit.*, no. 698.

30. James G. Roney. "Paleopathology of a California Archeological Site." *Bulletin of the History of Medicine*, 1959, vol. 33, pp. 97-109.

31. Rosemary Keupper Valle, *op. cit.*, p. 162.

32. *Ibid.*, p. 158.

33. *Ibid.*, p. 165.

34. Mariano Payeras, La Purísima, 2 February 1820, AGN, Historia de México, Primera Serie, Tomo 2. Cited in Francis Florian Guest, *op. cit.*, pp. 51-2.

35. Edith Buckland Webb, *op. cit.*, p. 35.

36. *Ibid.*, pp. 33-4.

37. Ivan Petrovitch Pavlov. "Normal and Pathological States of the Hemispheres," December 1925 lecture in Paris. *Lectures on Conditioned Reflexes*, vol. 1. New York: International Publishers, 1928, pp. 354-5.

38. Pavlov, "A Physiological Study of the types of Nervous Systems, i.e., of Temperaments," December 1927 lecture in Russia, *op. cit.*, pp. 374-5.

39. Edith Buckland Webb, *op. cit.*, p. 105.

40. Jean Francois de Galoup de La Pérouse, *op. cit.*, pp. 207-8.

41. Louis Choris, *op. cit.*, pp. 8-9.

42. Frederick W. Beechey, *op. cit.*, p. 32.

43. Francis Florian Guest, *op. cit.*, p. 15.

44. La Pérouse, *op. cit.*, pp. 211-12.

45. *Ibid.*

46. Sherburne F. Cook, *op. cit.*, p. 126.

47. Jacob Baegert. "An Account of the Aboriginal Inhabitants of the California Peninsula," as given by Jacob Baegert, a German jesuit missionary. Smithsonian Institution, p. 369.

48. Francis Florian Guest, O.F.M. "The Indian Policy Under Fermín Francisco de Lasuén, California's Second Father President." *The California Historical Quarterly*, vol. 45, no. 3, Sept. 1966, pp. 202, 206.

49. Francis Florian Guest, "Cultural Perspectives on California Mission Life." *Southern California Quarterly*, spring 1983, p. 20.

50. Sherburne F. Cook, *op. cit.*, p. 12.

51. *Ibid.*, p. 14.

52. *Ibid.*, pp. 11-12.

53. *Ibid.*, p. 415.

54. Rosemary Keupper Valle, "Medicine and Health in the Alta California Missions," *op. cit.*, p. 185.

55. Sherburne Cook, *op. cit.*, pp. 427, 445. Florence Connolly Shipek's study of population statistics for mission San Diego also shows a very low female-to-male ratio among Indian adults during the later mission period. (Shipek, "Saints or Oppressors: The Franciscan Missionaries of California," *The Missions of California: A Legacy of Genocide,* edited by Rupert Costo and Jeannette Henry Costo, San Francisco: Indian Historian Press, 1987, p. 40).

56. Rosemary Keupper Valle, *op. cit.*, pp. 188-9.

57. Edith Buckland Webb, *op. cit.*, pp. 284-5.

58. Vicente de Sarría to governor Solá, 28 June 1815. Taylor Papers no. 441, Archbishop's Archives, San Francisco.

59. Fermín de Lasuén, Monterey, 1 March 1795. Cited in Sherburne Cook, *op. cit.*, p. 110.

60. Fermín de Lasuén, Monterey, 12 November 1800. Cited in *Ibid.*

61. James J. Rawls and Walter Bean. *California: An Interpretive History.* New York: McGraw-Hill, 1983, p. 38.

62. Donald Worcester. "The Significance of the Spanish Borderlands to the U.S." Reprinted in *New Spain's Far Northern Frontier: Essays on Spain in the American West, 1540-1821.* Edited by David Weber. Albuquerque: University of New Mexico Press, 1979, p. 8.

63. Francis Florian Guest, "The Indian Policy Under Fermín Francisco de Lasuén, California's Second Father President," *op. cit.*, p. 200.

64. *Ibid.*

65. Louis Choris, *op. cit.*, pp. 6-7.

66. Francis Florian Guest, *op. cit.*, p. 208.

67. Joseph Park. "Spanish Indian Policy in Northern Mexico, 1765-1810." 1962. Reprinted in *New Spain's Far Northern Frontier: Essays on Spain in the American West, 1540-1821.* Edited by David Weber. Albuquerque: University of New Mexico Press, 1979, p. 228.

68. *Ibid.* Also, James J. Rawls and Walter Bean, *op. cit.*, pp. 34-5; and *The Works of Hubert Howe Bancroft*, vol. 18, *History of California, 1542-1800*, Santa Barbara: Wallace Hebberd, 1963, pp. 363-4, 370. Rawls and Bean write that the Yuma warriors killed 30 soldiers and 4 friars; Joseph Park writes that the Yumas killed a total of 104 people; Bancroft gives the number of dead as "at least 46, probably more." Maynard Geiger, in *The Life and Times of Fray Junípero Serra* (Washington DC: Academy of American Franciscan History, 1959, vol. 2, p. 269), writes that the Yumas killed a total of 50 people. The number of *Yuma* people killed in the *Spaniards'* punitive expeditions, also uncertain, seems to have been a lot higher than the number of Hispanics killed by the Yumas: Bancroft cites Arricivita as a primary source, who said that 108 Yumas were killed and 85 taken prisoner; a later expedition by captain Romeu, lasting three days, took many Yuman lives.

69. Thomas Temple. "Toypurina the Witch and the Indian Uprising at San Gabriel." *The Masterkey*, vol. 32, no. 5, Sept.-Oct. 1958, pp. 137-8. The following account is based entirely on Temple's carefully researched article.

70. *Ibid.*, p. 150.

71. *Ibid.*, p. 148.

72. Randy Milliken, "Ethnohistory of the Rumsen," *op. cit.*, p. 35.

73. Lasuén to Nogueyra, mission Carmel, 21 January 1797. Cited in Francis Florian Guest, "The Indian Policy Under Fermín Francisco de Lasuén,...", *op. cit.*, p. 209.

74. Sherburne Cook, *op. cit.*, p. 61.

75. Francis Florian Guest, *op. cit.*, pp. 210-16, 219.

76. James A. Sandos. "Levantamiento! The 1824 Chumash Uprising Reconsidered." *Southern California Quarterly*, Historical Society of Southern California, vol. 67, no. 2, summer 1985, p. 119.

77. Sherburne Cook, *op. cit.*, pp. 149-51.

78. Fermín de Lasuén, letter of 30 October 1800. Cited in Sherburne Cook, *op. cit.*, p. 152.

79. Louis Choris, *San Francisco 100 Years Ago, op. cit.*, pp. 9-10.

80. Edith Buckland Webb, *op. cit.*, p. 43.

81. Rosemary Keupper Valle, *op. cit.*, p. 213. Translation by Maynard Geiger.

82. Sherburne Cook, *The Conflict Between the California Indians and White Civilization, op. cit.*, p. 76.

83. Francis Florian Guest, O.F.M. "An Examination of the Thesis of S.F. Cook on the Forced Conversion of Indians in the California Missions." *Southern California Quarterly*, Historical Society of Southern Califonia, spring 1979, vol. 61, no. 1, pp. 28, 34.

84. Sherburne Cook, *op. cit.*, p. 303.

85. Robert Schuyler, "Indian/Euro-American Interaction: Archeological Evidence from Non-Indian Sites," *Handbook of North Americans Indians,* Volume 8: *California,* edited by Robert Heizer: Washington, DC: Smithsonian Institution, 1978, p. 74. Also, David J. Weber, editor, *New Spain's Far Northern Frontier: Essays on Spain in the American West, 1540-1821,* Albuquerque: University of New Mexico Press, 1979, p. xi.

86. Sherburne Cook, *op. cit.*, pp. 82-3, 75.

87. Frederick W. Beechey, *Narrative of a Voyage to the Pacific and Beering's Strait in 1825-28,* London: Henry Colburn and Richard Bentley, 1831, vol. 2, p. 19.

88. Rosemary Keupper Valle, *op. cit.*, pp. 212-3. Translation by Maynard Geiger.

89. Manuel Patricio Servín. "California's Hispanic Heritage: A View into the Spanish Myth." Reprinted in *New Spain's Far Northern Frontier: Essays on Spain in the American West, 1540-1821.* Edited by David Weber. Albuquerque: University of New Mexico Press, 1979, p. 128.

90. James A. Sandos. "Levantamiento! The 1824 Chumash Uprising." *The Californians*, San Francisco, vol. 5, no. 1, Jan./Feb. 1987, p. 13.

91. Campbell Grant. "Eastern Coastal Chumash." *Handbook of North American Indians*, volume 8, edited by Robert Heizer. Washington, DC: Smithsonian Institution, 1978, p. 513.

92. James A. Sandos. "Levantamiento! The 1824 Chumash Uprising Reconsidered." *Southern California Quarterly*, Historical Society of Southern California, vol. 67, no. 2, summer 1985, p. 118.

93. James Sandos, "Levantamiento!...," *The Californians, op. cit.*, p. 17.

94. *Ibid.*

95. *Ibid.*, p. 19.

96. 15 June 1832—after entry no. 4749, mission San José death register. Archbishop's Archives, San Francisco.

97. José Viader, 12 January 1830 report to missions president José Bernardo Sánchez. California Mission Documents, no. 984, Santa Barbara Mission Archives.

98. Narciso Durán, letter from mission San José, 23-26 September 1830. Santa Barbara Mission Archives.

99. George H. Phillips. "Indians and the Breakdown of the Spanish Mission System in California." 1974. Reprinted in *New Spain's Far Northern Frontier: Essays on Spain in the American West, 1540-1821*. Edited by David Weber. Albuquerque: University of New Mexico Press, 1979, pp. 266-7.

100. James Rawls and Walter Bean, *California: An Interpretive History, op. cit.*, pp. 50-1.

101. Richard Levy. "Costanoan." *Handbook of North American Indians*, volume 8, edited by Robert Heizer. Washington, DC: Smithsonian Institution, 1978, p. 487.

102. James J. Rawls. *Indians of California: The Changing Image*. Norman, Oklahoma: University of Oklahoma Press, 1984, p. 20.

103. Edith Buckland Webb, *op. cit.*, p. 300.

104. James Rawls, *op. cit.*, p. 21.

105. Sherburne Cook, *op. cit.*, pp. 287-8, 483-4.

106. Sherburne F. Cook. "Historical Demography." *Handbook of North American Indians*, volume 8, edited by Robert Heizer. Washington, DC: Smithsonian Institution, 1978, p. 93.

107. James Rawls, *op. cit.*, pp. 91-4, 101.

108. Sherburne Cook, *The Conflict Between the California Indians and White Civilization, op. cit.*, pp. 314-15.

109. *California Police Gazette*, 26 September 1865. Cited in James Rawls, *op. cit.*, p. 104.

110. Cited in James Rawls and Walter Bean, *California: An Interpretive History, op. cit.*, p. 137.

111. James Rawls. *Indians of California: The Changing Image, op. cit.,* p. 185.

112. *American Heritage Book of Indians.* Narrative by William Brandon. Editor in charge, Alvin Josephy, Jr. American Heritage Publishing Co., 1961, p. 305.

113. James Rawls and Walter Bean, *California: An Interpretive History, op. cit.,* p. 142.

114. *San Francisco Alta California,* 17 March 1851. Cited in James Rawls. *Indians of California: The Changing Image, op. cit.,* p. 175.

115. Fermín de Lasuén, 12 November 1800 letter. Cited in Sherburne Cook, *op. cit.,* p. 124.

116. *Humboldt Times,* 20 June 1860. Cited in James Rawls, *Indians of California, op. cit.,* p. 176.

117. Junípero Serra, letter to viceroy Marqués de Croix. Cited in Maynard Geiger, O.F.M. *The Life and Times of Fray Junípero Serra, O.F.M.: The Man Who Never Turned Back (1713-1784),* Washington DC: Academy of American Franciscan History, 1959, vol. 2, p. 165.

Chapter 4: Vatican *vs.* People's Movements

1. Interview with Mary Luke Tobin, Sisters of Loretto. *U.S. Catholic,* January 1987, p. 30.

2. Daniel Fogel. *Revolution in Central America.* San Francisco: Ism Press, 1985, pp. 185-6.

3. Sylvia Paggioli, National Public Radio report from Rome, 20 October 1986.

4. *National Catholic Reporter,* Kansas City, Missouri, 7 November 1986, p. 16.

5. Penny Lernoux, "New CELAM Head Another Right-Winger." *National Catholic Reporter,* 27 March 1987, p. 5.

6. Dawn Gibeau, "Papal Visit Symbols Grip Chileans." *National Catholic Reporter,* 17 April 1987, p. 22.

7. *Ibid.*

8. *National Catholic Reporter,* 8 May 1987, p. 4.

9. *National Catholic Reporter* editorial, 1 May 1987, p. 12.

10. National Public Radio report, 9 April 1987.

11. *National Catholic Reporter,* 9 May 1986.

12. *New York Times,* 7 October 1984, p. E7.

13. "Most Women Religious Resist Vatican's Retraction Demand." *National Catholic Reporter,* 28 December 1984, p. 5.

14. *Ibid.,* p. 16.

15. "Ad Signers Ask for 'Just' Measures," by Mary Fay Bourgoin. *National Catholic Reporter,* 18 January 1985, p. 2.

16. Rosemary Radford Ruether. "Why the Nuns, on Abortion, at This Time?" *National Catholic Reporter*, 11 January 1985, p. 12.

17. Janine Wedel. *The Private Poland*. New York: Facts on File Publications, 1986, pp. 155-6.

18. Rosemary Ruether, "The Flaw in the Weave of the Seamless Garment." *National Catholic Reporter*, 15 February 1985, p. 17.

19. *National Catholic Reporter*, 8 February 1985, p. 19.

20. *National Catholic Reporter*, 15 August 1986, p. 20.

21. "Don't Sign the Abortion Ad." *National Catholic Reporter* editorial, 27 September 1985, p. 12.

22. "Seven More Ad-Signing Sisters Cleared." *National Catholic Reporter*, 4 April 1986, p. 20.

23. "Nuns Take Rome to Task in New Abortion Ad Flap," by Patricia Scharber Lefevere. *National Catholic Reporter*, 15 August 1986, pp. 1, 20.

24. *National Catholic Reporter*, 1 August 1986, p. 16.

25. "Vatican Catches Up with Maryknoll Nun," *National Catholic Reporter*, 19 September 1986, p. 7.

26. *National Catholic Reporter*, 5 June 1987, pp. 24-5. This letter was distributed to U.S. bishops in May 1987.

27. "U.S. Navy Kept Files on Bishop Hunthausen." *National Catholic Reporter*, 3 April 1987, p. 5.

28. *National Catholic Reporter*, 19 September 1986, p. 24.

29. "Letter to the Bishops of the Catholic Church on the pastoral Care of Homosexual Persons," dated 1 October 1986, issued 30 October. *National Catholic Reporter*, 14 November 1986, p. 18.

30. "AIDS Ministers Angered by New Vatican Guidelines." *National Catholic Reporter*, 14 November 1986, p. 7.

31. "Letter to the Bishops of the Catholic Church on the pastoral Care of Homosexual Persons," *op. cit.*

32. *National Catholic Reporter*, 14 November 1986, p. 1.

33. *Ibid.*, p. 6.

34. *National Catholic Reporter*, 21 November 1986, p. 3.

35. *National Catholic Reporter*, 3 April 1987, p. 18; 29 May 1987, p. 3; and 17 July 1987, p. 7.

36. "Dignity Punches Back at Miami Meeting," by Bill Kenkelen. *National Catholic Reporter*, 14 August 1987, p. 28.

37. *National Catholic Reporter*, 17 April 1987, p. 3.

38. *National Catholic Reporter*, 24 April 1987, pp. 18-19.

39. Canadian Broadcasting Corporation, "Sunday Morning" radio program, 28 June 1987.

40. *National Catholic Reporter*, 24 May 1985, p. 22.

41. *National Catholic Reporter*, 19 June 1987, p. 3.

42. *National Catholic Reporter*, 24 April 1987, p. 3.

43. *National Catholic Reporter*, 7 November 1986, p. 16.

44. *The Essays of Michel de Montaigne*, vol. 1. Translated and edited by Jacob Zeitlin. New York: Alfred A. Knopf, 1934.

Bibliography

American Heritage Book of Indians. Narrative by William Brandon. Editor in charge, Alvin Josephy, Jr. American Heritage Publishing Co., 1961.

Baegert, Jacob. "An Account of the Aboriginal Inhabitants of the California Peninsula," as given by Jacob Baegert, a German jesuit missionary. Smithsonian Institution (undated).

Barthel, Manfred. *The Jesuits: History and Legend of the Society of Jesus.* Translated from the German by Mark Howson. New York: William Morrow and Co., 1984.

Beechey, Frederick W. *Narrative of a Voyage to the Pacific and Beering's Strait in 1825-28.* London: Henry Colburn and Richard Bentley, 1831, volume 2.

The California Indians: A Source Book. Edited by Robert F. Heizer and M.A. Whipple. Berkeley: University of California Press, 1962.

Cavin, Susan. *Lesbian Origins.* San Francisco: Ism Press, 1985.

Chandler, Wayne B. "The Moor: Light of Europe's Dark Age." *African Presence in Early Europe*, edited by Ivan van Sertima. New Brunswick, New Jersey: Transaction Books, 1985, pp. 144-175.

Choris, Louis. *San Francisco 100 Years Ago.* Translated from the French by Porter Garnett. San Francisco: A. M. Robertson, 1913.

Conley, Frances. "We All Lived Together at the Presidio." *The Californians*, Jan./Feb. 1987.

Cook, Sherburne Friend. *The Conflict Between the California Indian and White Civilization.* Berkeley: University of California Press, 1976.

Fages, Pedro. *A Historical, Political, and Natural Description of California by Pedro Fages, Soldier of Spain.* Herbert Priestley, editor. Berkeley, 1937.

Geiger, Maynard, O.F.M. *The Life and Times of Fray Junipero Serra, O.F.M.: The Man Who Never Turned Back (1713-1784).* Washington DC: Academy of American Franciscan History, 1959. Two volumes.

Geiger, Maynard. "Fray Junípero Serra: Organizer and Administrator of the Upper California Missions, 1769-1784." *The California Historical Quarterly*, vol. 42, no. 3, September 1963.

Giménez Fernández, Manuel. "Fray Bartolomé de las Casas: A Biographical Sketch." *Bartolomé de las Casas in History: Toward an Understanding of the Man and His Work*, edited by Juan Friede and Benjamin Keen. Dekalb: Northern Illinois University Press, 1971.

Guest, Francis Florian, O.F.M. "Cultural Perspectives on California Mission Life." *Southern California Quarterly*, Historical Society of Southern California, spring 1983.

_____. "An Examination of the Thesis of S. F. Cook on the Forced Conversion of Indians in the California Missions." *Southern California Quarterly*, Historical Society of Southern Califonia, spring 1979, vol. 61, no. 1.

_____. "The Indian Policy Under Fermín Francisco de Lasuén, California's Second Father President." *The California Historical Quarterly*, vol. 45, no. 3, Sept. 1966.

Handbook of North American Indians, volume 8. Edited by Robert Heizer. Washington, DC: Smithsonian Institution, 1978.

Hanke, Lewis. *All Mankind is One: A Study of the Disputation between Bartolomé de las Casas and Juan Ginés de Sepúlveda in 1550 on the Religious and Intellectual Capacity of the American Indians.* Dekalb: Northern Illinois University Press, 1974.

Kroeber, Alfred L. "Elements of Culture in Native California," 1922; "The Native Population of California"; "The Food Problem in California"; "Yurok Law and Custom." Reprinted in *The California Indians: A Source Book*, edited by Robert F. Heizer and M. A. Whipple. Berkeley: University of California Press, 1962.

Kroeber, Alfred, and Spott, Robert. "Yurok Shamanism." *The California Indians: A Source Book.*

La Pérouse, Jean Francois de Galoup de. *The Voyage of La Pérouse Round the World in the Years 1785-88.* Translated from the French. London: John Stockdale, 1798, vol. 1.

"Las Casas, Bartolomé de." *Enciclopedia Universal Ilustrada* vol. 29. Madrid, 1916.

Lerner, Gerda. *The Creation of Patriarchy.* New York: Oxford University Press, 1986.

Margolin, Malcolm. *The Ohlone Way: Indian Life in the San Francisco-Monterey Bay Area.* Berkeley: Heyday Books, 1978.

Milliken, Randy. "Ethnohistory of the Rumsen" (comb-bound monograph). *Papers in Northern California Anthropology*, No. 2, April 1987, Northern California Anthropological Group, Berkeley.

The Missions of California: A Legacy of Genocide. Edited by Rupert Costo and Jeannette Henry Costo. San Francisco: Indian Historian Press, 1987.

Moholy, Noel Francis, O.F.M., and DeNevi, Don. *Junípero Serra: The Illustrated Story of the Franciscan Founder of California's Missions.* San Francisco: Harper & Row, 1985.

National Catholic Reporter, weekly newspaper. P.O. Box 419281, Kansas City, Missouri 64141.

New Catholic Encyclopedia. Washington, DC: Catholic University of America, McGraw-Hill, 1967.

New Spain's Far Northern Frontier: Essays on Spain in the American West, 1540-1821. Edited by David Weber. Albuquerque: University of New Mexico Press, 1979.

O'Brien, Eric, O.F.M. "The Life of Padre Serra." *Writings of Junípero Serra.* Antonine Tibesar, O.F.M., editor. Washington, DC: Academy of American Franciscan History, 1955, vol. 1.

Rawls, James J. *Indians of California: The Changing Image.* Norman, Oklahoma: University of Oklahoma Press, 1984.

Rawls, James and Bean, Walter. *California: An Interpretive History.* New York: McGraw-Hill, 1983.

Redd, Danita. "Black Madonnas of Europe: Diffusion of the African Isis." *African Presence in Early Europe, edited by Ivan van Sertima.* New Brunswick, New Jersey: Transaction Books, 1985, pp. 108-133.

Sandos, James A. "Levantamiento! The 1824 Chumash Uprising Reconsidered." *Southern California Quarterly*, Historical Society of Southern California, vol. 67, no. 2, summer 1985.

––––––––––––––. "Levantamiento! The 1824 Chumash Uprising." *The Californians*, San Francisco, vol. 5, no. 1, Jan./Feb. 1987.

Scobie, Edward. "African Popes." *African Presence in Early Europe*, edited by Ivan van Sertima. New Brunswick, New Jersey: Transaction Books, 1985, pp. 96-107.

Serra, Junípero. *Writings of Junípero Serra.* Antonine Tibesar, O.F.M., editor. Washington, DC: Academy of American Franciscan History, 1955. Four volumes, English translations alongside Spanish originals.

Sheehan, Thomas. *The First Coming: How the Kingdom of God Became Christianity.* New York: Random House, 1986.

Soustelle, Jacques. *Daily Life of the Aztecs on the Eve of the Spanish Conquest.* Translated from the French by Patrick O'Brian. Stanford University Press, 1961.

Temple, Thomas. "Toypurina the Witch and the Indian Uprising at San Gabriel." *Masterkey*, vol. 32, no. 5, Sept.-Oct. 1958.

Valle, Rosemary Keupper. "Medicine and Health in the Alta California Missions, 1769-1833, as exemplified by a study of mission Santa Clara de Asís." Doctoral dissertation (unpublished), University of California at San Francisco, History of the Health Sciences, 1976.

Webb, Edith Buckland. *Life at the Old Missions.* Lincoln: University of Nebraska Press, 1952.

Index

Abella, Ramón: 122.

abortion: 3, 167; among California Indians, 103; punished by death in Aztec state, 35; defined as homicide in Spanish empire, 123; at missions, 134-5; controversy within U.S. church, 173-5; in Poland, 174-5; in Italy, 175; in Peru, 177; in Canada, 184*n*.

adultery: among California Indians, 99-102; punished by death in Aztec state, 35; at missions, 136.

AIDS (acquired immune deficiency syndrome): 179, 182.

Aldama, Juan de: 28, 32; urges Hidalgo to go into hiding, 29.

Alfonsín, Raúl: 171.

Alfonso 6 (Spanish christian king): 13.

Allende, Ignacio José: 28-9, 30, 32; wants to march on Mexico City, 31.

Amorós, Juan: 142.

Andrés (Chumash mission mayor): 153.

Augustine (black saint): 7*n*.

Ayala, Juan: 72.

Aztecs: 15-17, 26, 36*n*, 158; Sahagún's attitude towards, 25; victims of inquisition, 27; belief system and catholicism, 33-35.

Baegert, Jacob: 131*n*.

Balke, Victor: 182.

Baltazar (Rumsen Indian leader): 75.

Banco Ambrosiano: 186.

Barrenche, Juan: 138.

Beechey, Frederick: 119, 130, 150.

Benedict (black saint): 7*n*.

Bernardin, Joseph: 174.

Bernier, Sandra: 184.

Berrigan, Daniel: 179.

birth control: 177, 178; among California Indians, 103. *see also* abortion *and* contraception.

Boff, Clodovis: 168.

Boff, Leonardo: 168, 172.

Bouchard, Hippolyte de: 152.

Bucareli y Ursua, Antonio María de: 57, 58, 59, 68, 72, 121, 123; pardons Rivera and Kumeyaay rebels, 67.

Burnet, Peter: 161.

Cachum (Pame goddess): 45.

Cahuilla (Indians of southern California): 91-2, 157.

Californios (Hispanic residents of Mexican California): 157, 158; expropriated by Yankees, 160.

Caligula (Roman emperor): 8.

Calleja y Flon, Félix María: 31, 32.

Cambón, Pedro: 62.

capitalism: 94, 110.

Caprio, Giuseppe: 184-6.

Carlos (Kumeyaay Indian rebel): 63, 64, 69; seeks asylum, 66; Serra urges pardon for, 67; is confirmed a catholic, 68; 'recidivism', 68.

Carlos 1, king of Spain: 21; approves new laws of Indies, then backs down, 22; equivocal colonial policy, 25.

Carlos 3, king of Spain: 1, 71; expels jesuits from his empire, 48-9; campaign to end smallpox, 121; orders cesarian operations, 123.

Carrillo, José: 69.

Carter, G. Emmet: 184.

catholic church: 7, 9-10, 165. *see also* christianity; people's church; *and* Vatican.

Catholics for a Free Choice: 173.

211

Cayetana (Mexican woman denounced to inquisition): 46, 47-8.

cesarian section: 122-3.

Charles 5, holy Roman emperor: *see* Carlos 1, king of Spain.

Chichimecas (Indians of central Mexico): 44.

Chile: 169-71.

Chochenyo (Indians east of San Francisco bay): 158; *see also* Ohlones.

Choris, Louis: 117, 118, 130, 136, 142; paintings by, **143-5.**

christ (messiah): 4, 5. *see also* Jesus of Nazareth.

christianity: 5-10, 165; false start by elevating Jesus to messiah, 5; as radical movement in Roman empire, 6; co-opted by Constantine, 7; adapts to 'pagan' religions, 8; elevates Jesus to god, 9; slides into racial bigotry, 10.

Chumash (Indians along Santa Barbara channel): 59, 62, 91, 117, 118, 141; and shell-bead money, 93; sexual freedom, 102, 154; postpartum sex taboo, 103; abortion and infanticide, 103; cosmology, 113; as seen by Serra, 70, 80; cultural resistance within missions, 152; uprising, 153-5; surviving rebels hit by malaria, 156.

Chupu (Chumash earth goddess): 141, 152.

Clement 13, pope: 49.

Columbus, Christopher: 17.

Communion and Liberation: 167-8.

communism: 110.

Connery, Vincent: 183.

Constantine (emperor): 7.

contraception: 3, 167, 175, 177, 184; sterilization, 178.

Cook, Sherburne: 127-8n, 132; forced conversion thesis, 148n.

Córdoba, Pedro de: 18.

Cortés, Hernando: 15, 36n.

Crespí, Juan: 42, 52, 75.

criollos (Mexican-born whites): 28, 29, 30, 31, 54; turn against Mexican revolution, 31.

Cuomo, Mario: 173.

David, king: 168.

declaration of independence (1776): 38-9.

Díaz, Juan: 137.

Diderot, Denis: 28, 43.

Diego, Juan (Mexican Indian): 30n.

Dignity (gay catholic organization): 178, 182; repressed by Vatican, 182-183; radicalizes, 183.

divorce: 178; among California Indians, 97; restricted in Aztec state, 35; banned in Spanish catholic system, 135; legalized in Argentina, 171-2.

dominicans: 18, 80; advocate freedom for Indians, 19; give refuge to Las Casas, 20; attempt to enforce new laws of Indies, 22. replace jesuits in Baja California, 50. *see also* Córdoba; Las Casas; Montesinos; *and* Tuite.

dormitory, female: 118, 131, 133-4, 136.

Dorn, William: 182.

Dumetz, Francisco: 62.

Durán, Narciso: 118; views Indians as incorrigible, 156.

El Salvador: 30n, 167.

encomienda ('trusteeship') system: 18, 53; in Cuba, 19; abolition proposed by Las Casas, 20; modified by new laws of the Indies, 22.

Engels, Frederick: 96, 187.

enlightenment liberals: 164.

Enriquillo (Indian leader in Española): 21.

epidemics: 17, 76-7, 120-2, 141, 156, 162; *see also* measles, smallpox, *and* syphilis.

Esselen (Indians of California): 115.

Estanislao (Miwok rebel): 155-6.

eucharist: 35.

Fages, Pedro: 54, 62; exploits Mexican soldiers, 56-7; on Chumash transvestism, 102; punishes Yumas, 138; becomes governor of California, 73; and Gabrielino revolt, 138, 139.

father-right (patrilineage): 96-7, 99.

FBI (Federal Bureau of Investigation): 178.

Fernando 7, king of Spain: 29, 30, 31.

Figueroa, José: 156, 157.

Francis of Assisi, saint: 42; contempt for own body, 51.

franciscans: 1, 25, 39, 42, 43, 47, 70, 75-6, 80, 114, 132, 138, 139, 150, 156, 163; campaign for immaculate conception, **19**; first arrive in Mexico, 17; support to Las Casas, 22; provoke Pueblo Indian uprising, 35-6; build Florida missions as refuge from slavery, 38; of Mallorca, 41; side with Pame Indians in land dispute, 45; approach to self punishment, 48; replace jesuits in Baja California, 50; attract Indians into California missions, 52-3, 115; act as trustees for mission Indians, 53; lament soldiers' abuse of Indian women, 59; but need soldiers' protection, 62, 69, 74; orthodox policy towards mission Indians, 71; oppose pueblo San José, 73; oppose Indian self government, 74-75; exclude Indians from priesthood, 77; mission language policy, 118-19, 164; immune to epidemics, 120; give smallpox vaccinations, 121; perform cesarian sections, 123; dramatize catholic teaching, 129; allow sweat lodges at missions, 133-134; repressive sexual policy, 135; controversy over Yuma mission, 137; psychological warfare, 140; policy towards shamans, 141-2; towards dancing, 142; dress code, 142-7; engage in commerce, 149; paternalism, 151, 164, 186; drive to root out Chumash customs, 152-3;

(franciscans, *cont'd.*)
treated kindly by Chumash rebels, 155; and secularization of missions, 157; embrace Serra as saint, 1, 165. *see also* Abella; Amorós; Barrenche; Boff; Cambón; Crespí; Díaz; Dumetz; Durán; Fuster; Garcés; Jayme; Kaelin; Lasuén; Murguía; Palóu; Payeras; Peña; Ripoll; Rodríguez; Sahagún; Sarría; Señán; Serra; Solano; Viader; Viñals; *and* Zalvidea.

Ferraro, Barbara: 177.

Ferraro, Geraldine: 173.

Fiedler, Maureen: 174.

Francisco (Kumeyaay Indian rebel): 63, 64, 68.

Fresno, Juan Francisco: 171.

Fuster, Vicente: 62-3, 64, 67; analyzes Kumeyaay rebellion, 64-6; declares Rivera excommunicated, 66.

Gabrielinos (Indians of southern California): 104; blood feuds, 108; revolt inspired by Toypurina, 138-40.

Gálvez, José de: 50.

Garcés, Francisco: 137; death, 138.

gay and lesbian rights movement: 3, 179-80; within catholic church, 165, 175, 178, 179-80. *see also* Dignity *and* New Ways Ministry.

Gelasius (black pope): 7n.

gente de razón ('people of reason'): 46, 73, 151, 163; defined, 46n.

gold rush: 158-60.

Gordon, Humberto: 171.

Gramick, Jeannine: 175, **176**.

Greeley, Andrew: 184.

Gruel, Nate: 183.

Guadalupe, virgin of: 30. *see also* Madonna.

Guaraní (Indians of Paraguay): 49.

Guatemala: 167, 172.

Guest, Francis Florian: 131-2; disputes forced conversion thesis, 148n.

Gutiérrez, Gustavo: 168.

Haiti: 129, 172.

Heizer, Robert: 161.

Hickey, James: 175.

Hidalgo y Costilla, Miguel: 27-32, 186.

homosexuality: 3, 99, 135, 152; among California Indians, 102-3; punished by death in Aztec state, 35; and catholic church, 165, 178, 182, 183; denounced by Vatican, 179-80.

Horus (son of the virgin mother Isis): 8.

Huchnom (Indians of northwest California): 96.

human nature: 110.

Hunthausen, Raymond: 178-9.

Hupa (of northwest California): 106.

Hussey, Patricia: 177.

iconoclasm: 8-9.

immaculate conception: 19.

Inca peoples: 158; beliefs, 33.

India: 95*n.*

Indians of California: 1, 2, 3, 51-2, 58-59, 62, 72, 73, 74, 75, **55**, **82**, **87-9**, **100-1**, 112-13, 114, 140, **162**, 163; linguistic and cultural diversity, 83; acorn gathering and processing, 86-90; varied food sources, 90, 91; hunting, 90-1, 92; fishing, 90, 92; tobacco cultivation, 91, 92; agriculture, 91-2; controlled burning, 92; flint mining, 92; property relations, 93-4; money, 93; social responsibility among, 59-62, 91, 92, 105; kinship systems, 94; *moieties*, 94; menarche rite, 134; marriage practices, 94-6, 97-8; polygamy, 97, 135; divorce, 97; sex separation, 98; child rearing, 98, 104, 131*n*; sweat lodge, 98-9, **100-1**, 133-4; adultery, 99-102, 136; transvestism, 102, 103; homosexuality, 102-3; childbirth, 103; abortion, 103; infanticide, 103, 135; justice systems, 105; chiefs, 59-62, 105-6; councils of elders, 105-6; shamans, 106-7, 141-2; sorcery, 106, 107, 138, 140, 147; warfare, 107-8;

(Indians of California, *cont'd.*)

dance, 98, 105, 109, 142, **144-6**; music, 109; gambling games, 98, 109, 113, 142-7, **143**, 154, 157; mythology, 109; communal impulse, 110; taboo *vs.* mentioning names of the dead, 111-112; view Spaniards as sons of mules, 70; lured into missions, 52-3; mission living arrangements, 54; fail to spread Kumeyaay rebellion north, 66; mission work routine, 115-17, **116**, **124-5**; food sources at missions, 117-118, 127; vulnerable to disease, 120; and syphilis, 122; and depression, 127-8; shock of forced labor, 128-9, 136; humiliating punishment, 130-2, 134, 139; resistance and rebellion, 51-52, 64-6, 75, 137-40, 152-6; preserve cultures at missions, 142-7, **143-6**, 152, 156; under Mexican rule, 151-2; and secularization of missions, 156-8; population reduction, 159, 160; enslaved in wake of gold rush, 159, 160-161; suffer genocide, 161-3, 164. *see also* Cahuilla; Chumash; Esselen; Gabrielinos; Huchnom; Hupa; Ipai; Kumeyaays; Maidu; Miwok; Mohaves; Nisenan; Ohlones; Patwin; Pomo; Rumsen; Salinans; Tipai; Tubatulabal; Wappo; Yahi; Yana; Yokuts; Yumas; *and* Yurok.

inquisition, catholic: in Spain, 14, 23; in the Yucatán, 26-7; in Mexico, 33, 45-7; Serra's participation in, 45-7; tries Hidalgo, 28.

Ipai (Indians of southern California): 69, 103, 111.

Iroquois confederation: 38.

Isabel (queen of Spain): 14, 18.

Ishi (Yahi Indian survivor): **162**.

Isis (African mother goddess): 8.

islam: 10, 11, 12.

James (disciple of Jesus): 15.

Jayme, Luis: 62-3, 67, 70; laments soldiers' rape of Kumeyaay women, 63; death of 64, **65**.

jesuits: 48, 53; build mission in Paraguay as refuge from slavery, 49; mission work in Baja California, 50; expelled from France, 49; expelled from Spain and Mexico, 48-50; expel John McNeil, 180-2. *see also* Baegert; Berrigan; McNeil; *and* Novak.

Jesus of Nazareth: 3-5, 6, 35n, 180; worldlier than John the baptist, 4; embraces the poor and outcast, 10; no military protection, 169; his martyr's despair, 5; elevated to god, 9.

Jews: 23, 112; of Roman-occupied Palestine, 4; of Spain, 11, 12, 14.

Jiménez de Cisneros, Francisco: 14, 20.

Joffe, Roland: 49n.

John the baptist: 4.

John 23, pope: 166.

John Paul 2, pope: 1-3, 21n, 167; rejects people's church at Puebla, 167; supports Communion and Liberation, 167-8; in Chile, 169, **170**, 171; in Argentina, 171-2; on liberation theology, 172; approves Ratzinger's anti-gay letter, 179; declares Serra 'venerable', 1; delays beatification of Serra, 2; praises Serra, 2, 3.

Kaelin, Jerry: 173.

Kane, Jack: 183-4.

Kroeber, Alfred: 111.

Kumeyaay (Indians of southern California): 63, 91; attack mission San Diego, 64-6; repressed in wake of revolt, 67, 69.

land disputes between mission Indians and soldier/settlers: 140; in Sierra Gorda, 45; around San José, 72-3; in Yuma territory, 137; after secularization of missions, 158.

language policy: 118-19, 164; in Sierra Gorda, 44.

La Pérouse, Jean Francois de Galoup de: 117, 129.

Las Casas, Bartolomé de: 17-25.

Lasuén, Fermín Francisco de: 62, 68, 134-5; friend of Rivera, 67; and punishment of neophytes, 130; laments Indians' distaste for mission life, 141; denounces dancing, 142; contempt for Indian societies, 163.

laws of the Indies: 21, 25, 45, 71, 76. *see also* new laws of the Indies.

Lenin, Vladimir Ilyich: 167.

Leo (Byzantine emperor): 8.

Lerner, Gerda: 99.

lesbianism: 3; among California Indians, 102-3. *see also* gay and lesbian rights movement.

liberation theology: 3, 168, 186; promoted at Medellín bishops' conference, 167; and pope John Paul's tactical shift, 172. *see also* Boff; Gutiérrez; *and* Muñoz.

Lizana, Francisco de: 30.

López Trujillo, Alfonso: 169.

Los Angeles (pueblo): 80, 149, 157.

Louis 15, king of France: 49.

Madonna: 8-9, 131, 165; black, 8, 10, 165; brown, 30, 31, 165; white, 9, 31, 165.

Maidu (Indians of northeast California): 92.

Mao Zedong: 167.

Margolin, Malcolm: 109.

Mark (disciple of Jesus): 5n.

Marx, Karl: 31, 187.

marxism-leninism, 166-7.

Mary Magdalene: 5, 185.

Mary, mother of James: 5, 185.

Mary, mother of Jesus: 8. *see also* Madonna.

Maryknoll Missioners: 177.

Maxentius (Roman emperor): 7.

Mayas: 17, 158; Sahagún's attitude towards, 25; victims of inquisition, 26-7; and catholic masochism, 129.

McNeil, John: 180, **181**, 182.

measles: 120, 121n, 133.

Meirose, Carl: 179.

messiah: 5.

Miltiades (black pope): 7.

mission Carmel: 1-2, 76, 115, 117, 120, 129, 142; founded, 52; Baltazar's rebellion, 75; Toypurina's marriage, 139; visited by pope John Paul, 3.

mission La Purísima: 118, 123; military training for neophytes, 152; Chumash uprising, 153-4.

mission San Antonio: 76, 136.

mission San Buenaventura: 117; and Chumash uprising, 153.

mission San Diego: 62-3, 66, 69, 70; founded, 51; attacked by local Indians, 51-2; burned by Kumeyaay rebels, 64-6; rebuilt, 68; measles erupts, 120.

mission San Francisco de Asís: 80, 117, 119; founded, 39; female dormitory, 118, 136; measles epidemic, 120; coercive church services, 130; mass flight, 141, 150.

mission San Francisco Solano: 120.

mission San Gabriel: 56, 120, 135; Indian revolt, 138-40.

mission San José: 118, 156.

mission San Juan Capistrano: 136.

mission San Luís Obispo: 120.

mission Santa Barbara: 80, 141, 154, 155; military training for neophytes, 152; Chumash uprising, 153.

mission Santa Clara: 72-3, 80, 119n, 132, 147, 151, 156; epidemics, 77, 120; female and youth mortality, 133; cesarian operation, 123.

mission Santa Ynez: 153.

mission system: 80, 136, 147; in Spain during the christian reconquest, 13; in Mexico's Sierra Gorda, 44; in California, 52-4; coercive nature, 114; work routine, 115-17; religious instruction, 118-19, 129-30; medical conditions, 121-3, 133-4; conflictive social conditioning, 125-8; female dormitory, 118, 131, 133-4, 136; degrades Indian women, 132-6; physical punishment, 130-2, 134, 135; and shamans, 141-2, 152-3, 155;

(mission system, *cont'd.*)
forced conversion controversy, 148n; becomes more commercial, 149; provokes clashes between neophytes and pagan Indians, 150; secularization, 156-8; historical impact, 164.

Miwok (Indians of California): 155-6, 157.

Moctezuma (Aztec emperor): 15.

Mohaves (Indians of southeast California): 91-2; warlike, 108.

moieties (halves of Indian societies): 94, 187.

Montaigne, Michel Eyquem de: 187.

Montesinos, Antonio de: 19.

Moors (of north Africa and Spain): 11-12, 13, 14, 15, 41.

Morgenthaler, Henry: 184n.

mother-right (matrilineage): 96, 99.

Muhammad: 10.

Muñoz, Ronaldo: 169.

Murguía, Joseph Antonio: 73.

Murphy, Thomas: 179.

Musa Nosseyr: 11.

Muslims: 23, 112; in Spain, 11-12, 13, 14.

Napoleon Bonaparte: 28, 29.

Naranjo, Domingo: 36.

nervous breakdown: 127, 135.

Neve, Felipe de: 69, 147; and pueblo San José, 72-3; withholds food from missions, 74; pushes mission self-government, 74-5; challenges Serra's right to confirm, 77.

new laws of the Indies (1542): 22, 26, 73, 118.

Nicaragua: 167.

Nicolás José (Gabrielino Indian rebel): 138-9.

Nisenan (Indians of California): 107.

Notre Dame de Namur: 177.

Novak, Joseph: 183.

Obando y Bravo, Miguel: 169.

O'Connor, John: 168; elevated to cardinal, 175-7; expels Dignity, 182-3.

Ohlones (Indians of California): **60-1**, 91, 93, 96*n*, 111, 115, 118, 132, 187; post-partum sex taboo, 103; restrained warfare, 108; gambling games, 109.

Oñate, Juan de: 35.

Ortega, José: 69.

Ovando, Nicolás de: 18.

Palma, Salvador (Yuma chief): 137.

Palóu, Francisco: 77, 137; student of Serra, 42; works with Serra in Sierra Gorda mission, 43-4; on depopulation of Baja California Indians, 50; tries to dissuade Serra from journeying to San Diego, 50-1; stresses need for military escorts, 62; founds mission San Francisco, 39; takes Serra's final confession, 81; biographer of Serra, 46-7, 48.

Pames (Indians of central Mexico): 44-5.

Patwin (Indians of California): 108, 158.

Paul, the apostle: 6, 171-2.

Paul 3, pope: 21.

Pavlov, Ivan Petrovitch: 126-7.

Payeras, Mariano: 118; laments collapse of Indians' health, 123; military training for neophytes, 152.

Peña, Thomás de la: 73.

people's church: 166-167, 168, 172, 187. *see also* liberation theology.

Pequot Indians (of Connecticut): 39.

Peter's Pence: 184.

Philippines: 95*n*, 166, 167, 187.

Pico, Pío: 158.

Pinochet, Augusto: 169, **170**, 171.

pious fund (used to finance missions): 53, 157.

Pizarro, Francisco: 21.

Pomo (Indians of California): 96, 98, 107, 108.

pope (bishop of Rome): 7. *see also* Clement 13; Gelasius; John 23; John Paul 2; Miltiades; Paul 3; *and* Victor 1.

Popé (Pueblo Indian leader): 36-8.

Portolá, Gaspar de: 50.

Prat, Pedro: 121.

presidio (Spanish frontier fort): 54, 57, 80, 137, 139, 148, 149, 152, 154, 155; of Monterey, 56-7, 59, 121, 139; of San Diego, 64-6, 136.

Pueblo Indians: 35-8.

Puga, Mariano: 169.

rape: 107, 133; and marriage, 96*n*; of Indian women by Hispanic soldiers, 56, 63, 122; of Indian women by Yankee invaders, 159, 160, 161; of children in civilized society, 104.

Ratzinger, Joseph: 182, 183; denounces liberation theology, 172; rebukes archbishop Hunthausen, 178; denounces homosexuality, 179-80.

resurrection: 8, 129.

Reyes Acosta, Melchora de los: 46.

Ripoll, Antonio: 152; and Chumash uprising, 153; tries to persuade rebels to return, 155.

Rivera y Moncada, Fernando Javier: 59, 62, 68; informs Serra of disaster at San Diego, 70; excommunicated by Fuster, 66; pardoned by Bucareli, 67; opposes founding new missions, 71-2; violent death, 137.

Roderick (Visigoth king of Spain): 11.

Rodríguez, Antonio: 154.

Ruether, Rosemary Radford: 174-5.

Rumsen (Indians along Monterey bay): 52. *see also* Ohlones.

Sahagún, Bernardino de: 25-7.

Salinans (of central California coast): 132-3, 136.

Salome (disciple of Jesus): 5, 185.

San José, pueblo: 72-3, 80, 149, 157.

Santiago (saint James of the *conquistadores*): 15, **16**, 138.

Sarría, Vicente Francisco de: 119, 122; and Chumash uprising, 155.

scalp bounties: 161; issued by English colonial governments, 39.

School Sisters of Notre Dame: 175.

Señán, José: 117; drives to root out Chumash customs, 152-3; death, 153.

Sepúlveda, Juan Ginés de: 22-3.

Serra, Junípero: 39, **40**, 53, 64, 73, 115, 121, 129, 186; born and baptized, 41; becomes a franciscan novice, 41; assumes name Junípero, 42; decides to become a missionary, 42; his 'happy death' theology, 42, 43, 68, 69, 71, 76, 186; arrives in Mexico, 43; Sierra Gorda mission, 44-5; works for inquisition, 45-7; punishing self-discipline, 47-8; heads Baja California missions, 50; pushes into Alta California, 50-1; founds mission San Diego, 51; founds mission Carmel, 52; distraught over soldiers' abuse of Indian women, 56, 57; returns to Mexico City to reform mission/presidio system, 57-9; returns to Monterey, 59; promotes interracial marriage, 163; urges pardon for Kumeyaay rebels, 67; reverts to stern discipline, 68, 69; his zeal and practical sense, 70-1; opposes colonial settlements in California, 72; opposes Indian self government, 74-5, 77; paternalism towards Indians, 75-6, 164, 186; sanguine in face of epidemics, 76; confirmation campaign, 77-80; death, 81; campaign for sainthood, 1-2, 165; praised by pope John Paul, 2, 3.

sex ratios: 132-3, 135.

shamans: 99, 152-3, 155; among Pueblo Indians, 36; and transvestites, 102; 106-7; and mission system, 141-2.

Sheehan, Thomas: 5n.

Simon Peter (disciple of Jesus): 5.

Sisters of Loretto: 174.

smallpox: 17, 121.

Sodano, Angelo: 171.

Solá, Pablo Vicente de: 122, 152.

Solano, Francisco (saint): 47.

Soustelle, Jacques: 17.

Soviet Union: 166.

Stallone, Sylvester: 168.

Sullivan, Walter: 183.

syphilis: 122; ravages Baja California Indians, 50; at missions, 134.

Talavera, Hernando de: 14.

Tarik ibn Ziad: 11.

Tecumseh (Shawnee Indian chief): 113.

Tekakwitha Conference: 2.

Theodosius (ruler of eastern Roman empire): 11.

Tipai (Indians of southern California): 103, 111.

Tlaxcalan Indians (of Mexico): 36n.

Tlazolteotl (Aztec goddess): 33.

Tomasajaquichi (Gabrielino chief): 139.

Toypurina (Gabrielina Indian sorceress): 138, 139-40, 148n.

Trapasso, Rose Dominic: 177.

Traxler, Margaret Ellen: 175.

Tubatulabal (Indians of south central California): 107.

Tuite, Marjorie: 177.

Valladolid, Mexico: 27, 28, 32, 47; Hidalgo creates government at, 30.

Valladolid, Spain: 23.

Valle, Rosemary Keupper: 121n.

Vallejo, Mariano: 156.

Vatican: 2, 3, 165, 166, 175, 183; turns against black Madonna, 8; resorts to mass coercion, 10; declares Indians have souls, 21; law of asylum, 66; second council, 166, 174; vs. liberation theology, 172; stifles dissent over abortion, 173-4, 177; rebukes

(Vatican, *cont'd.*)

archbishop Hunthausen, 178; re-presses gay catholic movement, 175, 178, 183; represses John McNeil, 180-2; appeals for dona-tions, 184-6; underpaid employees, 184n; financial worth, 184-6. *see also* pope.

Velázquez, Diego: 18.

Verdugo, José María: 138.

Viader, José: 123, 156.

Victor 1 (black pope): 7n.

Viñals: Josef: 123.

Visigoths: 11, 12, 13.

vulgar marxists: 164.

Wappo (Indians of California): 108.

Webb, Edith Buckland: 114.

Wojtyla, Karol: 167. *see also* John Paul 2, pope.

women's struggles: 3; for equality within catholic church, 165, 173-7; for ordination as priests, 183, 185.

Wuerl, Donald: 178, 179.

Yahi (Indians of north central Cali-fornia): 161-2. *see also* Yana.

Yana (of north California): 91, 161.

Yokuts (of central California): 91, 96n, 111, 158; and Chumash upris-ing, 154, 155.

Yumas (of southeast California): 91-2; warlike, 108; revolt against Span-iards, 137-8; repressed, 138, 201.

Yurok (of northwest California): 97; transvestism, 102; legal system, 105, 106; restraints against war, 108; female shamans, 106; taboo against uttering names, 111.

Yusuf ibn Tashifin: 13.

Zalvidea, José María: 135.

ORDER FORM

Amount

☐ Send me _____ copy/ies of
    Junípero Serra... at $9.00 each . . . . $_____

☐ Send me _____ copies of
    Africa in Struggle at $8.00 each . . . . $_____

☐ Send me _____ copies of *Revolution in*
    Central America by Fogel at $6.00 each . . . . . $_____

☐ Send me _____ copies of
    Lesbian Origins by Cavin at $9.00 each . . . . . . $_____

Add postage: $1 for one book,
    25¢ for each additional book . . . . $_____

California residents add 6.5% sales tax
    ('Who says life's fair?') . . . . $_____

Total payment . . . .   **$**_____

Name _____

Address _____

City, State & Zip _____

Make check or
money order out to: **Ism Press, Inc.**
    P.O. Box 12447
    San Francisco, CA 94112

Multiple order discount on book price:
10% discount if 5-9 books ordered.
20% discount if over 10 books ordered.